P9-CSW-113

The Question of Imperialism

THE
QUESTION
OF
IMPERIALISM

The Political Economy of
Dominance and Dependence

BENJAMIN J. COHEN

Basic Books, Inc., Publishers

NEW YORK

For the memory of

Aeneas

Maps on pages 24–29 adapted
from © Rand McNally & Co., R.L. 73Y61.

© 1973 by Basic Books, Inc.
Library of Congress Catalog Card Number: 73–81036
SBN: 465–06780–8
Manufactured in the United States of America

77 10 9 8 7 6 5 4

ACKNOWLEDGMENTS

A number of my colleagues gave me the benefit of their comments and criticisms as I was writing this book. I am deeply grateful to them all. I especially wish to thank: Professor Robert G. Gilpin of Princeton University, Professor Alan K. Henrikson of the Fletcher School of Law and Diplomacy, Mr. John R. Karlik of the Joint Economic Committee of the Congress, Professor Peter B. Kenen of Princeton University, Professor Charles P. Kindleberger of the Massachusetts Institute of Technology, Professor James R. Kurth of Harvard University, Mr. Anthony M. Lanyi of the International Monetary Fund, Professor Arthur MacEwan of Harvard University, Mr. Harry Magdoff of *Monthly Review*, Professor Joseph S. Nye of Harvard University, Mr. Keith Pavitt of Sussex University (England), and Mr. Ernest H. Preeg of the United States Department of State. None of them, of course, bear responsibility for any errors of fact or logic that may remain in this book. I alone am accountable for the substance of the study as it now stands.

1973   B.J.C.

CONTENTS

The Question of Imperialism

INTRODUCTION

This book is about the relations between rich and poor countries. Specifically, it is about the problem of how to *explain* the relations between rich and poor countries. The focus is on one particular word which, according to many, explains it all — *imperialism*.

In recent years as a teacher of international economics, I have found that many of my students have been becoming increasingly reluctant to accept at face value the traditional analysis which I myself learned just a few years ago. Not for this newer generation the hoary tenets of capitalism. Not for them the conventional wisdom of comparative advantage and free trade, derived from the writings of Adam Smith and David Ricardo, John Stuart Mill and John Maynard Keynes. What they wanted was a newer, more unconventional wisdom distilled from the likes of Marx, Lenin, and Mao Tse-tung. What they wanted was a *political economy* of international economics, not mere technical jargon or dry supply and demand curves. They demanded: What about the role of politics in international economics? What about the part that power plays in the relations

3

between the rich and the poor? What about dominance, dependence, and exploitation? In short, what about imperialism?

I believe these are legitimate questions. Certainly these issues are rarely, if ever, treated satisfactorily in the conventional literature of international economics. In my opinion, they ought to be treated systematically and comprehensively. Politics *does* have a role in international economics, after all. Power does play a part in the relations between the rich and the poor. There *is* dominance, dependence, and exploitation. There *is* imperialism. If one is *really* interested in understanding what international economics is all about, then one must also try to understand what imperialism is all about.

That is the objective of this book—to understand what imperialism is all about. Necessarily, this is an exercise in *political economy*. To the extent possible, the economics and politics of relations between rich and poor countries will be combined and integrated within a single analytical framework. Also, to the extent possible, all important aspects of the problem will be included for consideration—conflicts of interest as well as allocation of resources, income and welfare as well as struggles for power. The immediate focus of the analysis will be on connections of trade, investment, and foreign aid. The ultimate purpose of the analysis will be, if humanly possible, to explain the meaning and implications of these connections. A proper prescription for any of the ills of the world must necessarily begin with proper diagnosis.

Before starting, I should perhaps make my own ideological position clear. I would not describe myself as either a marxist or a radical; neither would I describe myself as a conservative or a reactionary. Intellectually, I fall between the extremes, somewhat more to the left than to the right of center. While I am not particularly enamored of capitalism, I would still rather reform it than overthrow it. More important, I believe that capitalism is *capable* of being reformed. This is what distinguishes my attitude from most of those discussed in this book. Most writers on the subject of imperialism happen to be marxist or radical. Why this field should have been left to them alone for so long is not exactly clear. What is clear is that marxists and radicals have remarkably little faith in the reformative capacity of capitalist society. Virtually all of their theories of imperialism can be traced back to this single fundamental conviction, which is widely shared and has a powerful emotional sway in many parts of the world.

I mention all this in order to warn the reader that my own view of these marxist and radical doctrines is, to say the least, highly skeptical. I find their premises dubious, their logic questionable, and their conclusions improbable. I also find in them a reliance on faith and dogma that is perhaps more appropriate to discussions of religious belief than to the study of political economy. Most marxist or radical theories of imperialism offer little inherent superiority over other possible interpretations of international economic relations. In many respects they remind me of the study of the heavenly constellations. Certainly the stars are there, and certainly one might imagine that a group of them does look like, say, Ursa Major, the Great Bear. But one might also imagine that it looks like a great sheepdog, to say nothing of a Degas ballerina or a drunken chicken. Likewise, certainly the facts are there—rich countries and poor countries, trade and investment, dominance and dependence—and certainly one might imagine that marxist or radical interpretations account for them all. But one might also imagine very different explanations of at least equal, if not superior, merit.

One young marxist has written that rejection of marxist or radical theories of imperialism "often exists on no better ground than emotion and prejudice." [1] That is like the pot calling the kettle black. Marxists and radicals are hardly innocent of the same intellectual delinquencies. Besides, the glaring deficiencies of many of their own discussions—their propensity for overstatement and tendentious reasoning, their lack of humor and subtlety, their arguments which frequently throw out the baby along with the bathwater—provide more than enough ammunition for any scholarly critic to bring them down. Here I try not to allow my own emotions and prejudices to interfere with objective analysis (though obviously they do color my normative judgments). It is up to the reader to decide whether I succeed.

Chapter 1 is devoted to a terminological discussion of just what the word "imperialism" means. An objective and ethically neutral definition is offered which will hopefully ensure that the concept can be useful for an analysis of the political economy of international relations. Chapter 2 turns to the classical imperialism of the late nineteenth century, discussing alternative theories that were developed then and later to discuss that momentous historical event. The transition to modern imperialism is discussed in Chapter 3, along with some political forms of imperialism on the contemporary scene. The next three chapters concentrate on modern economic forms of imperialism. Chapter 4 focuses on the question of whether allegedly "neocolonial" trade and investment relations with poor countries are either necessary to the capitalist rich or an inevitable outcome of their mature growth. Chapter 5 asks whether these same relations retard or distort the economic development of the poor. Chapter 6 examines the issues of dependence and exploitation.

The final chapter draws together all the strands of the argument in order to suggest an alternative approach to the explanation of imperialism. One of the most useful laws of science is the Law of Parsimony, or Occam's Razor. This dictates that one cannot explain a behavioral phenomenon by a higher, more complex process if a lower or simpler one will do. The difficulty with marxist or radical theories of imperialism is that they tend to be more highly complex than they have need to be. A much less complex theory will do—a theory based simply on the competition of sovereignties inherent in the anarchy of the international political system. This theory is outlined and defended against possible objections in Chapter 7.

NOTE

1. Tom Kemp, *Theories of Imperialism* (London: Dobson, 1967), p. 163.

I

THE MEANING OF IMPERIALISM

Imperialism—what does it mean? For purposes of serious analysis, it is important first to know what one is talking about. Unfortunately, imperialism is one of those words, like liberal or communist (or beatnik or hippie), whose meaning has long since been lost. Once it was used to describe a specific historical phenomenon; currently it means virtually all things to all men. One well-known book has traced no less than twelve separate changes of meaning through the evolution of the word's use.[1] As a technical tool of analysis it no longer seems to have much utility at all. "Imperialism is no word for scholars," wrote one scholar.[2] The word has become too emotive and value-laden, too tied up with partisan politics and propaganda as a catchword or slogan. Indeed, for some it has actually become an epithet, a term of abuse or invective exceeded in opprobrium only by some of the very choicest among the famous four-letter words of the English language.

Under such circumstances, it might seem wisest in a scholarly study to drop the word altogether, in favor of a more technical— if less colorful—means of expression. But that would be self-defeating. The word is part of the common language and pre-occupies a large and growing part of the world's population. To

9

avoid its use would be, in a sense, to avoid the issue itself. A more appropriate procedure would be to retain the term, but at the same time to attempt to give it a well-defined meaning, ethically neutral and objective, that would make it useful for analysis of the political economy of international relations. That is the purpose here.

Originally, the term imperialism was connected with the Latin word *imperator*, and was usually associated with the ideas of dictatorial power, highly centralized government, and arbitrary methods of administration. In modern times it was first employed in France in the 1830s as a label for the ideas of partisans of the one-time Napoleonic empire; after 1848 it developed into a popular expression of abuse for the Caesaristic pretensions of Napoleon III. In the 1870s its use spread to Britain: supporters, as well as critics, of Prime Minister Disraeli began to describe his policy of strengthening and expanding the British colonial empire as imperialistic. In the decades that followed, use of the term imperialism accelerated along with colonial expansion by Britain and others. Toward the end of the century the meaning of the term was relatively clear; it was equivalent to "colonialism"—the establishment and extension of the political sovereignty of one nation over alien peoples and territories.

Curiously, this did not usually include the extension of political sovereignty over *contiguous* land areas. Czarist expansion into central and east Asia was not typically labeled imperialistic (even though the Czars themselves referred to their rule as "imperial"), nor was the westward march of the United States across North America (at least until it reached the Pacific shore). These were simply instances of "nation-building," albeit on a continental scale. At the close of the nineteenth century the term imperialism was specifically reserved for the colonialism of *maritime* powers—the extension of political sovereignty *overseas*, first by the Portuguese and Spanish, then by the British, French, and other Europeans, and finally by the Americans and Japanese.

After the turn of the century came the critics of capitalism—radical liberals like the Englishman John Hobson and marxists like Rosa Luxemburg, Rudolph Hilferding, and V. I. Lenin. Emphasis soon shifted from straightforward political relationships to more subtle economic forces and motivations—from simple colonialism to more complex forms of economic penetration and domination of markets, sources of supply, and investment outlets. The shift of emphasis was further stimulated in the post-World War II period by the gradual disappearance of most maritime empires of the more traditional political kind. Today many writers find it impossible to speak at all of imperialism without putting great emphasis on the economics of the matter.

An English author, for example, describes imperialism as

a complex of economic, political and military relations by which the less economically developed lands are subjected to the more economically developed. . . . [I]mperialism remains the best word for the general system of unequal world economic relations.[3]

A French author describes imperialism as "clearly an economic phenomenon, implying certain relationships in the international division of labor, in trade and the movement of capital."[4] One American likens imperialism to "the network of means of control exercised by one economy (enterprises and government) over another,"[5] while another, a marxist following Lenin's example, defines it as a specific "stage in the development of [the capitalist] world economy."[6] A third American source simply identifies it with "the internationalization of capitalism."[7]

Other contemporary writers still prefer more political definitions. Some continue to stress just the *direct* extension of sovereignty, as for instance the author who equates imperialism with "the process of founding an empire beyond the nation's natural frontiers, with the aim of subjecting the population outside these frontiers to the political rule of the dominating country. . . ."[8] Others are willing to extend the term to more *indirect* mechanisms as well, such as military or diplomatic pressures or economic penetration. Thus a pair of analysts describe imperialism as "the extension of sovereignty or control, whether direct or indirect. . . ." [9]

Certain writers have limited the term to attempts by states to reverse an existing state of affairs: imperialistic policies are those with explicitly expansionist ambitions, but not those which seek merely to conserve an existing empire. One scholar defines imperialism simply as "a policy devised to overthrow the status quo." [10] Others distinguish between "dynamic" and "static" imperialism.

What sense is one to make from all these approaches to the meaning of imperialism? The basic problem is that acceptance of most such definitions is tantamount to accepting a particular line of argument. About model-building in economic or political theory it is often said: Tell me your assumptions and I will tell you your conclusions. The same may be said of many writers on imperialism—definition anticipates analysis.

Consider briefly just two prominent historical examples. Joseph Schumpeter in 1919 defined imperialism as "the objectless disposition on the part of a state to unlimited forcible expansion." [11] The key word here was "objectless," which denoted the absence of a clearly defined rational interest, thus suggesting that imperialistic expansion could be explained by neither economic nor political motivations. The basic reason, accordingly, could only be found in the sociological structure of states—which, not surprisingly, Schumpeter then purported to do. Similarly Lenin, writing three years before Schumpeter, claimed to find the main reason for imperialistic expansion in the nature of the capitalist system—but this was also not surprising, in view of his *definition* of imperialism as "the monopoly stage of capitalism." [12] The two, he said, were identical. But did this not imply that his analysis amounted to not much more than a tautology?

The difficulty with such definitions is that they are too restrictive. So also are definitions which limit themselves only to certain countries (e.g., maritime powers but not continental powers), or certain mechanisms of control (e.g., direct but not indirect), or countries with certain economic systems (e.g., capitalism but not socialism), or countries at a certain stage of expansionist ambitions (e.g., dynamic imperialism but not static imperialism). Narrowing the focus in this way does have one advantage, at least from the author's point of view: it often permits exclusion of all possible interpretations of imperialism other than his own. It is a useful means for prejudging explanations, and can also be employed to attack the policies of particular groups or states. All this is consistent with the polemical and ideological tone that usually surrounds most discussions of imperialism.

A distinct disadvantage to narrowing the focus in this way is, obviously, the risk of failure to include all the relevant variables. If a definition of imperialism is to be useful for general analytical purposes, it must first of all be comprehensive—that is, sufficiently broad to exhaust all possible subtypes or special cases. At the same time it must remain sufficiently concrete so as not to get lost in ambiguity or vague generalities.

Formally speaking, imperialism refers to a *relationship*. The relationship itself is *international*—between nations. But what is a nation? The meaning of this word, too, is notoriously elusive, at least in the English language. Essentially the term refers to a sociocultural or perceptual phenomenon. Nations are historical groups, social collectivities which have developed and continue to exhibit a strong sense of group belonging or homogeneity—feelings of cohesion, separateness, oneness. This is quite distinct from the idea of "country," which has basically geographical connotations; nations do not always occupy the particular territory considered peculiarly their own. It is also quite distinct from the idea of "state," which has essentially legal connotations. A nation may comprise part of a state or extend over several states. There are many nations lacking the legal organization and authority to participate in international politics. (In some respects nations are indistinguishable from tribes or certain religious sects.) Nevertheless, in popular parlance the words country, state, and nation are usually used synonymously (or in combination, e.g., nation-state), and for most analytical purposes it is not illegitimate to adhere to that practice. For the purposes of this study imperialism can be treated as a relationship among countries-cum-states-cum-nations. (Only occasionally will it be necessary to refer to relations between national groups within single countries or states as well.) It should be kept in mind, however, that it is especially in their guise as *nations* that these social collectivities are of importance to the general analysis.

It should also be noted that precisely because they are collectivities, nations are not unitary actors. Governments (even if they are representative) are not the only participants in world activities. Individual citizens of a nation also engage in international relations, and so do groups, organizations, and corporations. Obviously these are not all the same thing, even if they are all part of the same nation. To speak of relationships between nations as if they were monolithic entities, therefore, is really to indulge in a kind of verbal shorthand, justifiable solely on grounds of convenience. In fact, it matters a great deal whether a given relationship arises from interactions at the government level or at some lower level, as students of international relations are becoming increasingly aware.[13] Any analysis of imperialism must keep this distinction clear. As we shall soon see, it is not always easy to avoid the practice of simply referring to relations between nations. But the familiar figure of speech should never be allowed to obscure key differences among various levels of international interaction.

What particular kind of international relationship is imperialism about? The word can hardly refer to *all* relations between nations. Manifestly, it can refer only to a particular subset of relations. Specifically, imperialism refers to that kind of international relationship characterized by a particular *asymmetry*—the asymmetry of *dominance and dependence*. Nations are inherently unequal. Some are big, others are small. Some are industrial, others are agricultural. And some are rich while others are poor. International inequality is a fact of life. For the purposes of this study, what is most important about this fact of life is that it frequently, though by no means always, results in the effective subordination of some nations by others; that is, in the imposition of some sort of rule or control. Here we approach the irreducible core of meaning in the ambiguous word imperialism. Imperialism refers to those particular relationships between inherently unequal nations which involve effective subjugation, the *actual* exercise of influence over behavior. The concept is basically operational. Inequality is the necessary condition; *active* affirmation of superiority and inferiority is the logical condition of sufficiency. As George Lichtheim has written, "What counts is the relationship of domination *and* subjection." [14] Or as A. P. Thornton put it, "At its heart is the image of dominance, of power *asserted*." [15]

Conceptually, imperialism has to do not only with *form* of dominance, but with the *force(s)* giving rise to and maintaining the particular relationship as well. Definitionally, however, imperialism is indifferent as between alternative variations of such forms and forces. For example, given the existence of international inequality and the interactions of specific groups and organizations, imperial control may be imposed directly, through the extension of formal political sovereignty; or it may be accomplished indirectly, through informal diplomatic or military pressures or economic penetration. Likewise, the factors underlying and motivating this control may be economic in nature, in pursuit of material gain; or they may be something else, such as the pursuit of political power or influence or the securing of strategic outposts. Properly defined for analytical purposes such as ours, imperialism allows for all these potential forms and forces. It simply refers to *any relationship of effective domination or control, political or economic, direct or indirect, of one nation over another.*

This is not meant to suggest that the alternative variations of forms and forces are unimportant. In fact, they are the very meat of analysis. Some of the potential forms of imperialism may in practice be much more prevalent than others. Some of the forces underlying and motivating imperial relations may have much greater practical potency than others. And some particular forms may be much more closely associated with certain forces than with others. The problem is precisely this: to determine which forms are the most prevalent, which forces the most potent, and what their connections really are. That is what we shall be concerned with in the remainder of this book.

NOTES

1. Richard Koebner and Helmut D. Schmidt, *Imperialism: The Story and Significance of a Political Word, 1840–1960* (Cambridge: Cambridge University Press, 1964).

2. W. K. Hancock, *Survey of British Commonwealth Affairs*, vol. II, part I (London: Oxford University Press, 1940), p. 1.

3. Michael Barratt Brown, *After Imperialism*, rev. ed. (New York: Humanities Press, 1970), p. viii.

4. Pierre Jalée, *The Pillage of the Third World* (New York: Monthly Review Press, 1968), p. 15.

5. Richard D. Wolff, "Modern Imperialism: The View from the Metropolis," *American Economic Review* 60, no. 2 (May 1970): 225.

6. Paul M. Sweezy, *The Theory of Capitalist Development* (1942; reprint ed., New York: Monthly Review Press, 1968), p. 307.

7. Richard C. Edwards, Michael Reich, and Thomas E. Weisskopf, *The Capitalist System* (Englewood Cliffs, N.J.: Prentice-Hall, 1972), p. 408.

8. Hans Neisser, "Economic Imperialism Reconsidered," *Social Research* 27, no. 1 (Spring 1960): 63.

9. George H. Nadel and Perry Curtis, "Introduction," in Nadel and Curtis, eds., *Imperialism and Colonialism* (London: Macmillan, 1964), p. 1.

10. Hans J. Morgenthau, *Politics Among Nations*, 3rd ed. (New York: Alfred A. Knopf, 1960), p. 53.

11. Joseph Schumpeter, "The Sociology of Imperialisms," in Schumpeter, *Social Classes and Imperialism* (Cleveland: World Publishing Co., 1968), p. 6. See also chap. 2, this volume.

12. V. I. Lenin, *Imperialism, The Highest Stage of Capitalism* (Peking: Foreign Languages Press, 1965), p. 105. See also chap. 2, this volume.

13. See, e.g., the various essays collected in Robert O. Keohane and Joseph S. Nye, eds., *Transnational Relations and World Politics* (Cambridge: Harvard University Press, 1972).

14. George Lichtheim, *Imperialism* (New York: Frederick A. Praeger, 1971), p. 9. Emphasis supplied.

15. A. P. Thornton, *Doctrines of Imperialism* (New York: John Wiley & Sons, 1965), p. 2. Emphasis supplied.

II

CLASSICAL IMPERIALISM

•

Serious analysis of imperialism began almost as soon as the term itself first came into widespread use, toward the end of the nineteenth century. Interest was stimulated by one of the most singular events of recent history—the sudden and momentous expansion of European colonial empires after 1870. In the three decades before 1900 the major states of Europe added to their direct political control overseas more than ten million square miles of territory and nearly 150 million people—about a fifth of the world's land area and perhaps a tenth of its population. This was the "new imperialism," and its importance for Europeans and non-Europeans alike was never in doubt. What *was* in doubt were the reasons for the event: a number of alternative interpretations were developed to explain the origin and nature of this maritime colonial expansion and the motivations of its various participants. These were the classical theories of imperialism, which even today, despite the fact that they tended to be less than fully comprehensive—they excluded, for example, parallel cases of colonial expansion over contiguous land areas (see Chapter 3)—still form the basis for most thinking on the imperialist phenomenon. It is to this subject that we will now turn.

The Background

If there was a "new" imperialism, there must also have been an "old" imperialism. This was the European colonialism which had its origin in the "Age of Discovery" and persisted throughout most of the sixteenth and seventeenth centuries. The old imperialism peaked after the middle of the eighteenth century. By the middle of the nineteenth century existing formal empires seemed mostly in decay. Hence when the colonial impulse reignited in Europe after 1870, it seemed natural to label it "new" to distinguish it from the older phenomenon.

The Old Imperialism

Imperialism was never a European monopoly; the history of empires is as old as the history of man himself. But in modern times the master empire-builders have been most strikingly the Europeans.

The first great wave of European empire-building was based on the extension of military and naval power and was essentially commercial in nature. It began with the sea explorations of the Portuguese and Spanish in the second half of the fifteenth century. A number of innovations in the sciences of navigation, geography, and astronomy, as well as in shipbuilding and firearms, combined to alter significantly the technological balance between the European and non-European worlds. Adventurers and *conquistadors* went forth, and in their wake went Europe's merchants, quickly seizing upon opportunities to increase their business and profits. In turn, Europe's governments perceived the possibilities for increasing their own power and wealth. Commercial companies were chartered and financed, with military and naval expeditions frequently sent out after them to ensure political control of overseas territories. Gradually great colonial empires were established by the various maritime powers of western Europe.

At the heart of these developments was the doctrine of *mercantilism*—the philosophy and practice of governmental regulation of economic life to increase state power and security. This was the era of the rise of the nation-state. Throughout western Europe political authority was, for the first time, effectively gathered into the hands of central governments; monarchs and ministers were preoccupied with the question of how to increase the power of the state. Since national wealth was viewed as the foundation of national power, governmental controls soon dominated nearly every sector of the state's domestic economy. And since gold and silver were viewed as the most important form of national wealth, regulation was soon extended to the foreign-trade sector as well. Unless a country had gold or silver mines of its own, bullion could be accumulated by only one means—a surplus of exports over imports, a favorable balance of trade. Colonies were desirable in this respect because they afforded an opportunity to shut out commercial competition; they guaranteed exclusive access to untapped markets and sources of cheap materials (as well as, in some instances, direct sources of the precious metals themselves). Each state was determined to monopolize as many of these overseas mercantile opportunities as possible.

The first great mercantile state was Portugal, which rose to brief commercial ascendancy in the first half of the sixteenth century, conquering the Moluccas (Spice Islands) in the East Indies, Angola and Mozambique in Africa, Brazil in South America, and other scattered possessions. Portuguese sea power proved unequal to the task of maintaining such a far-flung empire, however, and a good number of the country's colonial monopolies were soon lost. Spain conquered most of the New World, as well as various Pacific Islands, but Spanish power also tended to decline after the second half of the sixteenth century. In the seventeenth century a large share of the trade with Spain's colonies was taken over by other Europeans.

In the first half of the seventeenth century the Netherlands rose to a position of global commercial and naval supremacy, conquering most of Portugal's possessions in the East Indies and establishing settlements on the Atlantic coasts of North and South America. Later France entered the contest as well, establishing colonial footholds in North America and India. But both the French and the Dutch were eventually bested by British sea power, with the result that by the middle of the eighteenth century it was Great Britain that held the most impressive collection of colonies, including much of North America, India, and the West Indies, as well as parts of Africa and the Pacific. The Dutch colonial empire was confined to the East Indies and the southern tip of Africa. The French colonial empire had all but disappeared.

This was the high-water mark of Europe's old imperialism. If there was a distinct turning point, it was 1776. That was the year of the American Declaration of Independence, when Britain's number of colonies overseas was suddenly reduced by the famous total of thirteen. In the ensuing decades this example was followed elsewhere. Spain and Portugal rapidly lost virtually all of their remaining possessions in Latin America; in the Caribbean, France lost Haiti. The old formal empires were clearly decaying.

More importantly, so was the doctrine of mercantilism that lay at the heart of the old imperialism. Significantly, 1776 also was the year of publication of Adam Smith's monumental *Wealth of Nations*. Smith decisively exposed the basic fallacies of mercantilist foreign-trade policies. National wealth, he demonstrated, was not gold and silver but the abundance of goods capable of satisfying human wants; the gain from trade was not the accumulation of bullion but the opportunity to take advantage of an international division of labor. Monopolistic regulation of foreign trade therefore was misguided. A more appropriate policy, according to Smith, would be one of free trade.

Smith also stressed the so-called "price-specie-flow mechanism" first described by David Hume in 1752. Mercantilist emphasis on a favorable trade balance, Hume had shown, was self-defeating. Any inflow of gold and silver (specie) was bound in time to inflate the level of prices at home, adversely affecting the relative competitiveness of exports and import-competing production, and eventually eliminating any surplus in the nation's balance of trade. Again the appropriate policy would be free trade rather than regulation.

Smith's laissez-faire doctrines soon caught on. By the middle of the nineteenth century, throughout northern and western Europe, the ascendance of the new liberalism was complete; mercantilist doctrines were in disrepute. In Britain the Navigation Acts and Corn Laws were repealed. On either side of the Channel public sentiment seemed to be running strongly in favor of free trade and against any further extension of colonial acquisitions. Many were convinced that the old imperialism had been neither justifiable nor worthwhile; political control of overseas markets and raw materials had simply been a wasteful and unprofitable extravagance. In some quarters there were even suggestions that the old formal empires be dissolved.

The New Imperialism

This period of relative disinterest did not last long. Suddenly after 1870 a new wave of empire-building began that was completely unprecedented in either speed or scope. Within the span of less than two generations the principal nations of Europe, later joined by the United States and Japan, partitioned virtually all of the Eastern Hemisphere among themselves. The new imperialism established the greatest empires in history.

The largest of these was the British. Britain had the most extensive empire to begin with, and in the end acquired the most new territory—some 4.75 million square miles populated by an estimated eighty-eight million people. Over three dozen

MAP 2–1.   British Empire—1914

Bermuda

Bahamas

Brit. Virgin Is.

Jamaica

Barbados

Tobago

Trinidad

Brit. Guiana

Gibraltar

Malta

Cyprus

Kuwait

Bahrain

Nepal

Sikkim

Egypt

India

Aden

Oman

Bhutan

Sudan

Hadhramaut

Somaliland

Gambia

Nigeria

Sierra Leone

Maldive Is.

Ceylon

Gold Coast

Uganda

Kenya

Zanzibar

Seychelles Is.

Nyasaland

Northern Rhodesia

Mauritius

Southern Rhodesia

Bechuanaland

Swaziland

Basutoland

This map includes colonies, protectorates, leaseholds, and other imperial arrangements, but excludes the self-governing dominions (Australia,
Canada, Newfoundland, New Zealand, and Union of
South Africa). Also excludes minor island dependencies.

*Condominium.

MAP 2–2.   Empires of France, Belgium, Italy,
Netherlands, and Spain—1914

Fr. Indochina

Neth. East Indies

New Hebrides* (Fr.)

New Caledonia (Fr.)

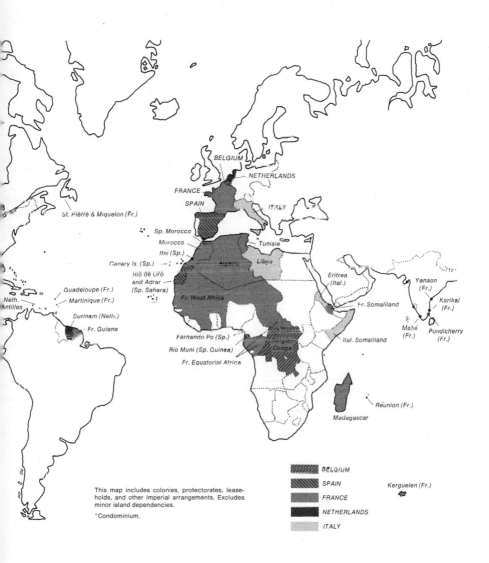

St. Pierre & Miquelon (Fr.)

BELGIUM

NETHERLANDS

FRANCE

SPAIN

ITALY

Sp. Morocco

Morocco

Ifni (Sp.)

Canary Is. (Sp.)

Rio de Oro
and Adrar
(Sp. Sahara)

Fr. West Africa

Algeria

Libya

Tunisia

Eritrea
(Ital.)

Fr. Somaliland

Ital. Somaliland

Guadeloupe (Fr.)

Martinique (Fr.)

Neth.
Antilles

Surinam (Neth.)

Fr. Guiana

Fernando Po (Sp.)

Rio Muni (Sp. Guinea)

Fr. Equatorial Africa

Belgian
Congo

Yanaon
(Fr.)

Karikal
(Fr.)

Mahé
(Fr.)

Pondicherry
(Fr.)

Réunion (Fr.)

Madagascar

This map includes colonies, protectorates, leaseholds, and other imperial arrangements. Excludes
minor island dependencies.

*Condominium.

BELGIUM

SPAIN

FRANCE

NETHERLANDS

ITALY

Kerguelen (Fr.)

MAP 2–3. Empires of the United States, Germany, Japan, and Portugal—1914

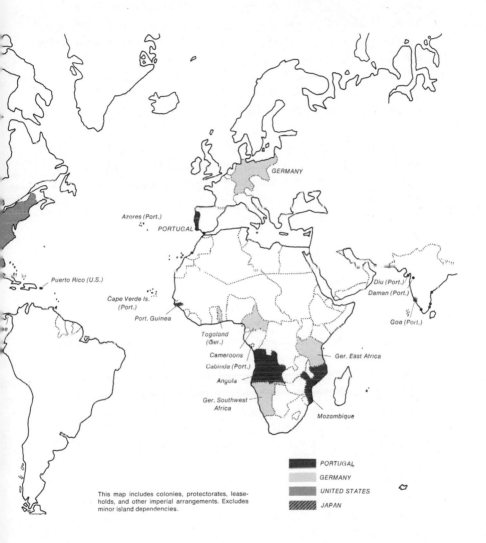

Azores (Port.)
PORTUGAL

GERMANY

Puerto Rico (U.S.)

Cape Verde Is.
(Port.)
Port. Guinea

Diu (Port.)
Daman (Port.)

Goa (Port.)

Togoland
(Ger.)
Cameroons
Cabinda (Port.)
Angola
Ger. Southwest
Africa

Ger. East Africa

Mozambique

This map includes colonies, protectorates, leaseholds, and other imperial arrangements. Excludes
minor island dependencies.

PORTUGAL
GERMANY
UNITED STATES
JAPAN

major acquisitions were involved, mostly in Africa, southern Asia, and the Far East. By 1900 the British Empire covered one-fifth of the land-area of the globe and included something like one-quarter of its population. This was truly an imperial domain on which the sun never set.

The second largest empire was created by the French, who gained control over 3.5 million square miles of territory with about twenty-six million inhabitants. Most of France's new dependencies were located in Africa and Indochina. Germany started late but managed to pick up a million square miles of territory with a population of thirteen million, mainly in Africa. Italy and Belgium also acquired African colonies. Toward the end of the century the United States and Japan also entered the contest, focusing their expansionist ambitions primarily in the area of the Pacific. By 1910 the rush was over. Maps 2–1 to 2–3 detail the holdings of the various imperial powers on the eve of World War I.

One of the most striking characteristics of the new imperialism was its belligerence and ruthlessness. The imperial powers typically pursued their various interests overseas in a blatantly aggressive fashion. Bloody, one-sided wars with local inhabitants of contested territories were commonplace; "sporting wars," Bismarck once called them. The powers themselves rarely came into direct military conflict, but competition among them was keen, and they were perpetually involved in various diplomatic crises. In contrast to the preceding years of comparative political calm, the period after 1870 was one of unaccustomed hostility and tension.

The principal prize in the struggle was Africa. This is where the new imperialism began. Indeed, in the minds of some the "Scramble for Africa" is what the new imperialism was all about, even though by the end of the nineteenth century Asia and the Pacific, and particularly China, were ultimately to displace the Dark Continent in Europe's ambitions and rivalries. In 1870 only a tenth of Africa was under European political control. Thirty years later barely a tenth (Liberia, Ethiopia) remained independent. The process began when Britain, France, Spain, and Portugal started to move inland from their scattered coastal footholds—essentially trading posts, relics of the old imperialism —to claim vast portions of the African interior. Soon Germany, Italy, and Belgium countered with rival claims. Clashes of interest were inevitable. In the west of Africa and in Egypt and the Sudan, Britain and France competed for predominance; in the east, Britain and Germany; in the north, France and Italy; in the northwest, France and Spain; in the Congo area, France and Belgium; and in the south, Britain, Germany, Portugal, and the Boer Republics. By 1898 most of these territorial conflicts were settled, mainly as a result of diplomatic bargains and with almost total disregard for the distribution of native populations. The South African question was finally resolved in the Boer War of 1899–1902.

In Asia and the Pacific, conflicts among the imperial powers were generally more open. Japan's colonies were gained principally through wars with China (1894) and Russia (1904–1905). Likewise, some of America's most important colonial acquisitions originated in the Spanish-American War of 1898. Britain, France, and Germany were also active rivals in southeastern Asia and Oceania, but the main arena of competition after the turn of the century was China. Here the great "battle of the concessions" took place, each of the major states trying to carve out as many spheres of influence as it could possibly manage. Perhaps the only thing that saved China from the fate that befell Africa was the stalemate created by the mutual jealousy and hostility of the imperial powers.

The Imperialism of Free Trade

Some writers have argued that the break in events around 1870 was more apparent than real—that the change was more in the methods of imperialism than in its substance. A main source of this viewpoint is a 1953 article by two English historians, Gallagher and Robinson.[1] According to them, the years prior to 1870 were no less disinterested in empire than the years following; the shift was only in the manner of colonial expansion, to formal from informal mechanisms of political control and influence. They called the earlier tactics the "imperialism of free trade."

The Gallagher and Robinson analysis focused explicitly on Britain, the home of the new doctrine of liberalism. What impressed them most was the seeming consistency of British imperial policy throughout the whole of the nineteenth century:

> Throughout, British governments worked to establish and maintain British paramountcy by whatever means best suited the circumstances of their diverse regions of interest. The aims of the mid-Victorians were no more "anti-imperialist" than their successors, though they were more often able to achieve them informally; and the late-Victorians were no more "imperialist" than their predecessors, even though they were driven to annex more often. British policy followed the principle of extending control informally if possible and formally if necessary. To label the one method "anti-imperialist" and the other "imperialist," is to ignore the fact that whatever the method British interests were steadily safeguarded and extended. The usual summing up of the policy of the free trade empire as "trade not rule" should read "trade with informal control if possible; trade with rule when necessary." [2]

There is much evidence for the Gallagher and Robinson thesis. Even at the height of free-trade sentiment the British government never completely observed laissez-faire principles. London was always prepared to intervene when necessary to open up commercial opportunities or to protect vital interests, using whatever means happened to be at its disposal. If possible, the government seemed to prefer indirect methods of influence. Treaties of free trade and friendship were a favorite tactic in South America, as well as in relations with the Ottoman Empire and with Persia; other instruments included cajolery, threat, the dangled loan, even occasionally blockade or bombardment. But in cases where all else failed, London was in fact willing to resort to outright territorial annexation. In the single decade 1841–1851 the British formally acquired New Zealand, the Gold Coast, Hong Kong, Natal, and three other new colonies. And in the next two decades control was extended as well to nine other major areas, including Kowloon, Sierra Leone, and the Transvaal. All of this empire-building occurred even before the new imperialism is supposed to have begun.

The British were not alone in this respect. Numerous parallel examples can be found in the history of Britain's main colonial rival, France. In 1815 French overseas possessions included just five Indian ports, French Guiana, and a few scattered islands. By 1870 control had been extended to Algeria, parts of Senegal and Indochina, New Caledonia, and Tahiti. Mexico might have been added, too, had Napoleon III been more competent at international intrigue. Even before the Scramble for Africa, France had begun to build the Second French Empire, just as the United States and Czarist Russia alike had begun their cross-continental thrusts prior to 1870. The only real exceptions were Germany and Italy, two recently united nations, and Japan, a new entrant on the international scene.

Thus there do seem to have been some elements of continuity as well as discontinuity in nineteenth-century imperial behavior, even though Gallagher and Robinson may have exaggerated the strictly commercial interest involved. The motives of power and prestige were of at least equal importance. The French, for instance, were animated first by an urge to rebuild their international status after the debacle of Waterloo, and the Americans and Russians were simply obeying the age-old impulse of strong nations to expand into a vacuum. Even the British had in mind considerations of a more general political or military nature. J. S. Galbraith has written of the imperialism of the "turbulent frontier." [3] British colonial governors in far-flung corners of the globe, charged with maintenance of order, could not remain blind to disturbances beyond their borders which threatened local security. Accordingly, pressures on them were intense to extend imperial authority and bring disorderly frontiers under control. However, this in turn created new border problems, calling for new territorial annexations. The result was a dynamism of expansion which had its own internal source of generation.

Even accepting this, the break in historical events around 1870 was quite extraordinary. The shift may have been more in the manner of expansion than in substance, but it was certainly spectacular. The problem of explanation has preoccupied several generations of historical analysts. Events of such sweep and magnitude could hardly be ignored. Over the years, and with a variety of motives, many writers have felt compelled to explain the renewal of formal empire-building after 1870—why it should have occurred at all, at that particular time, and to that great an extent. The result has been a proliferation of rival theories of the new imperialism.

The Economic Interpretation

From the beginning, most theories of the new imperialism tended to concentrate on economic considerations. All of the imperial powers, it was noted, shared a capitalist form of economic organization; moreover, all to a greater or lesser extent had begun to participate in the spreading industrial revolution. Since capitalism seemed to have reached a new stage of development, the source of the new imperialism seemed likely to lie in some flaw or dislocation within the capitalist system itself. The fundamental problem was in the presumed material needs of advanced capitalist societies—the need for cheap raw materials to feed their growing industrial complexes, for additional markets to consume their rising levels of production, and for investment outlets to absorb their rapidly accumulating capital.

The rush for colonies was supposed to be the response of these capitalist societies to one or another of these material needs. The new imperialism basically was supposed to be an economic phenomenon.

Two separate types of economic theory could be distinguished. One, the marxist type of theory, generally argued that the imperialist expansion was an inevitable product of capitalism, a necessary response to the internal contradictions generated by the capitalist mode of production. The other type, the so-called liberal (or, depending on one's point of view, radical) type of theory, generally denied this was so: the new imperialism was not a product of capitalism as such, but rather a response to certain maladjustments within the contemporary capitalist system which, given the proper will, could be corrected. Both themes were played in many variations. The best-known exponent of the marxist point of view was Lenin. Liberal theories had their origin in the writings of Hobson.

Until recently the economic interpretation of the new imperialism tended to dominate the field. Economic theories have certainly been the most influential of all historical explanations. Even today they remain dogma throughout a large part of the world, with many people still convinced that imperialism and economic imperialism are synonymous. With the wisdom of hindsight, however, we may be permitted to express a certain degree of skepticism about such narrow hypothetical constructs. Closer analysis reveals serious flaws in the economic interpretation as a general proposition; like most social theories which attempt to reduce reality to a single causative factor, it can be seriously faulted on grounds of excessive consistency and limited applicability. The truth was actually quite a bit more complex than many have thought. The details of the principal economic theories will be discussed and evaluated in the remainder of the present section of this chapter. Alternative interpretations of the new imperialism will be considered in the following two sections.

Intellectual Origins

All economic theories of the new imperialism, whether marxist or liberal, had a common intellectual source—the nineteenth-century doctrine of the *declining tendency of the rate of profit on capital*. Almost all economists of the nineteenth century assumed that the rate of profit in capitalist societies would tend to fall over the long term. They considered this a critical problem because, in their laissez-faire world, the progress of national economies was determined solely by the rate of private investment, which was in turn determined solely by the rate of private profit. If profits were high, savings would be invested and productive capacity would grow, but if profits were low, capital would not be accumulated and production would be static. A declining rate of profit therefore threatened a stagnation of all capitalist society. That threat hung over nineteenth-century discussions of political economy like a specter.

Significantly, the threat was always perceived just as a *tendency* of capitalism—not an inevitability. Potentially any number of counteracting forces might operate to sustain the rate of profit, at least temporarily. One of the most frequently mentioned was foreign trade and investment. Many economists of the nineteenth century recognized that the tendency of the profit rate to decline could be offset by gaining access to cheaper raw materials or foodstuffs abroad. Many also emphasized the usefulness of additional export markets or outlets for investments overseas. Few, however, insisted that trade or investment could take place only in *colonies;* no necessary connection was seen between the needs of capitalist society and the creation of colonial empires. Still, it should be clear just how easily the doctrine of the declining profit rate *could* eventually be transformed into a formal economic theory of imperialism.

Why should there have been this declining tendency of the

profit rate? Many different answers were offered by different nineteenth-century economists. Adam Smith attributed it to the excessive competition of capital within each country. Thomas Malthus blamed it on diminishing returns from investment on marginal lands as population growth strained food resources. John Stuart Mill put it down to limitations on each country's natural endowments. However, none of these arguments is directly applicable in the present context. From the point of view of later writers on the new imperialism, two other explanations tended to stand out more prominently. One has since become known as the underconsumption hypothesis. The other was Marx's unique contribution to the subject.

The *underconsumption hypothesis* was first developed by Simonde de Sismondi, a Swiss historian, and later elaborated by the German, Rodbertus.[4] The basic argument was really quite uncomplicated: highly developed capitalist economies simply tended to produce more than they could consume. The root cause of this tendency was the inadequate purchasing power of workers: labor was not paid enough by its capitalist employers to buy all that it produced. As population continued to grow, the expectation was that the real wages of workers would eventually tend toward some minimum level of subsistence. Capitalists, however, could not be expected to fill the gap in consumer demand, even though their purchasing power, based on profit income, was more than adequate. Since any individual's capacity to consume is limited, much of that income would necessarily be saved. But capitalists could be expected to seek to maintain the level of output, owing to the force of competition in the marketplace. Ultimately, therefore, there would be a tendency toward both oversaving and overproduction, and consequently a decline in the rate of profit over time.

One corollary of the underconsumption hypothesis should be obvious. If the root cause of underconsumption was inadequate wages for workers and oversaving by capitalists—in other words, a maldistributed income—then one possible solution might be redistribution of income. This much was clear even to Sismondi and Rodbertus, although neither was optimistic enough to think that such redistribution might occur spontaneously in their laissez-faire world. Sismondi laid much greater stress on the importance of finding new export markets overseas. Rodbertus thought the solution might lie in expanded foreign investment opportunities.

Marx, too, firmly believed in the doctrine of the declining rate of profit. His unique explanation emphasized what he called the *rising organic composition of capital*.[5] This referred to the increasing share of physical plant and equipment ("constant capital") and the decreasing share of wage payments to labor ("variable capital") in the total cost of production ("total capital"). Capitalists were driven by technological advance as well as by competition in the marketplace to reinvest profits continually in new physical capital. Accumulated capital, however, could not create economic value. Only labor could create value, and therefore profit. Accordingly, as total capital increasingly took the form of constant capital, and less the form of variable capital, which was the source of all profit, profit necessarily had to fall as a proportion of the total. Physical capital accumulation by definition meant a declining rate of profit.

For Marx, profit was defined as the difference between what workers were paid and the value of what they produced— "surplus value." The rate of profit was similarly defined as the ratio of surplus value to total production outlays; in Marx's notation,

rate of profit = s/C = $s/c + v$

where s = surplus value, C = total capital, c = constant capital, and v = variable capital. The tendency for the profit rate to decline as a result of a rising organic composition of capital followed directly from these definitions: with $c/c + v$ rising, and s derived from v alone, s/C had to fall.

Marx also incorporated the underconsumption hypothesis as a subsidiary theme in his general analysis of capitalism. But he specifically rejected this notion as the basis for his explanation of the declining rate of profit, because it implied that the fault lay with consumers within the general system of capitalism rather than with the capitalist system itself. The essence of the problem for Marx was the internal contradiction of the capitalist mode of production—the tendency for the physical stock of capital to grow too fast. This problem could not be solved simply by redistributing income; the distribution of income flowed directly from the essence of the capitalist process, so a maldistributed income was inevitable. Capitalism could not improve the purchasing power of workers and still remain capitalism.

Nevertheless, there were ways by which the capitalist system could manage, at least temporarily, to sustain the rate of profit on capital. Like other economists of the nineteenth century, Marx understood that the declining profit rate was just a tendency which could be offset for a long period of time by counteracting forces. One of these forces, he saw, might be trade with foreigners, and he specifically mentioned both access to cheap foodstuffs and the opportunity to sell profitably in overseas markets. However, Marx never carried through the logic of these arguments or of the alternative possibility of foreign investment, which he failed even to mention in this connection, to develop a formal economic theory of imperialism (understandably, since he died in 1883, only a short while after the new imperialism got started). This task was left to his socialist disciples.

Hobson

By all justice Marx's disciples, if not Marx himself, ought to have been the first to develop a formal economic theory of the new imperialism. Few were as eager to find fault with capitalism and imperialism; few had a greater sense of the economic interpretation of history. However, around the turn of the century marxists were still too preoccupied with the practical problems of socialist organization and tactics to turn their full attention to colonial expansion. Consequently, the field was left open for another—the English journalist and essayist John Hobson.

Hobson was no marxist disciple. He was, if anything, an economic heretic—radical from the point of view of prevailing orthodoxy, yet more in accord with the principles of liberalism than with the aims or ideas of socialism. Like any good nineteenth-century Englishman, Hobson believed in capitalism. But he refused to ignore what he considered distortions or maladjustments of the capitalist system. His major interest throughout his life was with the social and economic ills of Britain.

In 1900 Hobson went to South Africa as a journalist to cover the Boer War. The experience stunned him. Two years later he published his *Imperialism,* a passionate and forceful critique of the phenomenon of European, particularly British, empire-building.[6] Today this work is rightly regarded as a classic. In its own day, Hobson's became the most famous and influential of the many books then being written in the English language about the new imperialism. Essentially it was a tract for the times, rather than a serious study of the subject. Written with clarity and conviction, it struck a responsive chord in a public already profoundly disillusioned by Britain's bloody and rather shameful adventures in southern Africa. Liberal critics of capitalism and colonialism took it as the model for their own expositions; marxists also drew inspiration from its suggestive interpretation of events. In effect, Hobson invented the concept of economic imperialism. More than anyone else, he was responsible for the subsequent long pre-eminence of the economic interpretation of the new imperialism. His book offered the first general and systematic explanation linking late nineteenth-century colonial expansion with the dynamics of capitalist development.

The link, according to Hobson, was the problem of underconsumption. His intellectual heritage thus traced straight back to

Sismondi and Rodbertus. Capitalist powers were driven to become imperialist powers because of the tendency toward over-saving and overproduction.

Hobson dismissed the idea of any strong trade impulse behind the new imperialism. For him, the crucial issue was an undisposable surplus of capital. This was the "taproot" of imperialism.[7] "By far the most important economic factor in Imperialism is the influence relating to investments."[8] Capitalists were the source of all saving, but because of the inadequate purchasing power of the mass of workers, they had no place to invest it. Hence mature capitalist societies were doomed to stagnate unless they could assure themselves of sufficient outlets for investment. The renewed impulse toward colonial annexations, the Scramble for Africa, the Boer War—all were part of a global contest to monopolize markets for capital exports:

> It is not too much to say that the modern foreign policy of Great Britain has been primarily a struggle for profitable markets for investment. . . . What was true of Great Britain was true likewise of France, Germany, the United States, and of all countries in which modern capitalism had placed large surplus savings in the hands of a plutocracy or of a thrifty middle class.[9]

None of this was inevitable, however. In Hobson's view imperialism was not a necessary product of capitalism. It was merely a practical response to a certain maladjustment within the system at an advanced stage of development, namely the imbalance between savings and consumption arising from the unequal distribution of each nation's income—"the false economy of distribution," as he called it.[10] There *was* a remedy. If the problem lay in the inadequacy of labor's wages, then why not raise labor's share in the profits of capitalists?

> If the consuming public in this country raised its standard of consumption to keep pace with every rise of productive powers, there

could be no excess of goods or capital clamorous to use Imperialism in order to find markets. . . . [A]ll the savings that we made could find employment, if we chose, in home industries. . . .

The fallacy of the supposed inevitability of imperial expansion as a necessary outlet for progressive industry is now manifest. It is not industrial progress that demands the opening up of new markets and areas of investment, but maldistribution of consuming power which prevents the absorption of commodities and capital within the country. . . .

There is no necessity to open up new foreign markets; the home markets are capable of indefinite expansion. Whatever is produced in England can be consumed in England, provided that the "income" or power to demand commodities, is properly distributed.[11]

In the end, Hobson remained an optimist. The distortion of imperialism could be corrected within the framework of the capitalist system with a proper dose of rationality and reform. This was hardly likely to appeal much to marxist revolutionaries.

And the Marxists

Marxists have never denied their intellectual debt to Hobson, whose economic interpretation of the new imperialism gave them the key to their own approach to the problem. But marxists have never been able to share Hobson's optimism—not for them the temptations of the underconsumption hypothesis. Hobson's book and analytical outlook inspired a whole body of liberal theories of the new imperialism.[12] Marxist writers, however, drew their fundamental inspiration from a different source—Marx's notion of the rising organic composition of capital. For them, the new imperialism was not just a simple, reparable distortion in mature capitalism; it was an essential, inherent flaw. The only way to get rid of imperialism was to get rid of capitalism.

Unfortunately, beyond this fundamental proposition, marxists found it difficult to agree on a single explanation of the imperialist phenomenon. Almost as many theories were developed as there were marxists writing on the subject. In part this was because of Marx's failure to state a formal theory of his own, which left each of his disciples free to interpret events independently. Each, of course, regarded his own contribution as faithful to the way Marx himself would have viewed the situation. In time, two main traditions of marxist thought emerged—a minority view, best represented by the well-known German socialist Rosa Luxemburg, and a majority view, eventually codified in the writings of Lenin.[13]

The minority marxist view did not entirely reject the underconsumption hypothesis. Rather, elements of the notion were combined with Marx's rising organic composition of capital to lay principal stress on the *commercial* needs of capitalism. This approach received its fullest treatment in Rosa Luxemburg's *The Accumulation of Capital,* published in 1912. For Luxemburg, the main problem of capitalism was the lack of effective demand. How could the system continue to expand if workers lacked adequate purchasing power and capitalists limited their consumption of surplus value because of their ever-present drive for further accumulation of capital? Workers could not be expected to gain more in wages, nor could capitalists be expected to slow down their investments. The threat of overproduction, therefore, seemed chronic, with capitalism incapable of creating a sufficient market for itself within its own framework. The only solution appeared to be to seek markets elsewhere. The system could expand only if the surplus of production at home could be sold to noncapitalist economies abroad.

But would foreigners oblige to fill the gap in effective demand? By (marxist) definition, capitalist economies were characterized by a higher organic composition of capital than were less developed, noncapitalist economies. Since the manufactured products of the former, accordingly, embodied less value than the cheap foodstuffs and raw materials of the latter, why should the latter trade with the former? Why should the capitalist economies realize surplus value at their expense? Noncapitalist economies could not be expected to submit voluntarily to such a state of affairs; there was no advantage to it. Indeed, trade between them probably would not take place at all unless the capitalist economies took *control* of the noncapitalist economies and *forced* them to trade at these disadvantageous terms. Colonial annexation therefore had to be pursued if capitalism was to survive. Overseas empires had to be created in order to guarantee outlets for domestic overproduction. Here supposedly was the reason for the new imperialism.

Luxemburg's theory found support among a number of marxist writers (e.g., the German Fritz Sternberg and the Frenchman Lucian Laurat), but it was also severely attacked by many others. For the majority of Marx's disciples, underconsumption was beside the point. Marx's rising organic composition of capital alone sufficed to account for the new imperialist expansion. The principal reason lay not in the commercial needs of capitalism but in its *financial* needs—the requirement for profitable outlets for surplus capital.

The majority marxist view was largely the product of the Vienna school of socialists, which was active between the turn of the century and World War I. In particular it was the product of the writings of Rudolph Hilferding, who later rose to political prominence under the German Republic and was twice Finance Minister of Germany. His book, *Finance Capital*, published in 1910, was an immediate success, quickly becoming as famous and respected on the Continent as Hobson's *Imperialism* was in Great Britain. It was destined to become the decisive influence on Lenin's own thinking on the subject.

Hilferding's central concept was "finance capital"—a new stage of advanced capitalist development unforeseen by Marx himself. Marx had delineated only the earlier stages of capitalism. In its first stage, the system had been characterized by a comparatively high degree of competition in most industries. But this, according to Marx, was fated to change. The tendency for the rate of profit to fall, due to the rising organic composition of capital, would inevitably generate a two-sided consolidation of capital. First there would be the conventional accumulation of physical capital stock, as each capitalist attempted to rationalize production and make it more technologically efficient; this tendency toward larger-scale organization Marx called the "concentration" of capital. At the same time there would be a combination of capital stocks, as smaller capitalists were swallowed up by larger ones; Marx called this tendency toward fewer competitors the "centralization" of capital. Eventually only a minimum number of competitors, very large in size, would survive. At this point competitive capitalism would yield to monopoly capitalism, with the great industrialists playing the leading role. Marxists generally believe that this is an accurate description of what was actually happening in Europe and the United States at about the time of Marx's death.

Hilferding took the analysis one stage further, recognizing that the concentration and centralization of capital had meant the spread of the corporate form of organization, the development of securities markets, and, most importantly, an expansion of the role of banks in financing industrial growth. Marx had viewed banks merely as adjuncts to the production process. Hilferding, however, raised them to the very center of the picture. By virtue of their control over the sources of credit, he argued, banks had been able to set the direction of industrial development and to promote mergers and monopolies over which they themselves could establish dominance. Very soon they had actually replaced the great industrialists as the leading echelon of the capitalist class. Monopoly capitalism had quickly yielded to the new stage of finance capital—defined by Hilferding as "capital controlled by the banks and utilized by the industrialists."[14]

Since banks dealt in money rather than in commodities, their primary interest was in dividends rather than markets. What they wanted was the highest possible rate of profit on their capital. Since the rate of profit at home presumably tended to decline over time, finance capital was driven to find outlets for surplus capital abroad. The new imperialism was the natural result, as each country sought to establish exclusive domains for its own national investments overseas.

These ideas soon became the prevailing marxist orthodoxy. They were elaborated upon and refined by a variety of other writers, including Hilferding's fellow Viennese, Otto Bauer, the German Karl Kautsky, the Russian Nikolai Bukharin—and most importantly of all, the leader of the Russian Revolution, V. I. Lenin.

Lenin himself contributed relatively little to the evolution of imperialist theory. His analytical approach was taken almost entirely from Hilferding, as he ungrudgingly acknowledged. When his book [15] *Imperialism, the Highest Stage of Capitalism* was published in 1916, its dependence on Hilferding was clear:

> If it were necessary to give the briefest possible definition of imperialism we should have to say that imperialism is the monopoly stage of capitalism. . . . [A] definition of imperialism that will include the following five of its basic features: (1) the concentration of production and capital has developed to such a high stage that it has created monopolies which play a decisive role in economic life; (2) the merging of bank capital with industrial capital, and the creation, on the basis of this "finance capital," of a financial oligarchy; (3) the export of capital as distinguished from the export of commodities acquires exceptional importance; (4) the formation of international monopolist capitalist combines which share the world among themselves; and (5) the territorial division of the whole world among the biggest capitalist powers is completed.[16]

Despite its comparative lack of originality, Lenin's book soon surpassed Hilferding's in popularity among the faithful, eventually becoming the sole authority for most marxists everywhere. In part this was due to Lenin's extraordinary talent for exposition and polemics. Even more significantly, it was due to internecine conflicts within the international socialist movement, which in time left his writings as the only respectable source for marxist readers. After the Russian Revolution, Hilferding, Bauer, and Kautsky suffered the fate of denunciation as "rightists" and "revisionists," thus placing their printed works beyond the pale of discussion. And little was heard of Bukharin's ideas once he was purged at the hands of Lenin's successor, Stalin. Ultimately, only Lenin remained to represent the majority marxist view on the new imperialism. Today his book is doctrine in the world of socialist thought. Probably no other work on the subject —not even Hobson's—has had as great an influence.

Lenin's *Imperialism* was not conceived as an abstract scientific treatise. In fact, like most of his writings, its real purpose was quite a bit more practical—to set the disciples of Marx straight on the proper theoretical and tactical attitude to take toward the contemporary problem of imperialism. In effect it was a political pamphlet. Lenin saw the only purpose of theory as action. In 1916 the major European states were deep at war; his object was to pave the way for socialist revolution by correctly identifying the source of the conflict—supposedly the capitalist struggle for outlets for surplus capital. Over the previous half century the world had gradually been divided up among all the principal capitalist powers. But then, according to Lenin, pressures had begun to build up for repartition of investment domains, and ultimately these pressures had resulted in World War I—essentially a struggle for territory, an armed contest for hegemony and the redivision of colonial empires. For Lenin, such strife was an inevitable outcome of the process of capitalist development.

Marxists like Hilferding, Bauer, and Kautsky who had denied that this was the case were later denounced as rightists and revisionists. Their aim had been to suggest that imperialist struggle might not be a necessary *stage* of capitalist development; it might merely be a *policy* of the system, a matter of choice toward which the capitalist nations might be more or less inclined, depending on the circumstances. After Lenin this was considered heresy. (Ironically, Lenin and Luxemburg were on the same side on this issue.) Lenin used Kautsky as the chief foil for his argument. Kautsky had suggested in the German socialist newspaper, *Die Neue Zeit,* of which he was editor, that the capitalist nations were bound to recognize that such strife was a retrograde phenomenon which did not really serve their fundamental interests. They would see that rationality dictated a collective approach to the problem. Kautsky believed that capitalism did possess such rationality. He thought the system was perfectly capable of evolving toward a kind of global cartel among all the imperialist powers—a single world monopoly, or "ultraimperialism," as he called it. He asked:

> . . . Cannot the present imperialist policy be supplanted by a new, ultraimperialist policy, which will introduce the joint exploitation of the world by internationally united finance capital in place of the mutual rivalries of national finance capitals? Such a new phase of capitalism is at any rate conceivable. Can it be achieved? Sufficient premises are still lacking to enable us to answer this question.[17]

Lenin's answer was a definite no:

> It is sufficient to state this question clearly to make it impossible for any reply to be given other than in the negative; for any other basis under capitalism for the division of spheres of influence, of interests, of colonies, etc., than a calculation of the *strength* of the participants in the division, their general economic, financial, military strength, etc., is *in*conceivable. And the strength of these participants in the division does not change to an equal degree, for the *even* development of different undertakings, trusts, branches of industry, or countries is impossible under capitalism. Half a century ago Germany was a miserable, insignificant country, as far as her capitalist strength was concerned, compared with the strength of England at that time; Japan was the same compared with Russia. Is it "conceivable" that in ten or twenty years' time the relative strength

of the imperialist powers will have remained *un*changed? Absolutely inconceivable.[18]

This was Lenin's celebrated "law of uneven development," perhaps his only original contribution to the study of imperialism. Capitalism was incapable of evolving toward a stable ultra-imperialism, he said, because of the inherent characteristic of uneven development. Capitalist powers tended to grow at different rates; their balance of forces was constantly shifting. As a result, any alliances or understandings among them were bound to break down. Under the pressure of relative changes in their economic needs, periodic reallocation of their colonial empires would inevitably be required. But the claims of late-comers would naturally be resisted by older powers anxious to maintain the status quo, so imperialist war was inevitable. It was not a policy of capitalism which could conceivably be discarded, but a stage of capitalism that could not possibly be avoided.

Logical Validity

What a plethora of theories to choose from! Hobson, Luxemburg, Hilferding, Lenin—each had devoted followers; each painted a picture that seemed plausible in its content, profound in its insight. Together they ensured an enduring popularity for the economic interpretation of the new imperialism. Unfortunately, in most respects this popularity was not warranted. The elegance and simplicity of the economic interpretation are appealing, but the approach is superficial, unable to survive close analytical scrutiny. Validity is lacking at the levels both of logic and of empirical observation.

At the level of logic, what matters is the validity of either of the two alternative bases for the various economic theories—the underconsumption hypothesis or Marx's rising organic composition of capital.

The underconsumption hypothesis. The underconsumption hypothesis originated as a dissent from the prevailing liberal orthodoxy of the early and middle nineteenth century. Most economists following Adam Smith—the classical school of economists—subscribed to J. B. Say's famous "law of markets" which stated, in effect, that production always created its own consumers. Supply created its own demand; general overproduction was impossible. But why, asked observers such as Sismondi and Rodbertus, and later Hobson and his followers, was capitalism so prone to crisis and periodic unemployment? Perhaps production did not create its own consumers after all. Perhaps workers were not paid enough to buy up all they produced, and demand was *not* sufficient.

Expressed in this simplistic way, the underconsumption hypothesis was obviously fallacious and easily refuted. Effective demand included not just consumption expenditures by workers and capitalists, but capitalist investment as well. If capital accumulation was sufficient to absorb those resources not taken up by current consumption, then total output would be fully accounted for and employment would be sustained. Using modern notation:

$$Y = C + I = C + S$$

where Y = total production and income, C = consumption, I = investment, and S = saving. Production creates income. The sources of income are expenditures on consumption and investment, and the uses of income are consumption and saving. If capitalists choose to spend all their savings on capital goods (and workers are assumed to spend all of their meager wages on consumption, saving nothing at all), there can be no enduring problem of underconsumption or overproduction. Effective demand would be continuously sufficient.

Few underconsumption theorists were really quite so naive. Implicitly their analytical approach was rather more dynamic. They understood that capitalist investment was also a part of effective demand. But they also understood that capital accumulation created productive capacity, and if consumption expenditures failed to keep pace with it as total income grew, crisis and stagnation were inevitable. A widening gap between consumption and capacity could only be offset by an ever-rising level of investment. However, investment spending was hardly likely to keep up if prospects for sales were so poor. Capitalists were likely to hoard (i.e., not invest) their savings instead, and as a result aggregate expenditures would probably fall short of the total of aggregate output. Effective demand would *not* be continuously sufficient. This could be described as underconsumption, oversaving, or overproduction. In modern terminology it would be called a "deflationary gap"—a deficiency of desired spending relative to productive capacity, or, alternatively, a deficiency of desired investment relative to intended saving. Expressed in any of these ways, the underconsumptionists had a point.

The point can be rephrased as a question: What happens to consumption as income rises through time? Standard macroeconomic analysis assumes a stable functional relationship between consumption and income, both in the short term and in the long term. In the short term the connection is the marginal propensity to consume, the ratio of change of consumption to any associated change of income. (There is also a marginal propensity to save, defined similarly; the two add to unity.) In the long term the connection is the average propensity to consume, the ratio of total consumption to total income. (There is also a parallel average propensity to save; these two also add to unity.) The marginal propensity to consume is more important to Keynesian-type analysis of short-run stabilization problems. The average propensity to consume is more important to the kind of secular stagnation problem raised by the underconsumption hypothesis. What happens to the average propensity to consume through time in mature capitalist societies? If, as income grows, the level of consumption rises rapidly enough—that is, the average propensity to consume remains fairly stable or rises secularly —sufficient investment can be expected to be forthcoming to maintain the necessary total of effective demand. But if consumption rises too slowly—that is, the average propensity to consume tends to fall—investment will be inadequate and stagnation may set in. There is the nub of the issue.

For the underconsumptionists, consumption was indeed likely to rise too slowly, and the average propensity to consume likely to fall, because of the maldistribution of national income, thus making stagnation a very real threat. They have usually been stigmatized for this conclusion, but in fact, insofar as their strictly economic analysis of the question was concerned, they were probably correct. Assume a laissez-faire economy composed of capitalists (property-owning employers) and workers which is growing secularly. Capitalists and workers each earn wage and salary payments for productive labor. If total income consisted just of such "earned income," the distribution of income outstanding might never change over time. But total income includes property income ("unearned income") as well, which by definition here accrues only to capitalists. Moreover, also by definition, in a growing economy property income is constantly increasing, because the body of property is constantly increasing. The share of capitalists in total income, therefore, must necessarily rise. In the long run, the distribution of income will inevitably change to the detriment of workers.

Using formal notation,

$$Y = e_w + e_c + p$$

where Y = total income, e_w = the earned income of workers, e_c = the earned income of capitalists, and p = property income. The share of capitalists in total income is $e_c + p$. The proportionate share accruing to capitalists must necessarily rise as income grows, unless e_w increases more rapidly than $e_c + p$—an unlikely occurrence under laissez-faire conditions.

In the real world, workers also own some property. Formally, we should redefine total income as follows:

$$Y = e_w + e_c + p_w + p_c$$

where p_w = the property income of workers, and p_c = the property income of capitalists. However, this hardly affects the outcome of the argument. Owing to the markedly unequal distribution of property ownership in the real world, p_c is virtually certain to increase more rapidly than p_w; e_w, meanwhile, is not likely to increase very rapidly, if at all, in relation to e_c. Consequently, $e_w + p_w$ is almost certain to decline in relation to $e_c + p_c$. Other things being equal, the "natural" tendency of the income distribution in a capitalist world is to move strongly against workers.

Furthermore, it is reasonable to suppose that workers, being relatively poor, do not save much of their income, so it is unlikely that there can be much increase of their average propensity to consume as their share of income declines. At the same time we can expect that capitalists, being relatively rich, do save a considerable part of their income, and so as their share rises, their average propensity to consume will probably fall quite a bit. For the economy as a whole, consequently, the increasingly unequal distribution of income will probably mean a declining average propensity to consume. As income grows through time, consumption will tend to rise more slowly. The economy of a mature capitalist society will display an inherent tendency toward insufficient continuous effective demand—just as the underconsumptionists predicted.

The logic of the underconsumptionists' analysis was therefore perfectly valid, but only as strictly *economic* analysis. The underconsumptionists were good students of the economics of capitalism, and were correct in assuming that, left to itself, capitalism would tend to develop an increasingly unequal distribution of income. But they were poor students, unfortunately, of its politics: they failed to perceive that capitalism would not be left to itself. The underconsumption hypothesis implicitly assumed a significant *ceteris. paribus*—that the pattern of income shares would not be influenced by any noneconomic (political) factors. Yet in fact such factors did tend to operate, almost from the very beginning of the industrial revolution, to offset the capitalist system's "natural" maldistributive tendency. Capitalism proved to be quite amenable to reform of the income distribution.

Why should this have been so? It happened because the economic development of capitalism can—and usually does—influence the underlying power structure of capitalist society. There are two practical reasons for this extremely significant phenomenon. First, as industrial growth proceeds and total income rises, capitalists are not the only group to reap the ensuing benefits. Some other groups, such as farmers, skilled workers, independent professionals, and civil servants, also gain. Capitalists may benefit the most in absolute amount, but because of their initially inferior position other groups can improve their *relative* economic status. This in turn increases their relative bargaining strength within the system, political as well as economic.

Furthermore, as capitalism develops, the economic division of labor inevitably grows more intricate and specialized; the parts become ever more subtly interconnected and interdependent. As a consequence, total cooperation becomes increasingly vital if the system is to continue functioning smoothly. Those who benefit most from the system—presumably the capitalists—obviously have the most to lose if its operation is disrupted. Conversely, those with less to lose tend to gain a potential veto of sorts. This increases the relative bargaining strength of at least some interest groups within capitalist society.

For both of these reasons, changes in the power structure of capitalism do come about which are entirely endogenous to the operation of the political-economic system. In practice, strong internal pressures do arise to counter the "natural" tendency of the income distribution to move in favor of property-owning groups. Labor unions organize to fight for higher wages and social security legislation, farmers band together for higher prices and production subsidies, consumer-oriented groups lobby for antitrust and standards enforcement, and so on. Historically, workers and other nonpropertied groups in advanced capitalist economies did manage to maintain, and even increase, their share of aggregate income by such means. This was not accomplished without difficulty—capitalists were not philanthropists —but it *was* done. As a result, the average propensity to consume in such economies did not tend to decline significantly over long periods of time. All available evidence indicates that the consumption-income ratio in fact remained quite remarkably stable secularly.

In short, nineteenth-century capitalism did not show the marked tendency toward insufficient continuous effective demand expected of it by the underconsumptionists. This does not mean that the underconsumptionists were altogether wrong; indeed, as far as they went, they were quite right. They simply did not go far enough; their analysis was incomplete. Economic factors were considered, but the vital endogenous political consequences of the development of mature capitalism were overlooked. As a result, the conclusions of the underconsumptionist argument were off target. In a complete political-economic framework, the argument was logically invalid because too many important variables were left out.

For this reason, doubt is cast on the logical validity of the economic theories of the new imperialism that were derived from the underconsumptionist argument. Colonial annexation could not have been a response to a continuous insufficiency of effective demand if in fact demand was adequate (unless government perceptions were grossly erroneous). The imperialist rush abroad could not have been due to maldistribution of income at home if in fact strong domestic counterpressures were emerging. Liberal theorists such as Hobson at least admitted the *practicability* of internal income redistribution. They were not logically wrong in viewing imperialism and reform as alternatives; they simply miscalculated the probability of reform. Minority marxist theorists such as Rosa Luxemburg, however, were guilty of more than just miscalculating probabilities. For them reform was impossible, underconsumption inevitable. They were simply wrong.

But they were not alone. Lenin and others in the majority marxist view on imperialism, and even Marx himself, all denied the reformative capacity of capitalist society. In their view capitalism must necessarily grind down the workers and others like them; the system could not possibly operate to the benefit of the masses. However, this was only because they, like the underconsumptionists, insisted on concentrating exclusively on the economics of the matter, in which respect their insight was keen. With regard to the politics of the matter, they showed a real blind spot.

Marxist political analysis has always been based on a rather simple-minded theory of class. According to this tradition, government in any state exists solely for the purpose of guaranteeing a given set of property relations. In capitalist states this means that government is an instrument of the capitalist class, "a committee for managing the common affairs of the whole bourgeoisie," according to the Communist Manifesto. Furthermore, the capitalist class itself is perceived as a monolith, a united and integrated elite characterized by a common perception of its interests and objectives. This theory is the source of marxist pessimism concerning the reformative capacity of capitalist society. Capitalist government is by definition incapable of setting wrongs right.

Yet, historically, wrongs *were* set right. State power proved to be socially flexible, because the assumptions of marxist political theory simply were not realistic. The bourgeoisie was *not* a monolith, and the interests of different capitalists were not all the same, and were certainly not all identical with the interests of the various other, nonpropertied groups whose relative bargaining strength in the system gradually increased as capitalism developed. Moreover, governments did *not* concern themselves exclusively with the interests of just one class. They tended to concern themselves at least in equal measure with resolving and reconciling the conflicting interests of *all* groups with bargaining power within the system. Political rule, in short, was pluralistic. Governments were not the representative of a single elite; they were the mediator among all the elites. Marx and his disciples may have been good economic analysts, but they were poor political scientists.

Imperialism and the business cycle. One point about the new imperialism generally overlooked by the various economic theories was any possible relationship to the business cycles which were a regular feature of nineteenth-century life. Even if advanced capitalist societies showed no marked tendency toward insufficient *continuous* effective demand, there were certainly significant periods of *temporary* insufficiency and depression. Consequently, even if there was no inherent necessity in the system to offset a secular problem of underconsumption, there was often a need to offset a cyclical one. Something was needed to stabilize effective demand in the shorter term, and the solution might plausibly have been imperialism.

Even before the turn of the century, many economists understood the important function of overseas exports as an expedient to compensate for temporary deficiencies of effective demand at home. Foreign markets were recognized as a stimulant during periods of internal depression, a useful means for reviving capitalist expansion after a crisis. From this it might have been only a short step for liberal or marxist critics of capitalism to move to a theory of the new imperialism as a kind of regulator of the business cycle. The argument could have been quite simple: political control of markets assured their availability when needed, foreign colonies guaranteeing a convenient device for smoothing out domestic fluctuations. One could either have continued to emphasize the role of commercial exports, or have emphasized the role of exports of capital, with colonial empires serving as outlets for surplus savings temporarily unable to find profitable investment opportunities at home.

Such an argument would have been perfectly valid in logic, yet, surprisingly, no such theory was ever formally developed until as late as the 1950s. Perhaps this was because the logic was not strongly supported by the facts. On the other hand, similar difficulties hardly sufficed to deter other economic theories from being developed.

Commercial versus financial needs. One last point about the underconsumption hypothesis might be mentioned. Rosa Luxemburg used the idea to stress the commercial needs of capitalism: empires were guaranteed outlets for domestic overproduction. However, exports must be paid for. Where were the colonies to find the effective demand? They might have found it in their reserves of precious metals, but in the long run this was impossible except for colonies that happened to be producers of gold or silver bullion. Alternatively, they might make an equivalent sale of foodstuffs and raw materials to the imperialistic powers, but in the long run that was impossible, too. Certainly the imperialist powers wanted cheap foodstuffs and raw materials, but even more they presumably wanted a net export *surplus;* countries suffering from an excess of output owing to underconsumption at home would hardly have had an interest in *balance* of trade abroad. Accordingly, there was really only one possible way for colonies to get the necessary purchasing power —from capital imports. That is why Hobson and other liberal theorists, as well as the majority of marxist writers, stressed the financial rather than the commercial needs of capitalism. Ultimately it was capital export that was required by the logic of their arguments. Luxemburg chose to de-emphasize that particular theoretical point.

The rising organic composition of capital. If the underconsumption hypothesis was logically invalid, Marx's rival idea, the rising organic composition of capital, was even more so. Marx sincerely believed in the labor theory of value, which he borrowed from the early classical economists. But even by the time he was writing *Das Kapital,* most other analysts were already abandoning the notion. It was increasingly recognized that labor does not alone create value; wages represent just one of the components of total cost. In fact, *all* factors of production create value, physical capital included. The value of any commodity is simply a matter of exchange—the result of the conjunction of supply and demand in the marketplace. In similar fashion, the value of any factor, its rate of return, is also a matter of exchange. The rate of profit on capital depends on the effective demand for capital as well as on the available supply.

Marx concentrated exclusively on the supply side of capital, insisting that profit derived from labor alone. The rate of profit therefore had to decline over time. But if we admit that capital also creates value, then any such necessity logically disappears. It all depends on what is happening concurrently to the effective demand for capital. If technological change is occurring, or if population is growing, or if income is being redistributed to sustain the average propensity to consume, then demand for capital should rise at least as rapidly as supply. There should be no secular tendency toward a declining rate of profit. In fact, in the nineteenth century there was no such tendency precisely because just such demand influences were active. There was little practical justification for the pessimism of nineteenth-century economists about the profit rate on capital—and certainly none for Marx's. Accordingly, there was no logically valid basis for his disciples' later theories of the new imperialism.

Empirical Validity

At the level of empirical observation, it is the *predictive* value of any of the various economic theories of the new imperialism that is important for purposes of evaluation. How closely did their analyses correspond to fact? Although the two alternative bases used for rival liberal and marxist explanations were lacking in logical validity, the explanations themselves may have been perceptive. It is possible that imperialist expansion in the real world *was* motivated by commercial or financial needs, or both. Colonies *may* have been essential as export markets or as outlets for surplus capital, even if for causes *other* than underconsumption or the rising organic composition of capital. In other words, it is possible that the conclusions of the various economic theories *were* right—albeit for the wrong reasons.

Unfortunately, there is little evidence to back up such a line of defense. In the real world colonies rarely did assume the importance, either as markets or investment outlets, that the various economic theories would have us believe. The facts of history cast considerable doubt on the empirical validity of their analyses.

Commercial needs. Existing evidence does not suggest that colonies were ever of much importance for trading purposes. The economic theories assumed that the new imperialism was a direct reflection of the obsolescence of free-trade sentiment after the middle of the nineteenth century. Liberalism had proved to be a convenience mainly for the British, because of their head start in the industrial revolution; it was no accident that the greatest antimercantilist writers—Adam Smith, David Ricardo, John Stuart Mill—were all English subjects. But once such states as Germany and the United States, and later France and Japan, began to industrialize, competition for markets became increasingly keen. This not only accounted for the return to protectionism after 1870 in all the advanced capitalist countries (other than Britain); supposedly it was also responsible for the sudden return to colonialism. The new imperialism essentially is supposed to have been a revival of the old mercantilism. This was "neomercantilism." Colonial annexations would guarantee exclusive outlets for manufactured exports and access to cheap raw materials.

Unfortunately, the neomercantilism hypothesis is not supported by the facts. Most colonies were too poor to provide valuable markets for manufactured exports, and while some of them were suppliers of important industrial raw materials (e.g., metals, rubber, and fibers), their combined share of the world raw-materials markets always tended to remain relatively small. Trade rarely followed the flag, as even Hobson was forced to admit in the case of Britain:

> From the standpoint of the recent history of British trade there is no support for the dogma that "Trade follows the Flag." . . . Such evidence leads to the following conclusions bearing upon the economics of the new Imperialism. First, the external trade of Great Britain bore a small and diminishing proportion to its internal industry and trade. Secondly, of the external trade, that with British possessions bore a diminishing proportion to that with foreign countries. Thirdly, of the trade with British possessions the tropical trade, and in particular the trade with the new tropical possessions, was the smallest, least progressive, and most fluctuating in quantity, while it is lowest in the character of the goods which it embraces.[19]

The other imperial powers were no more dependent on colonial trade than Britain; in fact, because their imperial domains were less extensive than Britain's, they depended on it even less, as Table 2–1 demonstrates. Colonies never became the lucrative export markets that a revival of mercantilism might have suggested. Indeed, throughout the entire period of the new imperialism the major states continued to trade a good deal more with one another, and with other noncolonial areas (such as Latin America and Australasia), than they ever did with their own overseas territories. The reason was the inadequate purchasing power of most of the new acquisitions. As Hans Daalder has written: "Trade followed first of all not the flag, but effective demand."[20]

Colonies also never became *exclusive* markets (or sources). The major states never found it difficult to trade with the colo-

TABLE 2–1

Colonial Trade of the Main Imperial Powers, as a Share of Total Trade

	YEARS	IMPORTS (%)	EXPORTS (%)
Great Britain	1894–1903	21.27	30.42
	1904–1913	25.71	34.75
France	1894–1903	9.86	11.20
	1904–1913	10.58	12.61
Germany	1894–1903	0.10	0.35
	1904–1913	0.37	0.62
Italy	1894–1903	0.04	0.30
	1904–1913	0.21	1.55
Japan	1894–1903	1.66	2.72
	1904–1913	6.85	7.80

Source: Adapted from Grover Clark, *The Balance Sheets of Imperialism: Facts and Figures on Colonies* (New York: Columbia University Press, 1936).

nies of their rivals. Conversely, colonies always bought wherever cheapest, and sold their raw materials and foodstuffs freely to the highest bidder. Only two imperial powers, the United States and Japan, ever accounted for more than half the total trade of their overseas dependencies.[21]

Financial needs. There is also little evidence to suggest that colonies were ever of much importance for financial purposes, although massive capital exports were characteristic of the period.[22] The British alone invested abroad almost £2.5 billion ($12 billion) between 1870 and 1913. By the outbreak of World War I Britain's net foreign assets are reckoned to have reached a total of nearly £4 billion ($19.5 billion), representing something like a quarter of the total wealth of the country. After the early 1880s France and Germany also became substantial capital exporters. In the three decades before the war French foreign investments more than doubled, to forty-five billion francs ($8.6 billion), accounting for about 15 percent of national wealth. German foreign investments more than tripled, to perhaps twenty-eight billion marks ($6.7 billion), accounting for about 7.5 percent of national wealth. After the turn of the century the United States began to export capital on a significant scale as well. In 1914 American investments abroad totaled some $2.5 billion.

Hobson was the first to insist that there was a direct connection between these capital exports and the new imperialism. Focusing specifically on the British example, he listed all of Britain's colonial annexations between 1870 and the Boer War, and then drew attention to the outpouring of British foreign investments over the same period. The concurrence of the two phenomena, he suggested, must have been more than coincidence; the reason for the former surely must have originated in the requirement for the latter. In fact, this inference was not at all justified. It appeared to be plausible only because Hobson failed to distinguish carefully between the different destinations of British investments. Specifically, he made no attempt to determine approximately how much of the capital export had gone to colonies, and how much elsewhere. One scholar has called this an "intellectual conjuring trick":

> Convinced of the essential truth of his economic theory, he deceived the eye by the speed of his hand, creating the illusion that, of the two sets of statistics he held up, one was the cause of the other.[23]

Not much British capital was exported to colonies. Most went elsewhere—in particular, as Table 2–2 shows, to the United States and Latin America, and to the older self-governing dominions of the Empire (Canada, Newfoundland, Australia, and New Zealand). Of Britain's total of foreign investments outstanding in 1913, less than one-quarter was accounted for by the remainder of the British Empire, and of this, almost 90 percent was concentrated in just two areas, India and South Africa. These are hardly sufficient grounds for concluding that Brit-

TABLE 2–2

Geographical Distribution of British Foreign
Long-Term Investments, 1913

British Empire	47.3%
Canada and Newfoundland	13.7
Australia and New Zealand	11.1
South Africa	9.8
India	10.1
Other	2.6
Non-Empire	52.7
United States	20.1
Latin America	20.1
Europe	5.8
Other	6.7
Total	100.0

Source: Herbert Feis, *Europe, The World's Banker, 1870–1914* (New York: Norton, 1965).

ain's imperial drive was powered by a demand for new investment outlets, or for security for existing investments.

Speaking generally, there was really no close connection between capital exports in the nineteenth century and the new imperialism. Neither of the two other big capital exporters, France or Germany, invested much in their colonial empires. Table 2–3 indicates that other European states (in particular Russia, Austria-Hungary, and Turkey) received more than half of these two countries' total investments abroad; French and German colonies received probably less than a tenth. The United States also failed to invest significantly in its new overseas acquisitions (the bulk of American foreign investment went to Canada, Mexico, and Europe). On the other hand, some of the most aggressive imperial powers of the period were not capital exporters at all, but net capital importers. For Italy, Portugal, Russia, and Japan, the enduring pressure of an embarrassing surplus of capital could have played no role at all.

What about cyclical pressures of surplus capital? I suggested earlier that a plausible economic theory of the new imperialism

TABLE 2-3

Geographical Distribution of French and German
Foreign Long-Term Investments, 1914

	FRANCE (%)	GERMANY (%)
Europe	61.1	53.2
Russia	25.1	7.7
Austria-Hungary	4.9	12.8
Turkey	7.3	7.7
Other	23.8	25.0
Colonies	8.9	12.8 [a]
Other	30.0	34.0
Total	100.0	100.0

Source: Herbert Feis, *Europe, The World's Banker, 1870–1914* (New York: Norton, 1965).

[a] Includes other areas of Asia and Africa as well.

might have concentrated on the business cycle in nineteenth-century capitalism. In a 1953 article two economists, Zimmerman and Grumbach, did just that, arguing that colonial annexation provided a kind of automatism to compensate for temporary deficiencies of demand at home.[24] Their analysis stressed the role of capital exports, with statistical evidence taken mainly from the British experience between 1890 and 1910. Their findings were impressive: As such a hypothesis would predict, British home and foreign investment tended to be negatively correlated, and British foreign investments and foreign exports tended to be positively correlated. During depressions at home, when capital formation slowed down, investments tended to go abroad, and this led to additional exports, thus generating recovery of domestic activity. The only trouble with this analysis was that Zimmerman and Grumbach, like Hobson before them, failed to distinguish carefully between the different destinations of British capital and British exports. They did not differentiate between the Empire and other areas outside Europe and the United States generally, nor did they differentiate within the Empire between self-governing dominions and other constituents. In fact, as we have already seen, Britain's colonies never played an important role as importers of either home capital or home goods, so this analysis, too, was something of a conjuring trick.

Hilferding and Lenin attributed the alleged pressure of surplus capital to the arrival of capitalism at a new stage of development —the stage of finance capital, of industrial monopolies controlled and directed by the banks. This has been called a typically German theory; just as Hobson focused specifically on the British example, Hilferding and Lenin focused on Germany's. Their analytic construction was a fairly accurate description of the German economy after the turn of the century. However, Germany was hardly representative of the colonial powers. During the period of the new imperialism, neither Britain nor France was characterized by anything like the degree of industrial concentration in Germany; in neither country did the banking sector play anything like the role performed by the large German banks in financing national industrial development and overseas expansion. In both countries, in fact, financial interests were among the least favorably disposed of all domestic groups to further acquisition of colonies. Even in Germany itself the formation of domestic monopolies came mostly after the high point of imperialist expansion, rather than before. Here also the analysis has all the appearance of a conjuring trick.

Last Lines of Defense

The economic interpretation of the new imperialism has about it something of the *post hoc, ergo propter hoc* fallacy. The imperial powers were all *capitalist* countries, therefore capitalism must have caused the imperialist phenomenon. There is actually no support, either in logic or empirically, for the general proposition that advanced capitalist economies required colonies in order to sustain their long-term development. Neither Italy, Portugal, nor Russia, all active imperial powers, was at the time a mature capitalist society. None—nor even, in some respects,

France—was nearly so successful at development as Switzerland or the Scandinavian nations. Yet the Swiss and the Scandinavians managed quite well without benefit of colonial empires. All were able to locate markets and raw materials abroad without feeling compelled to monopolize them; the Swiss and the Swedes also made significant investments abroad without trying to secure them politically. Switzerland actually achieved the highest per capita foreign investment of any country in the world, and Sweden's foreign investments per capita were as high as France's.[25] These examples demonstrate that the new imperialism was hardly a *necessary* condition for capitalist development; the examples of Italy, Portugal, and other slow developers among the imperial powers suggest that it was not a *sufficient* condition, either.

Some authors have tried to save the economic interpretation by appeal to the "hypothetical alternative." So what if the Italians and Portuguese developed more slowly than the Swiss and the Swedes? Without colonies, they might have developed even more slowly; with colonies, Switzerland and Sweden might have grown more quickly. Plainly, there is no easy way to refute this kind of argument. It is like asking what history would have been had things been different. All that can be said is that the question of proof remains open.

The economic interpretation of the new imperialism has been called one of those "striking and colorful first approximations" that are a "besetting sin of economic historians."[26] Essentially the interpretation demonstrates the limits of historical gener-alization. Anyone so inclined can find examples of colonial annexation where commercial or financial interests predominated. Many times the object of conquest was manifestly to protect existing trading connections or investments, or else to open up fields for future trade and investment. Bismarck's takeover of the Cameroons in 1885, for instance, was a direct response to a request from two Hamburg trading firms for a colony in West Africa that would buy their excess output and supply them with needed raw materials. Similarly, France's protectorates over Tunisia (1881) and Morocco (1912) were established explicitly for the purpose of safeguarding the local investments of French financiers and bond holders. The British protectorate over Egypt, officially proclaimed in 1914 but informally initiated much earlier, also began ostensibly over the issue of debt default, and of course Britain's political involvement in southern Africa was essentially economic in origin. This involvement was the specific example that stimulated John Hobson's indignation. Leading investors in the Transvaal and Rhodesia—especially Cecil Rhodes himself—exerted a powerful personal influence on Britain's colonial policy. British gold and diamond interests were directly responsible for the outbreak of the Boer War, the "war for 45% dividends," as Lloyd George called it.[27] From this experience it was only a short step for Hobson to generalize about the phenomenon of the new imperialism as a whole.

It is equally easy to find evidence in the utterances of contemporary statesmen for an economic interpretation of the nineteenth-century expansion. King Leopold of Belgium repeatedly expressed his firm belief in the great profitability of colonies. (He had good reason, since he made millions from trade in rubber, ivory, and palm oil before his personal title over the Congo Free State, dating from 1885, was surrendered to the Belgian Government in 1908.) So did Joseph Chamberlain, for many years Colonial Secretary of Britain. Jules Ferry, twice Prime Minister of France, never tired of stressing the commercial and financial attractiveness of overseas territories:

> To rich countries colonies offer the most profitable field for the investment of capital. . . . France, which has always had a surplus of capital and has exported considerable quantities of it to foreign states—in fact, the export of capital made by this great and rich country must be counted in milliards of francs—I say that France has an interest in considering this side of the colonial question.
>
> But, gentlemen, there is another and more important side of this

question, which is far more important than what I have just been discussing. The colonial question is, for countries like ours which are, by the very character of their industry, tied to large exports, vital to the question of markets. . . . From this point of view . . . the foundation of a colony is the creation of a market.[28]

However, it is one thing to cite individual examples; it is quite another to elevate them into a universal law of history, as the various economic theories purported to do. There were just too many exceptions to disprove the rule. For every speech by a Chamberlain or a Ferry emphasizing the economic necessity for imperialism, there was another speech by some other statesman laying prior stress on diplomatic strategy or national prestige, or on the "white man's burden" or *"la mission civilisatrice."* Rudyard Kipling and the Christian missionaries were not unrepresentative of their time. Similarly, for every instance of a Cameroons or a Tunisia, for every Egypt or Rhodesia, there was some counter-example of annexation without the least claim of immediate economic value. Britain's takeovers in New Guinea and North Borneo, in Upper Burma and Bechuanaland, could hardly have been initiated in the expectation of instantaneous profit; neither could many of France's new colonial acquisitions in equatorial Africa, nor Germany's in the south Pacific. Such barren territories offered little in the way of current export or investment opportunities.

Of course, it may not have been current export or investment opportunities that mattered in these instances. A few authors have tried to save the economic interpretation as an historical generalization by appeal to more strategic considerations. Even if many of the territories acquired during the new imperialism were of little direct economic value, they can still be explained, it is argued, by economic considerations. Some were taken over simply to safeguard existing colonial holdings that *were* of economic value, as a defense against any encroachment by imperialist rivals. Paul Sweezy has called this the principle of "protective annexation." [29] Others were acquired simply to exploit any promise of *future* economic value, to pre-empt any imperialist rival, which Sweezy called the principle of "anticipatory annexation." Both principles are obviously reasonable, and such motives did often find expression in the context of nineteenth-century imperialism. Nevertheless, an attitude of skepticism is warranted. The evidence is strong that these motives frequently were used merely as a subterfuge to conceal more devious political or diplomatic objectives. Gallagher and Robinson have amply documented that often the "arguments of the so-called new imperialism were *ex post facto* justifications of advances, they were not the original reasons for making them." [30] Raymond Aron has observed:

> . . . [T]he actual relationship is most often the inverse of that accepted by the current theory of imperialism: the economic interests are only a pretext or a rationalization, whereas the profounder cause lies in the nations' will to power.[31]

Finally, as a last line of defense, other authors have tried to save the economic interpretation by appeal to the presumed class structure of capitalist societies. Even if capitalist economies per se did not require colonies for their development, the interests of certain individual capitalists, or groups of capitalists, or the bourgeoisie as a whole, may have depended on a policy of territorial expansion. The new imperialism thus may well have originated in the influence exerted by private pressure groups over their national governments. (Even Hobson was often prone to write in almost conspiratorial terms.) Plainly, there is no easy way to refute this kind of argument either. Class-based theories are notoriously difficult to subject to rational evaluation. Special interests were always involved in particular colonial adventures. The question is: Who used whom?

In some instances, profiteering capitalists seem to have been eminently successful in manipulating their governments into imperialist conquests; the Cameroons and other examples just cited come to mind. But such instances hardly suffice to prove that official policy was designed exclusively for the benefit of special interests. They could equally indicate that special interests were simply being used as convenient tools to accomplish the independent objectives of the state, and there is much evidence that this is actually the more accurate interpretation of the nineteenth-century experience. At times traders and investors were used as the instruments of diplomacy—rather than the other way around—by governments bent on empire-building for entirely different reasons. Commercial and, especially, financial connections were frequently promoted precisely in order to create pretexts for diplomatic or military intervention. A. J. P. Taylor has argued that French financiers were forced to invest in Morocco, for instance, much against their will, knowing they would lose their money, in order to pave the way for French political control.[32] And there is a strong possibility that British investments in Egypt were encouraged by the British government with much the same aim in mind. (Strategic concern with the Suez Canal was probably the paramount issue here.) At other times governments refused to extend their control over territories overseas despite intense lobbying by domestic interests. In 1884 the British Cabinet vetoed a proposed protectorate for Zululand: "I see the cabinet do not want more niggers," was one disappointed petitioner's reaction.[33] French traders and investors abroad often complained of a lack of cooperation from Paris. These examples indicate that, more often than not, the relationship between governments and capitalists was dominated by political rather than economic considerations. Where government and capitalist interests coincided, private profits were enhanced by public policy. But where government and capitalist interest diverged, it was ordinarily the state's purposes that ultimately prevailed. Eugene Staley concluded:

> Private investment interests have usually, in actual practice, been subordinated by governments to factors of general political or mili-

tary strategy which have a more direct bearing on power. Thus it is that private investors have received strong, even outrageously exaggerated governmental backing where they have been tools and agents of power and prestige politics; while other investors, whose projects seemed to run counter to the government's line of political endeavor, have experienced official indifference or even active opposition.[34]

The point is simply that economics cannot explain it all. It would be futile to deny that commercial and financial considerations were important in the new imperialism. But the importance of the economic variable should not be exaggerated. The fundamental explanation of nineteenth-century expansion lies elsewhere—as the citations above suggest, more in considerations of politics and of power. Here we approach the real heart of the matter.

The Sociological Interpretation

Before we delve into nineteenth-century politics, however, we must first make a brief detour to consider a possible alternative explanation of some major historical significance. This is the thesis initially proposed by the eminent Austrian (later American) economist, Joseph Schumpeter, in a classic essay entitled "The Sociology of Imperialisms," first published in the form of two long articles in 1918–1919.[35] Schumpeter's essay had the basic merit of assessing the new imperialism in the light of a longer view of history. What impressed him most was not the uniqueness of nineteenth-century expansion, but rather how much it shared with earlier, precapitalist experiences of empire-building. Capitalism could not have been the crucial factor; the determining cause must have been located elsewhere. For Schumpeter it was located in the social structure of nations.

In every nation, according to Schumpeter, there are remnants of classes which have long since lost their social function. Among the most important of these are the warrior classes in societies no longer seriously threatened by war. At a certain stage of national development a professional military is quite useful, as a means of establishing security both internally and at the borders. But beyond a certain point the need for a martial caste declines, even though a residue of its membership and, especially, of its mentality remains behind. Having outlived its role, the military, in casting about for a new purpose and activity, finds these in imperialism, in conquest and territorial expansion. It generates popular support for its imperialist impulse by capitalizing on culturally inherited attitudes—nationalistic memories of past military victories, the soldierly tradition, the pomp and glory of battle. Schumpeter saw imperialism as nothing more than an "atavism," a hereditary vestige of a past or passing age. Its explanation was sociological, not economic.

> The explanation lies . . . in the vital needs of situations that molded peoples and classes into warriors—if they wanted to avoid extinction—and in the fact that psychological dispositions and social structures acquired in the dim past in such situations, once firmly established, tend to maintain themselves and to continue in effect long after they have lost their meaning and their life-preserving function. . . . Imperialisms differ greatly in detail, but they all have at least these traits in common, turning them into a single phenomenon in the field of sociology. . . .
>
> Imperialism thus is atavistic in character. It falls into that large group of surviving features from earlier ages that play such an important part in every concrete social situation. In other words, it is an element that stems from the living conditions, not of the present, but of the past—or, put in terms of the economic interpretation of history, from past rather than present relations of production. It is an atavism in the social structure, in individual, psychological habits of emotional reaction.[36]

From this summary it is clear where Schumpeter's definition of imperialism, discussed briefly in Chapter 1, came from: if expansion was atavistic—nonrational, instinctive—then it was likely to be "objectless" and "unlimited" as well. However, this was a narrow conception of the problem, excluding all but the most virulent forms of empire-building. In the nineteenth century many colonies were acquired for quite explicit political or economic objectives; moreover, many of the imperial powers, and certainly the lesser among them such as Belgium or Portugal, had quite limited territorial ambitions. In fact, Schumpeter tried to account for too much. He did draw attention to a crucial contributory variable in the new imperialism. Undoubtedly a disposition to belligerence derived from a vestigial warrior-class social structure *did* figure prominently at the time. Military elements were able to gain an inordinate hold over public opinion, as well as governments, and thus created a jingoistic atmosphere in which a habit of colonial conquest could flourish. But the importance of this one variable should not be exaggerated. Schumpeter's approach cannot explain it all any more than the economic interpretation can.

Like the earlier books of Hobson and Lenin, Schumpeter's essay was essentially a tract for the times. One of its purposes was to warn the German people against considering any revival of militarism of the sort that had just brought on their defeat and humiliation. Another intention was to defend the liberal economic tradition, the classical school of capitalist economics, against the attacks of the Vienna school of socialists. The marxists were maintaining that capitalism inevitably produced imperialism, and Schumpeter vigorously disagreed. By arguing that imperialism was in reality an outgrowth of surviving precapitalist forms of social life, he tried to prove that capitalism could get along very well without such territorial expansion. Indeed, his argument was that capitalism was antithetical to imperialism, and fundamentally hostile to it. Capitalism was rationalistic, and since imperialism was irrational, a pure capitalist society would ultimately learn to reject it as costly and contrary to self-interest:

In a purely capitalist world, what was once energy for war becomes simply energy for labor of every kind. Wars of conquest and adventurism in foreign policy in general are bound to be regarded as troublesome distractions, destructive of life's meaning, a diversion from the accustomed and therefore "true" task.

A purely capitalist world therefore can offer no fertile soil to imperialist impulses. . . . [C]apitalism is by nature anti-imperialist.[37]

This sort of argument is bound to seem ridiculous to anyone dogmatically convinced of the symbiotic relationship between capitalism and imperialism. However, even to less categorical observers it is likely to appear overly sanguine. Certainly capitalism fosters rational inquiry and a predilection for cost accounting, but does this mean that what is rational for the system is rational for everyone in it? Not necessarily; that is the fallacy of composition. Capitalism means competition, which means uncertainty. A rational response to uncertainty is to seek security—security of markets, of sources of supply, and of outlets for investment. Colonial expansion may be perfectly consistent with logic and self-interest for the capitalists of any given country, even if it is not for the system as a whole. Capitalism therefore may indeed generate forces leading to imperialism and imperialistic conflicts. This is not meant to imply that capitalism *must* lead to imperialism; I have already made clear my belief that the evidence for such a proposition is seriously lacking. I only mean to deny that capitalism must lead away from imperialism. In this respect Schumpeter was, despite his acknowledged intellectual sophistication, just a bit naive.

The Political Interpretation

Schumpeter may have been wrong about the fundamental explanation of the new imperialism, but he was right to place it in a broader time perspective than did most of his contemporaries. Analysts writing more recently, with the advantage of a longer view of history, have recognized elements of continuity as well as discontinuity in nineteenth-century imperial behavior; Gallagher and Robinson have not been alone in stressing how much in common events after 1870 shared with preceding events. Today it is widely understood that the revival of formal empire-building had little to do with the presumed material needs of advanced capitalism. A new stage had been reached, not in the development of the economic system, but rather in the development of the *political* system. Here is the real heart of the matter.

Ever since the beginning of the mercantilist era, when the modern nation-state first made its appearance, Europe's political system had been characterized by a continuously shifting balance of power. The interests of each government were pursued within a general framework of ever-changing alliances and alignments; the independence of each government was assured by preventing any single state from so increasing its relative power as to threaten all the others. Nothing was immutable; combinations of countries were marked by shifting memberships, brief duration, and limited objectives. The significance of the balance-of-power system was that for the most part it managed quite successfully to resolve international conflicts—mainly because it was so strikingly flexible. This was especially true in the seventeenth and eighteenth centuries, when diplomatic influence and military strength were relatively evenly distributed among all the major states. Governments could change partners without radically upsetting the overall structure of relations. In fact, kings conducted foreign affairs as if they were playing a game of chess. This situation obtained into the nineteenth century, despite the fact that by the end of the Napoleonic Wars it was clear that industrial Britain had grown far beyond the capabilities of other powers. The flexibility of the traditional system could be maintained for a long time because the British played the role of "balancer," always ready to shift alignments temporarily in order to preserve the broader equilibrium of forces.

At the Congress of Vienna, for example, Britain joined with the other victorious powers—Austria, Prussia, Sweden, and Russia—in deflating the part of France in the European system. The French were obliged to renounce all claims of sovereignty outside their boundaries of 1792, as well as to cede a number of strategic posts to the allies. Yet by 1831 the British were joining with France, together with Russia, in intervening to assure the success of Greece's war of independence against the Ottoman Empire. In the 1830s and 1840s Britain and France cooperated in opposing Russia when the latter attempted to extend its power into the area of the Balkans. The British and French fought as partners in the Crimean War of 1854–1856. In this way Britain operated after 1815 to prevent the balance of forces from tipping too far in favor of any single European state.

This tactic could succeed only so long as Britain's position of pre-eminence within Europe continued unchallenged. Unfortunately, by midcentury that position was becoming increasingly precarious, owing to the rapid rise of the Kingdom of Prussia. Although the industrial revolution came late to the Prussians, they quickly developed the most powerful and dynamic economy on the continent, strong enough to provide a catalyst for unification of all the German states (apart from Austria) and to defeat in succession the Danes, the Austrians, and the French in a series of lightning wars. Pivotal here was the Franco-Prussian War of 1870, leading to the proclamation of the German Empire in 1871. That war's legacy—especially the problem of Alsace-Lorraine—imposed an irreconcilable strain on European relations, significantly reducing the flexibility of the alliance system. Other states were inevitably drawn into the political conflict between France and Germany, and this made it difficult for Britain to continue playing the role of balancer within a shifting set of alliances, since the British themselves were feeling menaced by the growing commercial and naval strength of the Germans. Gradually Europe divided into two fixed camps. The balance of power, once so fluid, became frozen.

With relations in Europe growing increasingly deadlocked, it was only to be expected that various states would look elsewhere for compensation or diplomatic advantage. Colonies grew more attractive as assets in the struggle for power. Territorial annexation could provide prestige, military bases, and pawns for diplomatic bargaining. Moreover, imperialist competition in the periphery could permit governments to confront one another without jeopardizing the integrity of the metropolitan center. It was a way of relieving tensions arising from stalemate nearer home. The evidence is strong that these considerations, more than anything else, accounted for the spectacular revival of empire-building after 1870. As Fieldhouse has observed, the main cause seems to have been the interaction of fears and rivalries in Europe:

> . . . [I]mperialism may best be seen as the extension into the periphery of the political struggle in Europe. At the centre the balance was so nicely adjusted that no positive action, no major change in the status or territory of either side was possible. Colonies thus became a means out of the impasse. . . . New worlds were brought into existence in the vain hope that they would maintain or redress the balance of the old.[38]

The French, in particular, were tempted to use colonial expansion to compensate for their defeat at the hands of the Germans: empire-building would help them to recover their sense of national glory and grandeur. The Germans and the Italians, both newly united and assertively nationalistic, were similarly determined to achieve equal status with the older imperial powers, their place in the imperial sun. And the Russians, too, unable to extend their hegemonic influence in the Balkans, turned to expansion in the direction of the Indian subcontinent and the Far East. In turn, all of these moves threatened longstanding British imperial interests at a time when Britain was also feeling increasingly isolated within Europe and threatened globally by the industrial and military development of Germany (and the United States). Not surprisingly, therefore, the British as well were driven into a renewed interest in empire, particularly in order to preserve the security of their sea routes around Africa to India. The contest for colonies became general.

What role did economic factors play in all this? Obviously, colonies were more than merely chips in a poker game; they offered potential advantages of a commercial or financial nature as well. Overseas annexations might help to promote the development of the domestic economy. However, as some of the citations above have suggested, and other sources tend to confirm,[39] in actual practice such considerations were usually subordinated to the broader requirements of political strategy. Colonial expansion was more a product of diplomatic rivalry than of the profit motive. The economic interest in empire generally succeeded the political motivation, rather than preceded it, material gain was conceived as a means of policy, not an end. It was in this sense that the new imperialism could truly be said to have been a revival of the old mercantilism. The overriding concern of the imperial states was not economics but national security—to use Richard Hammond's phrasing, "the good old game of power politics," in which the symbolic value of colonial ownership was no small element:

> If I were tempted to set up a rival doctrine of economic imperialism to that of Hobson and Lenin, my choice for prophet would be Veblen, the apostle of conspicuous consumption.[40]

The remark is apt. Preoccupation with national power and prestige can suffice to explain why even relatively immature capitalist countries like Italy, Portugal, and Russia chose to throw themselves into the imperial contest, while at the same time more highly developed but politically neutral states, such as Switzerland and Sweden, remained aloof. It can explain why

Britain annexed Upper Burma as well as Malaya; why France acquired numerous Pacific atolls as well as Indochina; why Germany and Italy were pleased to extend their sovereignty to barren stretches of Africa. It explains why the various economic theories fail as a general historical explanation. Economic considerations may have been important, but the new imperialism was much more fundamentally a political phenomenon.

NOTES

1. John Gallagher and Ronald Robinson, "The Imperialism of Free Trade," *Economic History Review*, 2nd ser., 6, no. 1 (August 1953): 1–15. See also Ronald Robinson and John Gallagher, *Africa and the Victorians* (New York: St. Martin's Press, 1961), chap. 1. For discussions, see Oliver MacDonagh, "The Anti-Imperialism of Free Trade," *Economic History Review*, 2nd ser., 14, no. 3 (April 1962): 489–501; D. C. M. Platt, "The Imperialism of Free Trade: Some Reservations," *Economic History Review*, 2nd ser., 21, no. 2 (August 1968): 296–306.

2. Gallagher and Robinson, "Imperialism of Free Trade," pp. 12–13.

3. John S. Galbraith, "The 'Turbulent Frontier' as a Factor in British Expansion," *Comparative Studies in Society and History* 2, no. 2 (January 1960): 150–168.

4. See E. M. Winslow, *The Pattern of Imperialism* (New York: Columbia University Press, 1948), pp. 77–91.

5. Marx's principal statements bearing on this subject are conveniently collected in Robert Freedman, ed., *Marx on Economics* (New York: Harcourt, Brace & Jovanovich, 1961), pp. 106–147. For discussions, see Winslow, *The Pattern of Imperialism*, chap. 6; Tom Kemp, *Theories of Imperialism* (London: Dobson Books, 1967), chap. 2. Winslow represents a nonmarxist point of view, Kemp one that is marxist.

6. John A. Hobson, *Imperialism: A Study* (Ann Arbor, Michigan: University of Michigan Press, 1965).

7. Ibid., p. 81.

8. Ibid., p. 51.

9. Ibid., pp. 53–54.

10. Ibid., p. 87.

11. Ibid., pp. 81, 85, 88.

12. See, e.g., Henry N. Brailsford, *The War of Steel and Gold* (London: Bell, 1914); Leonard S. Woolf, *Empire and Commerce in Africa: A Study in Economic Imperialism* (New York: Macmillan, 1919); Parker T. Moon, *Imperialism and World Politics* (New York: Macmillan, 1926).

13. For discussions of the various marxist schools of thought on imperialism, see Brynjolf J. Hovde, "Socialist Theories of Imperialism Prior to the Great War," *Journal of Political Economy* 36, no. 5 (October 1928): 569–591; E. M. Winslow, "Marxian, Liberal, and Sociological Theories of Im-

perialism," *Journal of Political Economy* 39, no. 6 (December 1931): 713–758; Winslow, *The Pattern of Imperialism*, chap. 7; Kemp, *Theories of Imperialism*, chaps. 4–5; George Lichtheim, *Imperialism* (New York: Frederick A. Praeger, 1971), chap. 7. Winslow's book also contains a useful bibliography of original sources.

14. As quoted in Winslow, *The Pattern of Imperialism*, p. 166.

15. V. I. Lenin, *Imperialism, The Highest Stage of Capitalism* (Peking: Foreign Languages Press, 1965).

16. Ibid., pp. 105–106.

17. As quoted in ibid., p. 142.

18. Ibid., p. 144.

19. Hobson, *Imperialism*, pp. 33, 39–40.

20. Hans Daalder, "Capitalism, Colonialism and the Underdeveloped Areas: The Political Economy of (Anti-) Imperialism," in Egbert de Vries, ed., *Essays on Unbalanced Growth: A Century of Disparity and Convergence* (The Hague: Mouton & Co., 1962), p. 141.

21. Frederick L. Schuman, *International Politics*, 4th ed. (New York: McGraw-Hill, 1948), p. 537.

22. The figures in this paragraph are consolidated from several sources, including A. K. Cairncross, *Home and Foreign Investment, 1870–1913* (Cambridge: Cambridge University Press, 1953), chap. 6; Herbert Feis, *Europe, The World's Banker, 1870–1914* (New York: Norton, 1965), pt. 1; Albert H. Imlah, *Economic Elements in the Pax Britannica* (Cambridge: Harvard University Press, 1958), pp. 70–75; Eugene Staley, *War and the Private Investor* (Chicago: University of Chicago Press, 1935), chap. 1.

23. D. K. Fieldhouse, "'Imperialism': An Historiographical Revision," *Economic History Review*, 2nd ser., 14, no. 2 (December 1961): 190.

24. Louis J. Zimmerman and F. Grumbach, "Saving, Investment, and Imperialism: A Reconsideration of the Theory of Imperialism," *Weltwirtschaftliches Archiv* 71, no. 1 (1953): 1–19.

25. Staley, *War and the Private Investor*, p. 14.

26. Richard J. Hammond, "Economic Imperialism: Sidelights on a Stereotype," *Journal of Economic History* 21, no. 4 (December 1961): 596.

27. As quoted in Schuman, *International Politics*, p. 519.

28. As quoted in D. K. Fieldhouse, ed., *The Theory of Capitalist Imperialism* (London: Longmans, 1967), p. 51.

29. Paul M. Sweezy, *The Theory of Capitalist Development* (1942; reprint ed., New York: Monthly Review Press, 1968), p. 303.

30. Robinson and Gallagher, *Africa and the Victorians*, p. 472.

31. Raymond Aron, "The Leninist Myth of Imperialism," *Partisan Review* 18, no. 6 (November–December 1951): 648.

32. A. J. P. Taylor, *Englishmen and Others* (London: Hamish Hamilton, 1956), p. 79.

33. As quoted in David S. Landes, "The Nature of Economic Imperialism," *Journal of Economic History* 21, no. 4 (December 1961): 507.

34. Staley, *War and the Private Investor*, pp. 361–362.

35. Joseph Schumpeter, "The Sociology of Imperialisms," in Schumpeter, *Social Classes and Imperialism* (Cleveland: World Publishing Co., 1968), pp. 1–98.

36. Ibid., pp. 64–65.
37. Ibid., pp. 69, 73.
38. Fieldhouse, " 'Imperialism': An Historiographical Revision," pp. 205–206.
39. See, e.g., Carlton J. H. Hayes, *A Generation of Materialism, 1871–1900* (New York: Harpers, 1941), chap. 6; Nicholas Mansergh, *The Coming of the First World War* (London: Longmans, 1949), chap. 3; Robinson and Gallagher, *Africa and the Victorians,* chap. 15.
40. Hammond, "Economic Imperialism," p. 596.

III

THE TRANSITION TO MODERN IMPERIALISM

The new imperialism did not last long. By the time World War I started, the expansion of colonial acquisitions was largely over; by the time World War II ended, most formal empires were in decay. Yet in the minds of many, imperialism is still characteristic of the relations between rich and poor countries. A vast body of literature has grown up in recent years to demonstrate the existence of modern imperialism, to explain its motivations and evaluate its effects. Separate issues raised by this literature will be considered here and in Chapters 4–6.

The Ebbing of the New Imperialism

The new imperialism was brought to an abrupt halt by World War I. The opening of hostilities marked the breakdown of the power balance in Europe, and attention quickly returned from the periphery to the metropolitan center. After the Great War, overseas colonies no longer seemed to have quite the same importance.

Of course, there was a considerable reshuffling of empires once the war was over. For the Central Powers one of the prices of defeat was loss of territory. The Ottoman Empire and Austria-Hungary both were stripped of their possessions as well as their pretensions. Their holdings in Europe were mainly granted independence. Former Ottoman territories in the Middle East were divided primarily between the French, who gained mandates over Syria and Lebanon, and the British, who were left in control of Palestine, Jordan, Iraq, and portions of the Arabian Peninsula, as well as Egypt and the Suez Canal. Germany lost all its overseas colonies. In Africa, Togoland and the Cameroons were divided between Britain and France; German East Africa was partitioned among Britain (the mandate of Tanganyika), Belgium (the mandate of Ruanda-Urundi), and Portugal (part of Mozambique); and German Southwest Africa was mandated to the Union of South Africa (which had gained self-governing dominion status within the British Empire only in 1907). In the Pacific, all German islands north of the Equator became Japanese mandates; all those to the south, mandates of Britain, Australia, and New Zealand. Kaiser-Wilhelmsland (German New Guinea) became an Australian mandate, and the port of Kiaochow, which had been seized by Japan in 1914, was returned to China in 1922.

Apart from these transfers there was really very little change in the status of colonial empires. During the next two decades the only significant acquisitions were made by Italy and Japan. The successful invasion and conquest of Ethiopia by the Italians in 1935–1936 avenged their earlier crushing defeat by the Ethiopians at the Battle of Aduwa in 1896—the one great African defeat of a European army during the era of the "sporting wars" —and resulted in the creation of a broad belt of Italian sovereignty in East Africa running from the Mediterranean to the Indian Ocean. Similarly, by invading China from 1931 on, the Japanese were able to add most of Manchuria to what was soon to become known formally as the "Greater East Asia Co-Prosperity Sphere." However, both of these expanding empires turned out to be remarkably short-lived, since all Italian and Japanese colonies were lost in World War II.

World War II proved to be a watershed for almost all of the old formal empires. The devastation of over half a decade of unrestrained hostilities had left most of the colonial powers exhausted and unable to sustain effective control over dispersed and distant dependencies. Local independence movements were encouraged by the demonstration that white imperialists did not possess inherent invincibility; the early victories of the Japanese had conclusively settled that question. Adding encouragement were the principles of self-determination learned in the universities of the mother countries and enunciated in the Charter of the United Nations, abetted by the spreading popularity of revolutionary ideologies. The result was a swelling tide of nationalism in Asia, Africa, and elsewhere. Gradually, over the course of the postwar period, this has become a virtually irresistible force in world politics. Imperial domains everywhere are being rapidly shrunk by decolonization.

In 1945 the largest imperial domain was still the British; it was also the first to be substantially reduced. As many as 600 million people—more than a quarter of the world's population—were ruled from London. Within three years almost two-thirds of them, living in the Indian subcontinent (India, Pakistan, and Ceylon) and Burma, were formally independent. Egypt and Iraq successfully asserted their freedom from British control during these same years; they were soon joined by Jordan and, after the partition of Palestine, by Israel. By the early 1950s the British could see the handwriting on the wall. In 1956–1957, the granting of sovereignty to the Sudan, Malaya, and Ghana (formerly the Gold Coast) began a series of largely peaceful emancipations which have since resulted in the addition of over three dozen new states to the world map. Today, apart from some scattered islands and primitive backwaters, not much remains of the empire on which, just a few years ago, the sun never set.

The second largest empire in 1945 was still France's, but this too was soon reduced—first by the departure of Syria and Lebanon, later by cession of French India to the new Indian Government, and then in 1954, after a disastrous struggle, by the loss of Indochina. In 1956 Tunisia and Morocco gained their independence following years of agitation, guerrilla fighting, and negotiations. By the time Charles de Gaulle came to power the necessary course was clear to many Frenchmen. A plebiscite in 1958 led to emancipation, first for Guinea (in 1958) and later (in 1960) for the rest of French Equatorial and West African possessions and Malagasy (Madagascar). In 1961 resistance to the Algerian independence movement was finally terminated as well. The second French Empire proved hardly more durable than the first.

The same story has been repeated elsewhere. Hardly any of the old empires has shown much evidence of durability. Japan's short-lived Co-Prosperity Sphere was divided up among Russia (southern Sakhalin, which had been lost to the Japanese in 1905, and the Kurile Islands), the United States (various Pacific islands), and China (Manchuria and other territories previously seized by Japan); Korea, partitioned, was given its independence. All of Italy's possessions eventually received their independence (Ethiopia, Libya, and Somalia). As early as 1946 the United States transferred formal sovereignty to a major dependency, the Philippines; two others, Alaska and Hawaii, have since been absorbed as states in the union. Okinawa and the other Ryukyu Islands were returned to Japan in 1971. Immediately after the war the Dutch lost the jewel of their empire, Indonesia (the East Indies). Later the Belgians gave up all their African holdings (Zaire, Burundi, and Rwanda), and more recently even the Spanish have begun the process of decolonization (Equatorial Guinea).

The expansion of colonial domains which began so suddenly a century ago seems now to be subsiding with even greater speed. It is difficult to exaggerate how extraordinary this transformation has been. After 1870 the new imperialism flooded the

The Remnants of the British Empire, 1972 [1]

AMERICA	AFRICA
Bahamas Bermuda British Honduras (Belize) British Virgin Islands West Indies Associated States 　(Windward and Leeward 　Islands)	Rhodesia [2] Seychelles Islands
	EUROPE
	Gibraltar
OCEANIA	**ASIA**
Brunei Gilbert and Ellice Islands New Hebrides (condominium) Solomon Islands	Hong Kong

The Remnants of the Other Maritime Empires, 1972 [1]

FRANCE	PORTUGAL
French Guiana Guadeloupe Kerguelen Martinique New Caledonia New Hebrides (condominium) Réunion St. Pierre and Miquelon French Territory of the Afars 　and the Isas (French 　Somaliland)	Angola Azores Cape Verde Islands Macao Mozambique Portuguese Guinea Portuguese Timor
	SPAIN
	Canary Islands Ifni Rio de Oro and Adrar (Spanish 　Sahara)
UNITED STATES	
Guam Midway Panama Canal Zone Puerto Rico Samoa U.S. Trust Territory of the Pacific 　Islands (includes Mariana, 　Marshall, and Caroline Islands) U.S. Virgin Islands	**AUSTRALIA**
	New Guinea Trust Territory Papua
	NETHERLANDS
	Netherlands Antilles Surinam
	SOUTH AFRICA
	South West Africa (Namibia)

[1] Includes colonies, protectorates, leaseholds, trust territories, and other imperial arrangements. Excludes minor island dependencies.

[2] Rhodesia (formerly Southern Rhodesia) unilaterally declared independence on November 11, 1965. Britain still considers Rhodesia a colony.

world like a tidal wave. Now it is swiftly ebbing, and in its wake more than 800 million people have won their independence, more than sixty new states have been created. Never in recorded history has there been such a spectacular political emancipation as in the past three decades.

To be sure, there are still numerous colonies (see the list on page 87). Portugal continues to stand fast against dissolution of its foreign empire, its only losses so far having been in India. South Africa refuses to loosen its grip over Southwest Africa (now called Namibia by many), and most of the other old imperial powers still do maintain their hold on various scattered possessions. But the great majority of these dependencies are really just fossil remnants. Some are so small and insignificant, or primitive, that the idea of giving them independence scarcely seems realistic; others are scheduled for emancipation as soon as it becomes practicable. Even the Portuguese and South Africans are finding it increasingly difficult to resist the force of rising nationalism. The moral is simple: the day of the overseas colony —the maritime empire—is over.

The Persistence of Imperialist Forms

Does this mean that imperialism is dead? Not at all; imperialism is still alive and well and living in almost every part of the globe. A large number of writers in recent years have emphasized the persistence of imperialist forms in the modern world.

The Political Form

Some writers object to the traditional emphasis on *maritime* empires, to the exclusion of other varieties of political subjugation. They argue—and I would agree—that it was only an historical accident that most of the great colonial domains of the last century happened to be extended over intervening bodies of water. It is equally imperialistic to extend political sovereignty over *contiguous* land areas; in the ancient world almost all empires were built up in this way. One could cite the Chinese, Persians, Incas, Arabs, Mongols, or Ottomans, among others, as practicing an elementary form of imperialism.

A modern example that is frequently cited is Russia.[1] Under the Czars during the nineteenth century, Russia's dominions were expanded to include nearly all of central and east Asia; when the revolution came in 1917, more than half of the population inherited by the new Soviet Government was non-Russian in origin. This expansion has been continued since 1917 under the Soviets themselves. During World War II Russia annexed large chunks of eastern Europe, including the formerly sovereign Baltic states of Estonia, Latvia, and Lithuania (all three had been Czarist domains before 1917). After the war, control was extended to Russia's new communist neighbors as well. Of course, control there has taken the form of indirect rather than direct political rule, but as the military interventions in East Germany in 1953, Hungary in 1956, and Czechoslovakia in 1968 served to demonstrate, Soviet dominance is nonetheless effective. The celebrated Brezhnev Doctrine gave the Russians no less authority in their eastern European empire than the old maritime imperial powers enjoyed in their own foreign domains.

Of course the Russians—as well as their supporters among marxists elsewhere—deny that any of their activities have been in the least imperialistic. By definition, imperialism is only what capitalists do. In fact, the Russians claim to be the leaders of a world-wide movement *against* all imperialistic vestiges. The various non-Russian peoples inherited by the Bolsheviks in 1917 were not denied national independence, according to the Soviet version of history; they chose voluntarily to remain within the new Union of Soviet Socialist Republics. And the same is supposed to apply to the Baltic states and other territories incorporated after World War II. Domination of eastern Europe since the war is justified on the grounds that a ring of buffer states is needed to protect the homeland of the communist revolution against any threat from the capitalist world. Military interventions and the Brezhnev Doctrine were necessary to counter any capitalist counterrevolution.

What we have here is plainly an ideological exercise. The Russians and their supporters are using imperialism to mean only what they prefer it to mean; this is propaganda, pure and simple. A more technical meaning of the term was offered in Chapter 1. By that definition, Soviet actions to prevent national self-determination or to limit the sovereignty of national groups, either domestically or in contiguous territories, must qualify for description as imperialistic.

Not that the Russians are alone in such behavior. There are numerous contemporary examples of similar imperialistic practices elsewhere. The tactic of dominating and subordinating buffer states is as old as the nation-state system itself. Nazi Germany used it to great effect in the interwar period; all the great powers use it today. Likewise, there have always been national groups either unable or unwilling to assimilate themselves within larger political entities. The Habsburgs and the Ottomans built their empires precisely out of such disparate nationalities. In the modern world, campaigns have been waged by a variety of domestic peoples against what they considered dependent or colonial status—the Kurds in Iraq, the Biafrans in Nigeria, the Tibetans in China, the Bengalis in Pakistan, and the Québécois in Canada, are a few examples.

Perhaps the country most like the Soviet Union in this respect is the United States. This country also spent most of the nineteenth century expanding into contiguous land areas; in our history we too have incorporated, though not assimilated, whole indigenous populations. How different was the fate of the Navajo or the Seminoles (or the blacks brought from Africa, for that matter) from that of the Kazakhs or the Uzbeks? Likewise, this country has always employed the principle of buffer states. In some respects the whole of the Western Hemisphere has been treated as one great buffer state. Following proclamation of the Monroe Doctrine in 1823, many of the new republics of Latin America were gradually reduced to the status of clients of the United States. Whenever North American dominance seemed in jeopardy, Washington did not hesitate to send in the Marines to take control. Santo Domingo in 1965 was only the latest of a long series of U.S. military interventions in the Caribbean or in Central America, usually justified on the grounds of ensuring law and order or preserving democracy and freedom. But the American Government has always denied any implication of U.S. imperialism. Has this country not always opposed the building of empires in the Western Hemisphere or anywhere else? Have we not always favored decolonization by the old maritime imperial powers? Our behavior has always been that of a good neighbor, helping others out in time of trouble.

This is again an ideological exercise with the ring of propaganda. The American Government, like Russia and its supporters, also tends to give imperialism only the meaning it prefers. Using the more technical definition offered in Chapter 1, U.S. behavior over the years in Latin America certainly qualifies for description as imperialistic.

In fact, today both the United States and Russia manage blocs of client states, spheres of influence, which can be described as imperialistic. Spheres of influence, areas dominated by the interests of a foreign power, have always been a familiar feature of the nation-state system. In this respect America and the Soviet Union are simply adhering to a long tradition. Following history's example, each has developed a variety of means for ensuring indirect political rule over smaller, potentially important states which are not necessarily contiguous. The United States relies heavily on instruments such as its foreign-aid program to promote interests abroad; the range of countries subject to America's hegemonic power stretches from Korea to Iran to Greece to Brazil. Many authors now take for granted the existence of an "American empire." [2] Russia's main instrument of dominance is its program of arms sales, by which means influence has been extended to a number of Arab states, and more recently to India. During the India-Pakistan war in late 1971, Communist China repeatedly charged the Russians with imperialism for their role in arming and backing India. Since Russia was a "socialist" state, this was "social imperialism." According to the Chinese ambassador to the United Nations:

> This is a naked revelation of the role played by Soviet social imperialism.
> This is exactly the same tactic it has used in the Middle East. The Soviet social imperialists are carrying out aggression, control, subversion and expansion everywhere.[3]

The point is simply that *any* action which involves the political domination or control of one country over another, or of one national group within a country over another, must for our purposes be labeled imperialistic. This is much more substantive than just an issue of semantics. If the term imperialism is limited to maritime empires, analysis runs the risk of being incomplete. Colonies overseas are but one special case of a much more general social phenomenon; political dependencies at home or beyond the borders, of which there seem to be numerous examples, are of equal importance. The problem is national oppression or subjugation, the subordination of one nation by another. No specific type can be ignored. From the point of view of the present study, what is significant about these alternative types is that they can all be readily accounted for within a single analytical framework. The underlying forces in all such cases are very much the same. The argument for this proposition will be made clear in the final chapter of this book.

The Economic Form

First, however, we must address ourselves to another, more controversial form of imperialism in the modern world—*economic* imperialism, the economic domination or control of one country over another. In the opinion of many, this is a virulent and persistent form of imperialism, perhaps the *only* form of imperialism. As mentioned in Chapter 2, a large number of writers still continue to treat imperialism and economic imperialism as synonymous.[4]

Most prominent among such writers are the marxists, but they are not alone. One also finds the "radical" economists, a comparatively new group of critics of the existing capitalist order. Modern radical economics originated after World War II. In the former colonial areas it developed under the pressure of demand for rapid economic growth; in the United States, Europe, and Japan, it grew out of the New Left movement of the later 1950s and early 1960s. Modern radical economics differs from the old left in a number of respects, especially in eschewing the marxists' traditional jargon and concepts; its inspiration is derived from a considerably broader range of sources than merely Marx and Lenin. At the same time the new radicals share much with the marxist tradition—in particular an inherent revolutionary bias and pessimism about the alleged evils of the capitalist system. Capitalism itself must be replaced. Certain consequences grow inevitably out of the contradictions of capitalism which cannot be remedied by ordinary reforms, and one of the worst of these consequences is the phenomenon of modern economic imperialism.

Radical and marxist authors attach no particular significance to the ebbing of the new imperialism after World War II. Like Gallagher and Robinson writing about the nineteenth century, they argue that the break in events since 1945 has been more apparent than real—that the change has been more in the methods of imperialism than in its actual substance. Behind the veil of nominal independence, imperial dominance continues with a different form. Control is now exercised informally, rather than formally, and the main form of this control is economic penetration—connections of trade and investment. For such writers this is the true essence of imperialism in the modern world.

Conventional analysis assumes that trade and investment relations between rich and poor countries are generally (though not always) mutually beneficial. Not so, however, marxist or radical analysis, which sees all of the gain necessarily going to the rich. Indeed, the only reason trade and investment take place at all is to satisfy the presumed material needs of advanced capitalist societies and their monopolistic corporations. The idea is to keep the poor in their place within the world capitalist nexus. Toward this end corporations and governments use trade and investment (and foreign aid) to subordinate the development of former colonies and make them so dependent economically that their newly won political sovereignty will remain more illusion than reality. *Effective* sovereignty still remains where it always has, with the former colonialists.

This is generally referred to as a policy of "neocolonialism" or "neoimperialism":

> [N]eo-colonialist policy is first and foremost designed to prevent the newly independent countries from consolidating their political independence and thus to keep them economically dependent and securely in the world capitalist system. In the pure case of neocolonialism, the allocation of economic resources, investment effort, legal and ideological structures, and other features of the old society remain unchanged—with the single exception of the substitution of "internal colonialism" for formal colonialism, that is, the transfer of power to the domestic ruling classes by their former colonial masters. Independence has thus been achieved on conditions which are irrelevant to the basic needs of the society, and represents a part-denial of real sovereignty, and a part-continuation of disunity within the society. The most important branch of the theory of neo-colonialism is therefore the theory of economic imperialism.[5]

Many writers cite with approval the definition proposed by Kwame Nkrumah:

> The essence of neo-colonialism is that the State which is subject to it is, in theory, independent and has all the outward trappings of

international sovereignty. In reality its economic system and thus its internal policy is directed from outside.[6]

The main neocolonialist power today is said to be the United States. We are by far the richest capitalist power in the world. Our network of trading connections is the broadest, our foreign investments the most extensive. Here supposedly are the bones and sinew of what is called the "American empire." What does it matter that we have few formal colonies? American imperialism has never depended on direct extension of political sovereignty. Our methods have always been mainly indirect, as in our relations over the years with Latin America. De facto, virtually all of the Western Hemisphere, and also some parts of the Eastern Hemisphere (e.g., the Philippines, Liberia), have traditionally been dependencies of the United States. Now it is said that much of the rest of the world is controlled from here as well, mediated in part through our influence on western Europe and Japan. The key to all of this is capitalist economics. By virtue of their relative commercial and financial strength, the Europeans and Japanese have been able to maintain a neocolonialist hold over their former imperial domains; by virtue of our overwhelming economic pre-eminence, we have been able to develop a neocolonialist hold over Europe and Japan as well as over poorer nations. Only the communist bloc has been able to escape the tentacles of what some writers describe as the American "octopus." The remainder of the globe is informally arranged into an international capitalist hierarchy, with this country at the top, other former colonial powers lower down, and former colonies at the bottom. In the words of one writer, the United States is the "organizer and leader of the world imperialist system."[7]

This describes the core of the theory of modern economic imperialism. Marxist and radical writers may differ on details, but on its basic substance, as outlined here, they seem more or less in agreement. This theory is a direct lineal descendant of the economic interpretation of the new imperialism of the late nineteenth century—Hobson and Lenin modernized—and as such is heir to a remarkably weak intellectual heritage. Its propositions ought to be earnestly questioned. As we shall see, apart from some serious flaws of logic, in many respects not even the facts are accurately represented. And even where the empirical evidence is unobjectionable, more plausible alternative hypotheses are possible. In fact, much of the radical and marxist literature on this topic, while often scholarly in appearance, is fundamentally propagandistic. Nevertheless, we must consider it carefully, if only because of its widespread popularity. Surprisingly large numbers of people believe that the theory of neocolonialism suffices to explain the nature of relations between rich and poor countries. This is an article of faith, a dogma. Insofar as there may be said to be a universally accepted theory of imperialism, this is it.

Analytically, the theory breaks into two separate aspects. One stresses the view from the metropolitan center, and concentrates on the alleged inevitability and necessity of economic imperialism for advanced capitalist economies. Neocolonialism is a natural outgrowth of the development of the capitalist order; it is also a basic requirement of capitalism if the order is to be capable of survival. The second aspect stresses the view from the periphery, and concentrates on the alleged detrimental consequences of capitalist trade and investment for the poorer economies of the world. Neocolonialism retards and distorts the process of economic development, and results in dependence and exploitation. Both of these aspects must be examined in detail. The first will be taken up in the following chapter, the second in Chapters 5 and 6.

NOTES

1. See, e.g., Hugh Seton-Watson, *The New Imperialism* (Chester Springs, Pa.: Dufour Editions, 1961); Thomas P. Whitney, "Russian Imperialism Today," in Barbara Ward et al., *The Legacy of Imperialism* (Pittsburgh:

Chatham College, 1960), pp. 23–42; Wlodzimierz Baczkowski, "Russian Colonialism: The Tsarist and Soviet Empires," in Robert Strausz-Hupé and Henry W. Hazard, eds., *The Idea of Colonialism* (New York: Frederick A. Praeger, 1958), pp. 101–109.

2. See, e.g., Ronald Steel, *Pax Americana* (New York: Viking Press, 1967); George Liska, *Imperial America: The International Politics of Primacy* (Baltimore: Johns Hopkins Press, 1967); Claude Julien, *America's Empire* (New York: Pantheon Books, 1971).

3. Quoted in *The New York Times*, December 7, 1971, p. 16.

4. For a representative sample of such writers, see the citations in chaps. 4 and 5, this volume.

5. James O'Connor, "The Meaning of Economic Imperialism," in K. T. Fann and Donald C. Hodges, eds., *Readings in U.S. Imperialism* (Boston: Porter Sargent, 1971), p. 40.

6. Kwame Nkrumah, *Neo-Colonialism: The Last Stage of Imperialism* (New York: International Publishers, 1965), p. ix.

7. Harry Magdoff, *The Age of Imperialism* (New York: Monthly Review Press, 1969), p. 40.

IV

THE VIEW FROM THE METROPOLIS

Modern marxist and radical discussions of imperialism raise a number of interesting questions. From the point of view of the metropolitan center, the most salient of these are: (1) Are neo-colonial trade and investment an inevitable outcome of capitalist development? (2) Is neocolonialism necessary to the survival of capitalism? (3) What is the role of the multinational corporation in modern economic imperialism?

The Old Line

There can be no doubt that the advanced capitalist economies have extensive trade relations with what are commonly regarded as the less developed countries (LDCs) of the world. (For a closer look at what constitutes an LDC, see Chapter 5.) In 1968 alone, exports from the main industrial nations to the LDCs amounted to some $31.7 billion, and imports came to nearly $35 billion (Table 4–1). The advanced capitalist economies also have extensive direct-investment relations with the LDCs. In 1966 the book value of the accumulated assets of the main industrial countries in the LDCs came close to $30 billion

(Table 4–2). However, the analytical significance of these various connections is open to question. In practice, it is not at all certain that they are as crucial to the presumed material needs of the rich countries as marxist and radical writers would have us believe.

Many such writers still hew to the straight Leninist line of argument first laid down more than half a century ago. Imperialism abroad is a reflection of the declining rate of profit at home; the declining rate of profit is a reflection of the rising organic composition of capital. Mature capitalist societies, dominated by monopolistic finance capital, seek to avoid stagnation domestically by gaining access overseas to cheap raw materials and foodstuffs, markets for manufactured exports, and, above all, outlets for investment of surplus capital. Wherever possible, security of access is sought through extension of national control.

The one new element in this traditional line concerns the form of control extended. Lenin, having died well before the ebbing of the new imperialism, could not have anticipated the wave of decolonization that has swept the world since World War II. But such an historic development could scarcely be ignored by his followers. The question had to be answered: How could capitalism continue to maintain itself in the absence of formal empires? The only answer that seemed possible was by the substitution of *informal* empires. Control must still exist, only now it must be exercised indirectly, through relations of trade and investment. Thus was the Leninist argument saved. Colonialism was simply replaced by neocolonialism:

> Thus modern capitalist imperialism comprises a complex of private corporate policies, supplemented by induced governmental support, seeking to develop secure sources of raw materials and food, secure markets for manufactures, and secure outlets for both portfolio and direct capital investment.[1]

Not surprisingly, most such analysis has tended to originate in the Soviet Union and eastern Europe, where Lenin is still

TABLE 4–1

Trade of Advanced Capitalist Countries
with Less Developed Countries, 1968

	EXPORTS (IN BILLIONS OF DOLLARS)	IMPORTS (IN BILLIONS OF DOLLARS)
United States	10.8	8.9
United Kingdom	3.6	4.8
France	2.9	3.2
Germany	3.2	3.9
Japan	5.5	5.2
Canada	0.8	1.0
Others [a]	4.9	7.9
Total	*31.7*	*34.9*

Source: Adapted from International Monetary Fund, *Direction of Trade.*

[a] Includes Austria, Belgium-Luxemburg, Denmark, Italy, Netherlands, Norway, Sweden, and Switzerland.

TABLE 4–2

Direct Investments of Advanced Capitalist Countries
in Less Developed Countries (Accumulated Assets), 1966
(in Millions)

	TOTAL	PETROLEUM	MINING AND SMELTING	MANUFACTURING	OTHER
United States	$16,841	$ 6,975	$1,827	$4,124	$3,915
United Kingdom	6,184	2,167	298	1,471	2,255
France	2,100 [a]	670	n.a.	n.a.	n.a.
Germany	845	65	38	645	97
Japan	605	222	71	270	33
Canada	n.a.	n.a.	202	332	n.a.
Others [b]	n.a.	n.a.	n.a.	n.a.	n.a.
Total	*29,970*	*11,892*	*2,801*	*8,047*	*7,230*

Source: Sidney E. Rolfe, "The International Corporation in Perspective," in Sidney E. Rolfe and Walter Damm, eds., *The Multinational Corporation in the World Economy* (New York: Praeger Publishers, 1970).

Note: n.a. = Not available.

[a] Estimate.

[b] Includes Austria, Belgium-Luxemburg, Denmark, Italy, Netherlands, Norway, Sweden, and Switzerland.

revered as prophet and leader. Much has also been produced by loyal communist party members elsewhere in Europe and in North America.[2] A good example was Maurice Dobb, for years the leading British marxist economist. Dobb's major work, *Political Economy and Capitalism,* published in 1937, differed little in its discussion of imperialism from Lenin's own treatment, except in acknowledging more explicitly the possibility of indirect as well as direct imperial control.[3] Colonies were defined not politically but in *economic* terms; colonization consisted of "a relation between two countries or areas involving the creation of superprofit for the benefit of one of them." [4] Otherwise the analysis was pure Lenin. The purpose of colonization was to create a "counteracting influence to the tendency of the profit-rate in the home country to fall." [5] This was accomplished "*either* by means of some form of monopolistically regulated trade between them, *or* by an investment of capital." [6]

> Capital thereby gains doubly: by the higher rate of profit it reaps abroad and by the higher "rate of surplus-value" it can maintain at home; and this double gain is the reason why, fundamentally, the interest of capital and of labour in this matter was opposed, and why a capitalist economy has a motive for imperialist policy which a socialist economy would not have.[7]

The fallaciousness of the straight Leninist style of analysis should be obvious. There is an element of circularity in its reasoning. Colonies in Lenin's time were offered as prima facie evidence of a tendency toward domestic stagnation in advanced capitalist societies. When formal colonies began to disappear, one might logically have concluded that perhaps there really was not such a conspicuous tendency toward domestic stagnation. But this would have been intolerable, denying the very foundation of all marxist thought. It was still necessary to prove that the profit rate in mature capitalism tends strongly downward over time. Therefore, something else had to be invented to perform the function allegedly served earlier by colonies. The most convenient device proved to be "informal empire"—modern economic imperialism.

The device was the most convenient, perhaps, but it was not the most convincing. In fact, there seems remarkably little evidence in mature capitalism today for any secular tendency toward a declining rate of profit. There is no logical basis for it in the marxist idea of a rising organic composition of capital (that notion's lack of validity has been discussed in Chapter 2), nor is there much empirical evidence for it in the development of the effective demand for capital. Technological change, population growth, the consumption-income ratio—all of these have operated in the postwar period to sustain, if not increase, the rate of return on capital. On the whole, there hardly seems any basis left for the traditional Leninist line of argument. It can prove neither the necessity nor the inevitability of economic imperialism in the modern world. Inherited doctrine has been adhered to. The result is only that it has become increasingly irrelevant and out of touch.

Two New Lines

Interestingly, a growing number of marxists and radicals have started to admit the truth of this contention. In Britain we find a young marxist criticizing Leninist-style discussions of imperialism as "deficient on the theoretical side"; they "suffer from the dead hand of orthodoxy." [8] In America a young radical suggests that "the Leninist thesis is open to criticism on several grounds," [9] and another American simply dismisses the Leninist line as "not very useful today . . . out-of-date." [10]

Younger marxist and radical writers have been casting about for a new theory to explain the alleged persistence of economic imperialism. Two related lines of argument have gradually been developed which, though divergent in their initial perspectives, are essentially convergent in their ultimate conclusions. One line takes its inspiration from the work of two American marxist economists, Paul Baran (now deceased) and Paul Sweezy—in particular from their major work, *Monopoly Capital*.[11] The other is perhaps best represented by the work of a third American marxist economist, Harry Magdoff—in particular by his major work, *The Age of Imperialism*, first published as a series of articles in 1966–1968.[12] The two approaches will be examined separately up to their point of convergence; thereafter they will be evaluated jointly.

Baran and Sweezy

The ambitious objective Baran and Sweezy had in mind in writing *Monopoly Capital* was no less than to provide a modern substitute for the traditional Leninist approach to analysis of capitalist development. Not for them the hoary doctrinal concentration on the rate of profit on capital. In their opinion, the proper focus should be on what they call the concept of *economic surplus*. The source of economic imperialism is not a tendency of the profit rate to fall, but rather a tendency of the economic surplus to rise.

The economic surplus. What is the economic surplus? Unfortunately, Baran and Sweezy never make this entirely clear. One has to practice a little exegesis. Although the concept is central to their analysis, they offer no more than what is, by their own admission, "the briefest possible definition": the economic surplus is merely "the difference between what a society produces and the costs of producing it," [13] "the difference between total output and the socially necessary costs of producing total output." [14] Beyond this they provide little of significance in the way of either elucidation or elaboration, simply referring the reader to Baran's earlier book, *The Political Economy of Growth*.

In that book, Baran distinguished between two different variants of economic surplus in capitalist societies. One he called *actual economic surplus*, which he defined as "the difference between society's *actual* current output and its *actual* current consumption." [15] The other he called *potential economic surplus*, and defined it as "the difference between the output that *could* be produced in a given natural and technological environment with the help of employable productive resources, and what might be regarded as essential consumption." [16]

There is really nothing particularly new about the first of these two variants, apart from the nomenclature. Actual economic surplus is simply the familiar national-income concept of aggregate saving. Ex post, it is identical to the total of capital accumulation —the sum of assets added to the nation's wealth during the period in question (including inventories and net foreign investment as well as productive plant and equipment). In other words, it is the S (and therefore, ex post, the I) in the Keynesian-type identity already introduced in Chapter 2:

$$Y = C + S = C + I.$$

The second of the two variants, by contrast, is less familiar, at least to nonmarxists. In fact, what it implies is the most fundamental of all marxist criticisms of the organization of capitalist society—that the production and distribution of output under capitalism are inherently irrational and wasteful. In effect, some part of capitalist output must necessarily be *lost*. By definition, some productive capacity must be unavailable to satisfy "essential" consumption needs. The loss is indicated by the potential economic surplus.

Criticism such as this clearly involves some powerful normative judgments. Who is to say what is or is not "essential" consumption? Who is to say what is irrational or wasteful? Surely these are matters on which honest men can honestly disagree. Nevertheless, the argument is not illegitimate. It does draw attention to two of the most vital problems of economic organization—efficiency and equity. No system can afford to ignore these problems for very long.

The loss indicated by the potential economic surplus appears under three main headings. First is the output diverted to the excess of nonessential consumption of upper-income groups—

"goods and services the demand for which is attributable to the specific conditions and relationships of the capitalist system, and which would be absent in a more rationally ordered society." [17] Examples include armaments, luxury articles, objects of conspicuous display, and marks of social distinction, as well as many services, such as those provided by the military establishment, tax evasion specialists, and public relations experts. Second is the output lost because of the supposedly unsound and unproductive organization of the existing industrial apparatus— "the waste of resources caused by various aspects of monopoly and monopolistic competition." [18] Examples here include underutilization of economies of scale stemming from excessive product differentiation, and distortion of scientific research owing to its control by profit-oriented business. Third is the output lost simply because of unemployment, "caused partly by the inadequacy of coordination of productive facilities, but mainly by insufficiency of effective demand." [19]

Obviously, it is the latter variant—*potential* economic surplus, the genuine marxist article—that Baran and Sweezy have in mind in *Monopoly Capital*. True, their "briefest possible definition" mentions costs of production rather than levels of consumption in relation to total output. Can these be the same? Yes, they can. Note the similarity of the concept of potential surplus to Marx's original idea of surplus value (see Chapter 2). If the only costs of production recognized are "socially necessary" costs —that is, wage payments to labor—and if the only consumption regarded as "essential" is the consumption of workers, then the two notions are equivalent. *Total surplus is identical to capitalist profit (surplus value)*.

Of course, some part of capitalists' consumption really ought to be included among outlays regarded as "essential," as should at least some of the spending by government. Conversely, if the capitalist system is truly as irrational and wasteful as supposed, then at least some wage payments to labor should not be treated as "socially necessary." Potential surplus, therefore, conceptually is really a bit more complicated than surplus value. Nevertheless, as a first approximation, the sum of capitalist profit (equal statistically to the sum of profits, interest, and rent) will do for most purposes. This is eventually the position taken by Baran and Sweezy: "We provisionally equate aggregate profits with society's economic surplus."[20] Despite use of the word provisional, in fact they never get around to modifying their position anywhere else in their book. Their entire analysis remains based on an implicit identification of surplus with profit.

This suggests that the Baran-Sweezy approach is really not so new. The pair have simply retreated from the *rate* of profit to the *total* of profit. In effect, what they have done is merely recast the traditional Leninist approach in familiar underconsumptionist terms. The tendency toward domestic stagnation is still there, as is the need to counteract it by any means possible. Only now the problem is caused by a rising mass of profit rather than a falling rate of profit; it is a secular deflationary gap, not a rising organic composition of capital. From the point of view of ideology, this comes close to being a major heresy, strikingly reminiscent of the minority marxist view of classical imperialism developed earlier in the century by such writers as Rosa Luxemburg (see Chapter 2); the analysis also owes much to the "new economics" of Keynes and his disciples. However, in the end apostasy is safely avoided (as it was by Luxemburg and other minority marxists) by asserting the *inevitability* of the systemic disorder. This is the true pessimism of traditional marxism. Effective demand at home must *necessarily* become increasingly insufficient to absorb the economic surplus and so maintain full employment. Imperialism abroad therefore must *necessarily* follow:

> Twist and turn as one will, there is no way to avoid the conclusion that monopoly capitalism is a self-contradictory system. It tends to generate ever more surplus, yet it fails to provide the consumption and investment outlets required for the absorption of a rising surplus and hence for the smooth working of the system. Since surplus

which cannot be absorbed will not be produced, it follows that the *normal* state of the monopoly capitalist economy is stagnation. . . . Left to itself . . . monopoly capitalism would sink deeper and deeper into a bog of chronic depression.[21]

Ultimately, Baran and Sweezy confirm their marxist credentials by casting the tendency of the surplus to rise as an iron law:

[W]e can formulate as a law of monopoly capitalism that the surplus tends to rise both absolutely and relatively as the system develops.[22]

This leaves two questions to be answered: (1) *Why* does the surplus tend to rise? (2) Why can it *not* be absorbed?

The tendency to rise. The surplus tends to rise, according to Baran and Sweezy, because capitalism has become monopoly capitalism. Competition has been replaced by a handful of giant corporations in each industry. Gone are the competitive industrialists of Marx's day, and the domination of the bankers of Hilferding's and Lenin's day. The capitalist system has progressed beyond the stage of finance capital. As Baran and Sweezy argue:

One can no longer today speak of either industrialists or bankers as the leading echelon of the dominant capitalist classes. The big monopolistic corporations, which were formed and in their early years controlled by bankers, proved to be enormously profitable and in due course, through paying off their debts and plowing back their earnings, achieved financial independence and indeed in many cases acquired substantial control over banks and other financial institutions. These giant corporations are the basic units of monopoly capitalism in its present stage; their (big) owners and functionaries constitute the leading echelon of the ruling class.[23]

Today's giants share perhaps only one characteristic with the competitive industrialists or bankers who preceded them—their basic interest in growth. As Baran and Sweezy accurately ob-

serve, under capitalism expansion is considered the most important criterion of genuine business success. In fact, expansion
is considered an imperative in dynamic capitalist society; it is
the only safe way to avoid being gobbled up by one's competitors.
At a more practical level, this concern about survival translates
into the objective of maximization of profit (over some relevant
time horizon). Profits provide the internal funds for investment
and offer leverage in gaining access to external funds when and
if needed. They are, in other words, the means to capital accumulation—which, in turn, is the key to enlargement of the enterprise.
The big corporation of the twentieth century undoubtedly has as
much interest in increasing its profits over time as did any small
competing firm in the nineteenth century.

But there is also the difference that the big corporation today
is more *able* to do this than was the traditional small competing
firm:

> The crucial difference between the two is well known and can
> be summed up in the proposition that under competitive capitalism
> the individual enterprise is a "price taker," while under monopoly
> capitalism the big corporation is a "price maker."[24]

The big corporation has market power; it can choose (within
a wide range) what prices to charge for its products. Allegedly,
it can also maintain whatever prices it chooses, because modern
capitalism characteristically avoids price competition. At the
same time, the corporation is supposed to be able to use its
market power to suppress and reduce costs to something ap-
proaching an absolute minimum. The result, consequently, is
that over time it can appropriate the lion's share of all productivity increases directly in the form of higher profits. Profit margins are continuously widening. "And continuously widening
profit margins in turn imply aggregate profits which rise not
only absolutely but as a share of national product."[25] Hence the
iron law of the ever-rising economic surplus.

Baran and Sweezy are right to emphasize the commanding position of the giant corporation in capitalist economies today. There is no question about its pre-eminence. In the United States, for instance, the twenty largest manufacturing corporations in 1962 held an estimated 25 percent of all assets of manufacturing companies; the 100 largest, nearly half. The twenty largest also received 38 percent of all profits after taxes; the 100 largest, nearly three-fifths (see Table 4–3). High degrees of concentration can be observed in almost all heavy industrial categories in America, such as motor vehicles, machinery, rubber, metals, petroleum, chemicals, instruments, tobacco, and al-

TABLE 4–3

Three Alternative Measures of Industrial Concentration in the United States, 1962

CORPORATE SIZE GROUP [a]	TOTAL ASSETS (%)	NET CAPITAL ASSETS (%)	PROFITS AFTER TAXES (%)
5 largest manufacturing corporations	12.5	15.3	19.8
10 largest manufacturing corporations	18.7	24.3	29.6
20 largest manufacturing corporations	25.4	31.3	38.0
50 largest manufacturing corporations	36.2	44.6	47.9
100 largest manufacturing corporations	46.8	55.1	57.6
200 largest manufacturing corporations	56.8	64.1	67.5
500 largest manufacturing corporations	68.9	75.8	79.0
1000 largest manufacturing corporations	76.0	82.2	86.4
Remainder (179,000)	*24.0*	*17.8*	*13.6*

Source: Willard F. Mueller, "Recent Changes in Industrial Concentration and the Current Merger Movement," in *Economic Concentration,* Hearings Before the Subcommittee on Antitrust and Monopoly of the Senate Judiciary Committee (Washington: Government Printing Office, July 1964).

[a] Corporations owned 98.4 percent of all assets of American manufacturing enterprises in 1962.

TABLE 4–4

*Industrial Concentration in Selected Industries
in the United States, 1962*

INDUSTRY	PERCENT OF TOTAL ACCOUNTED FOR BY 4 LARGEST FIRMS		
	TOTAL ASSETS	NET CAPITAL ASSETS	PROFITS AFTER TAXES
Aircraft	41.9	32.6	46.6
Alcoholic beverages	47.2	30.8	58.3
Bakery products	39.6	38.2	52.8
Basic industrial chemicals	45.5	44.6	64.6
Dairy products	48.8	47.4	73.9
Electrical machinery	35.6	41.5	44.4
Instruments	41.2	50.2	56.6
Lumber and wood products	31.0	41.5	48.6
Motor vehicles	79.7	83.1	89.1
Other machinery	24.3	31.5	39.6
Other transportation equipment	44.2	59.9	51.6
Paper	23.2	22.3	35.0
Petroleum refining	50.1	47.7	54.3
Primary iron and steel	48.0	48.8	44.3
Primary nonferrous metals	41.1	47.7	37.1
Rubber	55.0	56.4	51.6
Tobacco	72.7	69.8	72.5

Source: Federal Trade Commission, Bureau of Economics.

coholic beverages (see Table 4–4). The same story is evident in most other mature capitalist economies in Europe and Japan as well.[26]

Moreover, Baran and Sweezy are correct in stressing the administered-pricing policies of today's giant corporations. The big firms do try, wherever and whenever possible, to avoid direct competition in the form of price variations. But they are not always successful in this respect. Baran and Sweezy make no distinction between monopoly and oligopoly; the two market forms are treated casually as functionally equivalent.[27] However, in practice it makes a great deal of difference whether a firm faces no competitors or a few. If it faces none—if it is a *true* monopolist—then of course prices can be maintained without much difficulty. But if it *does* face some competitors within the framework of an oligopolistic market, matters become much more complicated. Though the firm can *try* to maintain its prices, it may not always *succeed*. And even if price competition *can* be avoided, competition will still continue along various dimensions other than price (e.g., by way of product differentiation, advertising, or credit schemes), all of which will affect the *cost* structure of the firm. In the end, therefore, firms may not be able to raise their profit rates quite so easily as Baran and Sweezy suggest.

In advanced capitalist societies today there are relatively few true monopolists. Concentration rates are high, but virtually all corporate giants are obliged to operate within the framework of some sort of oligopolistic market structure (e.g., see Table 4–4). Consequently, they are virtually all under some sort of pressure from competitors. Baran and Sweezy acknowledge the problem: "The abandonment of price competition does not mean the end of all competition: it takes new forms and rages on with ever increasing intensity." [28] But then they fail to draw the logical conclusion. Their conclusion is the iron law, while a more logical one would admit of greater uncertainty. It is *possible* that aggregate profits will tend to rise relative to national product through time. (In a growing economy aggregate profits will almost certainly rise in absolute amount.) It is even possible that profit *rates* will tend to rise. But it is equally possible that these trends will *not* appear. In oligopolistic markets we just cannot know a priori.

A posteriori, of course, we do know. Historically, the iron law has *not* prevailed in modern advanced capitalist economies. Neither in the United States nor in Europe or Japan have aggregate profits demonstrated any significant tendency to increase relative to national product through time. As Table 4–5 indicates, the share of America's GNP accounted for by the aggregate profits of corporations has actually remained on a fairly horizontal trend since at least 1929. Adding interest and rent to the figure, to approximate the total sum of capitalist profit, does not alter this observation, except for a sharp *drop* in the 1930s. (Adding some part of the category of proprietors' income to the figure would actually result in a decline of the trend throughout the whole of the last forty years.) This does not say much for the predictive powers of the Baran-Sweezy argument.

The problem of absorption. The law of the rising tendency of the economic surplus thus rests on some rather weak foundations, empirical as well as intellectual. For purposes of analysis, however, let us assume that such a tendency in modern capitalism does actually exist. The question still remains: Why can it not be absorbed?

At this point we are back in the world of underconsumption. If, as Baran and Sweezy argue, aggregate profits are rising as a share of national product, then only a smaller and smaller proportion of income can be available to the mass of workers for the purpose of current consumption. Consumption cannot keep pace as total capacity grows. Of course, the capitalists who appropriate the aggregate profits might raise their own expenditures for consumption, and thus fill the gap in effective demand. But since the economic surplus *ex hypothesi* is rising, capitalists would be required to increase their consumption spending not only absolutely but relative to national income; in other words, they would need to have a rising average propensity to consume—which is, to say the least, improbable. Accord-

TABLE 4–5

The Share of Profit in the Gross National Product
of the United States, 1929–1969

	1929 (%)	1939 (%)	1950 (%)	1960 (%)	1969 (%)
Corporate profits	10.1	7.0	13.2	9.9	8.5
+ Rent	5.3	3.1	3.3	3.1	2.4
+ Interest	4.6	3.9	0.7	1.7	3.2
= "Capitalist profit"	20.0	14.0	17.2	14.7	14.1

Source: Department of Commerce, *Survey of Current Business.*

ingly, domestic stagnation is inevitable, unless ever-rising outlays for investment are forthcoming. However, why should investments keep rising, and adding to capacity, if prospects for sales are so poor? It is likely that the rate of investment will eventually fall short of the level needed to sustain full employment. Consequently, aggregate expenditures will fall short of total productive capacity; effective demand will be insufficient. "Monopoly capitalism would bog down in a state of permanent depression." [29] Like the underconsumptionists of the last century, Baran and Sweezy have a point.

Where the pair go wrong is in suggesting that modern capitalism is incapable of finding any means for offsetting such a stagnationist tendency—apart from imperialism and its concomitant, militarism. They dismiss all other potential counteracting forces.

For example, consumption might conceivably be stimulated by means of price reduction. This would be one potential counteracting force, but the idea is quickly dismissed by Baran and Sweezy as altogether incompatible with the essential nature of the capitalist system. Since the pricing process is controlled by the most powerful vested interests in society, there is no reason to imagine that it might possibly be regulated for the broader public good. That vested interests might find in unsold inventories enough reason to cut prices—or, what is the same thing in an era of inflation, to restrain price increases—does not seem to have occurred to them. Again they are the victims of their own failure to draw the logical conclusion from the nature of oligopolistic competition.

Alternatively, consumption might be stimulated by means of subsidization through the fiscal mechanism. The government could transfer purchasing power to various individuals unable on their own to satisfy their basic consumption requirements. This could involve either those below some stipulated level of income, or those who can make some kind of a claim to special treatment, such as farmers, veterans, the aged or disabled, or college students. Baran and Sweezy dismiss this possibility, and Baran explained why: because it would be incompatible with the nature of the system.

> The principle that the ordinary man has to earn his bread in the sweat of his brow is cement and mortar to a social order the cohesion and functioning of which are predicated upon monetary penalties and monetary rewards. Reducing the necessity to work for a living, the distribution of a large volume of free goods and services would inevitably undermine the social discipline of capitalist society and weaken the positions of social prestige and social control crowning its hierarchical pyramid.[30]

This explanation reflects the traditional faith that all marxists share in the inability of capitalist society to redistribute income. Capitalism cannot correct a maldistributed income and remain capitalism. What the argument overlooks is the extremely significant fact, emphasized in Chapter 2, that for very practical reasons the system has proved to be quite amenable to reform along such lines. In practice, bourgeois governments have shown a remarkably high degree of social flexibility. Public subsidization of private consumption via transfers is now commonplace in mature capitalist economies, with the volume of transfer payments consistently growing over time. In the United States in 1939 government transfers accounted for less than 0.5 percent of all personal disposable income. By 1949 they were up to about 6 percent; by 1969, to nearly 10 percent. That same year we even had the experience of witnessing a (Republican!) President proposing a comprehensive national system of negative income taxation. Today both major American political parties stand in favor of some form of direct income maintenance for the poor. What could be more contrary to the traditional marxist thesis?

A traditional marxist might object that even with all these transfers, the overall distribution of income in this country remains strikingly unequal. Obviously he would be correct. In

1969, for instance, before taxes, the richest 20 percent of American families received more than seven times the income of the poorest 20 percent; as Table 4–6 shows, the top 5 percent alone received almost three times the income of the bottom fifth of the population. However, such an objection would really be beside the point. I have already conceded in Chapter 2 that the "natural" tendency of income shares under capitalism is largely to move in favor of the rich. The point is, as the table also shows, that despite this "natural" tendency the actual trend of the income distribution has been in the other direction. The lower three-fifths of the population have actually increased their share of total income over at least the last forty years. In part, this has been because of the strong endogenous counter-pressures which tend to arise in advanced capitalist societies (see Chapter 2). In equal measure it has been precisely because of the consistent growth of government transfers, which are included in the family income statistics reproduced in Table 4–6, and which of course tend to move mostly in favor of the poorer segments of the population. The pessimism of Baran and Sweezy regarding subsidization of consumption through the fiscal mechanism is not supported by the facts.

A marxist might still object that transfers do not represent subsidization of consumption through the fiscal mechanism if

TABLE 4–6

Distribution of Before-Tax Family Income
in the United States, 1929–1969

	1929 (%)	1947 (%)	1960 (%)	1968 (%)
Poorest fifth	12.5 {	4.5	4.9	5.6
Second fifth		11.9	12.0	12.4
Middle fifth	13.8	17.3	17.6	17.6
Fourth fifth	19.3	23.5	23.6	23.4
Richest fifth	54.4	42.8	42.0	41.0
Richest 5 percent	30.0	16.9	16.8	14.7

Source: Bureau of the Census.

Note: Detail may not add to 100 percent because of rounding.

the revenue system itself is regressive; that is, if the taxes raised to finance the transfer payments take a higher proportion of income from the poor than from the rich. Again he would be correct. Moreover, it is correct to say that many of the taxes in the American economy—sales and property taxes in particular—are often paid disproportionately by lower income groups. However, the single most important tax in the United States is the Federal income tax, which, despite its many loopholes, is still a strongly progressive source of revenue, taking considerably more income proportionately from the rich than from the poor. The income share of the top 5 percent of the population drops a full two percentage points after deduction of individual income tax payments.[31] Other taxes, such as estate and gift taxes and excises on luxuries, also tend to fall disproportionately on the rich. As a result, the revenue system overall tends to produce an impact that is at least mildly progressive. Since at the same time government transfer payments go principally to lower-income groups, the suggestion is that subsidization of consumption can and does occur through operation of the fiscal mechanism.

A third potential force to counteract any stagnationist tendency of modern capitalism would be direct civilian expenditure by the government sector. Fiscal spending for social needs is also a part of effective demand. However, this too is dismissed by Baran and Sweezy because it would be basically incompatible with the nature of the capitalist system:

> [I]n case after case the private interests of the oligarchy stand in stark opposition to the satisfaction of social needs. Real competition with private enterprise cannot be tolerated, no matter how incompetent and inadequate its performance may be; undermining of class privileges or of the stability of the class structure must be resisted at any cost. And almost all types of civilian spending involve one or both of these threats.[32]

Spending on low-cost housing and slum clearance allegedly would be opposed by real estate interests; public programs of medical care would be resisted by the medical profession; river valley development, promising cheap electric power, would be fought by the public utilities. The exceptions are few; Baran and Sweezy mention only highway construction in this regard. In virtually all other cases public civil expenditures would be contested and the amounts involved necessarily inhibited *"given the power structure of . . . monopoly capitalism."* [33] This argument reflects the traditional marxist theory of class, according to which the government is simply the instrument of the bourgeoisie—again an article of fundamental, if naive, faith. That the facts seem to denote the contrary does not appear to matter. As I argued in Chapter 2, governments historically have *not* concerned themselves exclusively with the interests of a single class. Political rule has been pluralistic, and consequently public spending for social needs has *not* been held down. True, many programs have encountered hostility and active opposition from specific vested interests, but in practice government social spending has risen to substantial levels in all advanced capitalist societies. In the United States, for example, federal expenditures in 1969 for social purposes (e.g., education, health) accounted for almost 10 percent of the entire GNP.

This is not to imply that 10 percent is high enough; a good case could be made for raising it considerably above that level. Government transfers could similarly be made considerably more generous and taxes considerably more progressive than they now tend to be, and oligopolistic prices could be considerably more flexible downward than they are at present. It is hardly my intention to suggest that the capitalist system is perfect—only that the Baran-Sweezy analysis of it tends to be imperfect. The pair are too cavalier in denying the reformative capacity of modern capitalism.

Militarism and imperialism. Having dismissed all other potential counteracting forces, Baran and Sweezy conclude that there is only one option left for offsetting the stagnationist tendency of modern capitalism. That is military spending:

Here at last monopoly capitalism had seemingly found the answer to the "on what" question: On what could the government spend enough to keep the system from sinking into the mire of stagnation? On arms, more arms, and ever more arms.[34]

As a means for absorbing a rising economic surplus, military spending allegedly has one great advantage: it poses no threat to the position or privileges of the capitalist oligarchy. In fact, a large military establishment coincides precisely with what is termed the class interest of the bourgeoisie.

What is that class interest? The traditional imperative of expansion in capitalism has already been referred to. In the context of modern capitalism, with its giant corporations, this tends to mean expansion on a much broader scale than ever before. Today's giants do not limit themselves to piecemeal export promotion or occasional overseas investment. For them the entire world capitalist system is becoming a single sphere of operations. Decisions on production, marketing, and research increasingly are being made in terms of strategies that are as nearly global in scope as possible. As a result, corporate interests are becoming truly international, even if corporate ownership and management still tend to remain essentially national. The big corporations are no longer simply *domestic* economic entities; increasingly they are becoming *multinational* corporations.

According to Baran and Sweezy, the class interest of these new multinational corporations is to make their operating universe as large and amenable as possible. Their objective is to fence off as much of the globe as they can, to make it their own private preserve, in order to conduct their business wherever they wish, on their own privileged terms. Ultimately, their aim is to dominate all of the world's markets and sources of raw materials. Toward this end they will attempt to enforce control informally through ties of trade and investment. When necessary, they will call in the support of their respective national governments.

The general policy which the multinational companies require of their government can thus be summed up in a single formula: to make a world safe for Standard Oil.[35]

This is what makes a large military establishment so useful to the oligarchy. Besides absorbing the rising economic surplus, it serves as well to protect the world-wide interests of the giant corporations. It helps to keep local ruling classes in power around the globe; it also helps to overcome local resistance to capitalist expansion, and to persuade local governments to keep their policies receptive to foreign business. In short, it preserves the free enterprise system. In the words of one young disciple of Baran and Sweezy:

> The growth and persistence of a high level of military spending is a natural outcome in an advanced capitalist society that both suffers from the problem of inadequate private aggregate demand and plays a leading role in the preservation and expansion of the international capitalist system.[36]

Baran and Sweezy are obviously right to stress the rise of the multinational corporation in recent years. Even most nonmarxist economists readily acknowledge the ascendancy of this new breed of institution. Harry Johnson, for instance, who has often been called the "economist's economist," has written: "We have evolved beyond international trade into a world in which the fundamental decisions of corporations are . . . to regard the international community of nations rather than one single nation as their sphere of operations." [37] (Sweezy and Harry Magdoff put the same point slightly differently: "The multinational corporation, in brief, is the key institution of finance capital in the second half of the twentieth century." [38])

Moreover, Baran and Sweezy are correct in emphasizing what they call the class interest of the multinational corporations. Most nonmarxist economists would undoubtedly acknowledge that point also; the welfare of the big corporations *is* best served in a world "safe for Standard Oil." According to the modern theory of oligopolistic competition, the dramatic rise of multinational operations is easily explicable in terms of rational strategy to defend or expand oligopoly power.[39] It is all part of the struggle to survive, to hold or increase market shares at home or abroad, in the face of ever intense competition and changing market conditions. After all, these are profit-making, opportunistic institutions. Like water seeking its own level, they will seek out the paths of least resistance to profit—the most lucrative markets and investment opportunities, the least costly sources of raw materials. They therefore do have a logical incentive to maximize the scope for their everyday business operations. John Gurley is a leading radical economist, yet few of his more orthodox colleagues could quarrel with his assertion that the "principal requirement of the foreign corporations is for a stable and highly favorable environment for their investment and trading activities." [40]

But does this warrant the conclusion that multinational corporations will call in the support of their national governments whenever they feel it necessary? Will they be *able* to call in this support? Is the relationship between business and state really so close? This is the crucial issue to consider, and we shall focus on it sharply in a moment. First, however, we must examine the alternative line of argument on economic imperialism that has been developed in recent years, since it is at the point of this issue that the two lines essentially converge.

Magdoff

This alternative line of argument has received its fullest treatment to date in Harry Magdoff's *The Age of Imperialism,* which practically from the day it was published gained wide popularity in radical and marxist circles. Magdoff's objective, no less ambitious than that of Baran and Sweezy, was to demonstrate the economic "taproot" (borrowing John Hobson's word) of United States foreign policy.[41] In his opinion, there is a close parallel between, on the one hand, the aggressive United States foreign policy aimed at controlling (directly and indirectly) as much of the globe as possible, and, on the other hand, an energetic international expansionist policy of U.S. business.[42]

By implication the same parallel prevails in other advanced capitalist economies as well. This is the "reality of imperialism": "the underlying purpose is nothing less than keeping as much as possible of the world open for trade and investment by the giant multinational corporations." The principal characteristic of the international capitalist system today is the "competition among groups of giant corporations and their governments [which] takes place over the entire globe."[43]

What accounts for the drive of the giant corporations to keep the world open for trade and investment? Here is where the Magdoff approach differs from the older Leninist line of argument, as well as from the newer line inspired by Baran and Sweezy. Abstractions such as a declining rate of profit or a rising mass of profit receive scant notice in his discussion. Neither, it appears, is needed. The reasons for the imperialist behavior of private enterprise are really much more concrete:

> The patterns . . . should be examined in their historical context, in light of the actual situations business firms deal with, rather than in the more usual terms of an abstraction. . . .[44]

In one stroke Magdoff frees himself from the obligation to undertake any sort of fundamental analysis of the structure of modern capitalism. He avoids any attempt to demonstrate a tendency toward either a rising organic composition of capital or a secular deflationary gap (not unwisely, in view of the rather weak empirical and intellectual foundations of both of these concepts). Instead he takes a shortcut, simply falling back on the traditional capitalist imperative of expansion, "the compelling behavior of monopolistic-type business organizations," as he calls it.[45] In effect, he takes his cue from the modern theory of oligopolistic competition rather than from more traditional marxist sources. His point is simply that the corporation's basic interest in survival leaves it no choice but to extend the scope of its market continually and to be looking always for new sources of supply. Its compulsion is to maximize its own market power in the grinding competitive struggle. "The urge to dominate is integral to business." [46]

This in turn is what leads business organizations to call for the support of their national governments, and allegedly leads governments to respond to their calls and play an active role on their behalf. "Where there are competing interests between the business organizations of different countries, the aim of each government's policy is to keep on extending its foreign influence." [47] Depending on the circumstances, this influence may be exercised through many different channels—manipulation of aid and commodity programs or tariff and trade policy, for instance, or application of political pressure or even diplomatic sanctions. Ultimately, however, it must be backed by the substance of military power. This alone suffices to explain the high level of military expenditure in advanced capitalist societies; there is no need to resort to such an abstraction as a rising economic surplus. In fact, Magdoff mainly stresses the economic waste involved in the maintenance of a large military establishment. He has written that most military spending must be regarded as "the price being paid to maintain the imperialistic network of trade and investment in the absence of colonialism . . . the skeletal framework of the imperialist system." [48]

This brings us back to the point of convergence with the Baran-Sweezy line of analysis. Though they start from differing perspectives, Baran and Sweezy and Magdoff end at essentially the same conclusion—that there is a close relationship between the giant multinational corporations of modern capitalism and their home governments. It will not be necessary to consider separately Magdoff's shortcut for arriving at that conclusion. The traditional imperative of expansion in capitalist economics cannot be denied. The question is whether this imperative can, and will, be translated into political and military actions, as we are told.

Business and the State

If one subscribes to the traditional marxist theory of class, then it is easy to believe in the symbiotic relationship of business and state. As one young radical, Arthur MacEwan, has written:

> We need to explain first why expansion is so important that the state is willing to use its power—diplomatic power, "aid"-giving power, military power—and often incur high costs in order to assure a free rein for expansion. . . . If one views the state as acting in a rational manner to further the general welfare of its nationals, without particular regard for their class, an economic explanation of the international activities of the state is not easily developed.
>
> On the other hand, if the state is viewed as using its power to serve the interests of capitalists as a class, then an economic theory of imperialism begins to make sense.[49]

The point is well taken, but unfortunately the marxist theory of class is not. I have already suggested that this theory is really much more naive than realistic. The evidence of history is not strong enough to support it. In fact, as indicated earlier, state power in advanced capitalist societies has *not* been employed exclusively on behalf of a monolithic bourgeoisie. The tendency has been for it to be used to reconcile the conflicting interests of *all* groups, bourgeois or otherwise, with bargaining power within the system.

Nonetheless, even with a pluralist model of politics, it is possible (if no longer easy) to believe in an economic explanation of the international activities of the state. (MacEwan did not say that it would be impossible to develop an economic theory of imperialism in the absence of the marxist theory of class, just that it would be more difficult.) Even if corporate welfare is not viewed as the exclusive objective of government policy, it may turn out in practice that corporate welfare is well served by government policy, at least insofar as foreign trade and investment are concerned, because of a strong tendency toward coincidence of interests between business enterprise and the state. In other words, the international objectives of multinational corporations and their home governments may be just about the same. In that case a close relationship would be bound to exist between them.

How coincidental are the international objectives of corporations and their national governments? They do of course overlap a great deal. Businessmen in this country are always arguing —and not always for self-serving reasons—that the expansionist interests of private enterprise are really identical with the American national interest. They stress the crucial importance of secure access to foreign markets and sources of raw materials, which they say is the only guarantee of the continued vitality of the domestic economy. Bernard Baruch stressed the "essential one-ness of United States economic, political and strategic interests." [50] Moreover, many government officials tend to echo these sentiments and even expand upon them. Radical writers never tire of citing the testimony given by Assistant Secretary of State Dean Acheson in 1944 before a special congressional committee on postwar economic policy and planning. Acheson argued that the projection of America's national power overseas was rooted in economic necessity. In the future the economy had to have expanding markets abroad to absorb its "unlimited creative energy" at home if stagnation was to be avoided.[51] Radicals also like to quote from a 1954 staff report of the President's Commission on Foreign Economic Policy (the Randall Commission) on the issue of raw materials:

This transition of the United States from a position of relative self-sufficiency to one of increasing dependence upon foreign sources of supply constitutes one of the striking economic changes of our times. . . . Both from the viewpoint of our long-term economic growth and the viewpoint of our national defense, the shift of the United States from the position of a net exporter of metals and minerals to that of a net importer is of overshadowing significance in shaping our foreign economic policies.[52]

According to some marxist and radical sources, such statements translate directly into policies of support for every foreign interest of private corporate enterprise. The influence of business is seen behind every act of the state. Individual examples are cited, such as the American Government's intervention in the domestic policies of Guatemala in 1954 on behalf of the United Fruit Company, or the Belgian Government's support of Katangan secession from the Congo (Zaire) in 1960–1961 on behalf of *Union Miniere*. Such examples are then elevated into a universal law of history.

More sophisticated marxist or radical writers, having learned the lesson of nineteenth-century imperialism, recognize the limits of such historical generalization. They know it is always possible to find some counterexample which is an exception to any rule. Consider United States policy in the Middle East, for instance, where it is virtually impossible to detect the hand of business behind the acts of state. Indeed, the American Government's traditional support of Israel against the Arab states runs in diametric opposition to the interests of major U.S. oil companies. Can United States policy in Vietnam possibly be explained in terms of concern for the economic advantages of American business? Some radical writers have tried to locate an economic motivation for our military involvement in Vietnam. One source sees it as an attempt to preserve Japan's access to the markets of Southeast Asia, without which the Japanese would allegedly become dependent on China and America's privileged commercial and financial position in the Pacific would gradually come to an end.[53] Others have seen it as an attempt to preserve access for American oil companies to offshore petroleum deposits that have recently come to light. Neither hypothesis is very persuasive. (I will have more to say about Vietnam in Chapter 7.)

All this is conceded by writers such as Magdoff or MacEwan. They profess not to expect anything like perfect correlation between specific interests of individual corporations and corresponding policies of national governments. What they see is a more subtle form of symbiosis. Capitalist governments, they say, do not make a cost-benefit analysis every time a specific interest is threatened. They are not simply tools in the hands of conspiratorial businessmen who misuse the powers of the state to further their own ambitions (though this is not entirely unknown). Nevertheless, the influence of business on the state is strong. What motivates the state to intervene overseas is concern over the *system*—not to protect a particular trade or investment relation, but rather, more fundamentally, to defend the whole arrangement of trade and investment relations, to preserve the entire world-wide structure that makes such trade and investment possible. In short, what is really at stake is global capitalism itself. As MacEwan has written:

[T]o explain the government's actions, from aid giving to military intervention, we need not point to any particular interests or sets of interests that are being served. It need only be argued that the system is being threatened, that the rules of international capitalist operation are in jeopardy.[54]

This is supposed to be the ultimate link between business and state—a link based on ideology, growing out of the traditional capitalist imperative of expansion. The economic system gives rise to a world view consistent with, and supportive of, the need for constant growth of markets, sources of supply, and investments; this view in turn shapes national political and military strategies to support the private economic system. Governments become convinced that it is their duty to promote a favorable business climate for their corporations, and corporations know that they can count on their governments to promote "economic freedom." Again to quote MacEwan:

> Thus, growing out of economic process, the capitalist ideology provides a basis for unifying the economic and political realms of the system and for facilitating their joint operation.[55]

The convenience of this type of formulation must be noted. Any number of examples can be cited in its defense, such as Guatemala or Katanga, yet it is invulnerable to the citation of counterexamples, such as Israel or Vietnam. (It is not necessary to point to any particular set of interests, MacEwan said.) In effect, therefore, it fails to meet squarely the issue with which this discussion began—namely, the coincidence of interests between business and state. Indeed, the issue is entirely begged. Areas of overlap are stressed, while areas of divergence are ignored or assumed to have no influence on the alleged unity of the "economic and political realms." No evidence is adduced for this assumption; no test of logical reasoning or empirical fact is proposed to justify it. The formulation is simply asserted as self-evident, the reader being asked to accept it on faith.

However, as in so many similar situations, faith is difficult to sustain in the face of conflicting fact. We have already seen in Chapter 2 how frequently private and government objectives came into conflict overseas in the nineteenth century. The objectives of twentieth-century multinational corporations and their home governments also diverge quite strikingly. Indeed, one of the main reasons why the giant corporations go abroad in the first place is to escape the jurisdiction and control of the national political authorities—to evade taxation or to circumvent antitrust or other types of domestic public regulation. Business wants no part of trade embargoes or other economic battles; it just wants to get on with the pursuit of profit. Its objectives are determined by the requirements of the corporation, not by the national identity or loyalties of its owners and management. Its standards of judgment are commercial, not political. Where these standards diverge, the corporation will do everything in its power to achieve its own objectives rather than those of the state.

Nonmarxist economists have for some time been stressing the many areas of conflict of interest between multinational corporations and their governments.[56] Now even marxist and radical writers are beginning to recognize these as well. One of the most astute of these students of the subject has written: "This trend towards multinational corporations breaks the simple connection between the nation state and the national bourgeois that characterized the old imperialism." [57] Whatever the connection may have been in the past, it has become quite tenuous in the present. As a prominent member of the radical left has written:

> The managers of these giant corporate units are becoming aware that their interests and the interests of the national security managers clash. Guided as they are by exclusively economic criteria, the corporate managers are coming to see that the pursuit of the national interest . . . threatens corporate property and corporate profits. . . . [T]he managers are coming to see themselves as a self-conscious class with a new transnational ideology. The nation-state is obsolete. Patriotism is old-fashioned and glory is much too expensive to purchase at the cost of sound money and corporate expansion.[58]

If this is the case, what *is* the relationship between business and state? What happens when the interests of corporation and government do come into conflict? This is the issue begged by the MacEwan-type formulation outlined above. The real question is: Who wins? Who uses whom?

Marxist and radical writers would argue that the corporation wins: business uses the state. Even if the government is opposed to the activity of some particular national corporation, it remains dedicated to its role as protector of the capitalist system in general. To accede to this argument, one must either accept the discredited marxist theory of class, or take at face value official statements such as that by Dean Acheson cited earlier. However, as Robert Tucker has asked:

> Why take this statement of Acheson's and not others which had a quite different emphasis, unless of course it is simply assumed that no other rationale can account for America's post-war policy? Indeed, why may we not argue that such statements as the one cited above obscure far more than they reveal the true sources of policy, that their purpose is largely to elicit support for a policy that is pursued primarily for quite different reasons? [59]

Just as was true in the nineteenth century, the relationship between business and the state today is as frequently dictated by political as by economic considerations. This is not to deny the influence of commercial or financial issues in determining government policy. But they are not all-important; economics cannot account for everything. Some writers like to stress the business background from which many officials of the government bureaucracy are recruited.[60] This is bound to influence their perceptions and prejudices once they become employees of the state. At heart, this is what the MacEwan-type formulation is all about. However, once such individuals do enter the government their perspective is bound to change, at least in part, to encompass broader and more long-range considerations. Governmental authorities cannot think merely in terms of profits and corporate performance. They tend rather to think in terms of politics, power, and national prestige, with national security, not material gain, their objective. Economic goals may figure in their calculations, but essentially as means rather than ends. When economic arguments are contained in their statements, it is more often as ex post justifications or a subterfuge for other purposes rather than as the prime moving force of policy. Their objective is to bend the corporation to serve the will and interests of the state, rather than the reverse. No one has summarized the relationship between business and state better than the radical, Richard Barnet:

> U.S. corporations operating abroad as multinational enterprises now seek maximum freedom from U.S. government control and surveillance. . . . In response to this challenge the nation-state in general and the number one nation in particular are asserting the prerogatives of sovereignty in stronger terms than ever before. . . . The U.S. government is continually seeking to make corporations serve political ends. . . . The competition is still in an early stage, and who will win it is by no means clear. The multinational corporation has certain crucial advantages. . . . Yet the nation still holds the strongest cards.[61]

Summary

One cannot be much impressed by either the Baran-Sweezy or Magdoff lines of argument. The two attempt to provide alternative explanations of the alleged persistence of economic imperialism in the modern world, but neither seems any more persuasive than the traditional Leninist approach to the subject. Both argue that capitalist society is imperialistic because it has to be. Baran and Sweezy stress a rising economic surplus which must somehow be absorbed; both lines stress the monopolistic position of expansionist giant corporations which must be protected. As Magdoff has summarized their joint position: "Imperialism is not a matter of choice for a capitalist society; it is the way of life of such a society." [62]

Unfortunately, neither of these lines of argument can stand up to detailed critical evaluation. As far as the Baran-Sweezy approach is concerned, there is no assurance that the economic surplus would tend to rise over time as a proportion of national product. A priori, we simply cannot know what would happen to the trend of aggregate profits. Furthermore, proof is lacking that a rising economic surplus—if there is one—would be so difficult to absorb. In practice, a variety of counteracting forces have operated to great effect in advanced capitalist societies, including progressive fiscal transfers to individuals and collective government expenditures for social needs. At the same time, as we can see from Table 4–7, most of the major capitalist countries have managed to sustain continuing prosperity and high economic growth rates without feeling compelled to devote more than a minimum of national product to military spending —including Japan, for many years the fastest growing nation in the world.

Finally there is the relationship between business and state, stressed by Magdoff as well as by Baran and Sweezy. Both lines of argument insist that the relationship is close; the joint view has probably been best formulated in the quotes by MacEwan. Yet in practice there seems to be as much conflict as coincidence of interest between today's multinational corporations and their national governments. It is not at all certain that the state would be as exclusively devoted to the welfare of business as we are told.

The Importance of Trade and Investment

The trouble with the modern economic theory of imperialism —old *or* new lines of argument—is that it tries to prove too much. Marxists and radicals do not simply accept that trade and investment in LDCs are *important* to advanced capitalist societies, a point in their favor already conceded at the outset of this chapter. There is no question that without such connections the profits in at least some industries of the metropolitan center would be lower, their costs higher, and their goods scarcer. Marxists and radicals unfortunately insist on trying to demonstrate much more—that trade and investment connections are *necessary* (in the sense that without them center countries would unavoidably sink into stagnation and unemployment), that economic imperialism is *inevitable* (in the sense that the capitalist system as a matter of course must generate behavior

TABLE 4-7

A Comparison of Economic Growth Rates and Shares of Military Expenditure in Domestic Production in Advanced Capitalist Countries, 1951–1968

	ANNUAL GROWTH RATES OF GROSS DOMESTIC PRODUCT			PROPORTION OF GROSS NATIONAL PRODUCT ACCOUNTED FOR BY MILITARY SPENDING			
	1951–1960 (%) (AVERAGE)	1961–1967 (%) (AVERAGE)	1968 (%)	1955 (%)	1960 (%)	1965 (%)	1968 (%)
Austria	5.7	4.0	4.1	0.7	1.2	1.2	n.a.
Belgium	3.0	4.5	3.8	3.3	3.2	2.9	2.9
Canada	3.9	5.3	4.8	6.9	4.7	3.2	2.9
Denmark	3.2	4.6	3.9	3.1	4.0	2.7	2.6
France	4.4	5.6	4.3	4.9	5.5	4.0	3.8
Germany	7.9	3.9	7.6	3.3	3.2	4.0	3.2
Italy	6.1	5.5	5.7	2.8	2.5	2.5	2.2
Japan	8.3	10.4	14.3	1.5	1.0	1.0	0.8
Netherlands	4.5	4.8	6.6	5.3	3.9	3.7	3.3
Norway	3.6	5.2	4.0	3.7	3.2	3.6	3.4
Sweden	3.4	4.5	4.7	4.6	4.5	4.1	3.9
Switzerland	4.4	4.3	3.4	2.6	2.5	2.5	2.1
United Kingdom	2.8	2.9	3.1	7.6	6.1	5.8	5.5
United States	3.3	4.8	4.8	9.8	9.0	7.5	9.2

Sources: Growth rates: International Bank for Reconstruction and Development, *World Tables*. Military spending: United Nations Statistical Office, *Yearbook of National Accounts Statistics, 1969*. For Japan: Japan Defense Agency, *The Defense of Japan* (October 1970).

Note: n.a. = Not available.

classified in this way). In terms of these more ambitious targets, they fail.

At the level of logic, there is little validity to any of the three lines of argument—the old marxist concept of a rising organic composition of capital, the refurbished underconsumptionist concept of a rising economic surplus, or the radicalized version of the modern theory of oligopolistic competition. None of these approaches can prove either that economic imperialism is an inevitable product of capitalist development, or that trade and investment connections in the poor countries are necessary to preserve the prosperity of the rich.

At the level of empirical observation there is equally little support for the modern economic theory of imperialism. As important as trade and investment connections with the poor countries may be for the rich, they are not decisive.

Exports

As markets for the exports of the rich, the poor countries undoubtedly matter considerably. Table 4–1 indicates the magnitude of sales involved—almost $32 billion in 1968. But compare this with sales in the same year among the main industrial countries themselves of more than $100 billion. Compare this with total export volume of more than $155 billion, and total gross product amounting to almost $1,650 billion (see Table 4–8). Placed in proper perspective, exports to LDCs are no more than a drop in the bucket. They account for a uniformly small percentage of the aggregate income generated in any of the advanced capitalist economies. In the United States, supposedly the leading imperialist power, they account for barely more than 1 percent of total gross national output.

Even if exports to LDCs are comparatively small overall, their *marginal* impact could be unusually significant, insofar as they stimulate growth in the advanced economies.[63] However, for this to be true the LDCs would have to show some signs of rapid growth of their own, and unfortunately the opposite is

TABLE 4–8

Relative Importance of Exports of Advanced Capitalist Countries
to Less Developed Countries, 1968

	EXPORTS TO LDCS AS A PERCENTAGE OF:		
	EXPORTS TO OTHER INDUSTRIAL COUNTRIES	TOTAL WORLD EXPORTS [a]	TOTAL GROSS PRODUCT
United States	51.9	31.3	1.2
United Kingdom	45.2	23.4	3.5
France	28.1	23.2	2.3
Germany	17.5	12.8	2.4
Japan	93.8	42.8	3.9
Canada	6.8	6.0	1.2
Others [b]	15.8	11.9	2.5
Total	*30.5*	*20.4*	*1.9*

Source: International Monetary Fund, *Direction of Trade;* OECD, *Main Economic Indicators.*

[a] Includes exports to industrial countries, other developed nations, LDCs, and the socialist bloc.
[b] Includes Austria, Belgium-Luxemburg, Denmark, Italy, Netherlands, Norway, Sweden, and Switzerland.

the case. As markets for the exports of the rich, the poor countries have actually been declining in relative importance. Their share of world trade has fallen sharply from above 30 percent in 1950 to under 20 percent by the late 1960s. The most rapid growth of exports has been in the markets of the advanced economies themselves, where the purchasing power lies. As in the nineteenth century, trade follows effective demand. Increasingly, growth in the mature capitalist countries is being sustained by intratrade *within* the metropolitan center—*not* by trade between the center and the periphery.

Investments

In similar fashion, the poor countries have been declining in importance as outlets for the investments of the rich, although they continue to matter considerably. Table 4–2 indicates a total of almost $30 billion of accumulated direct investment assets at the end of 1966. But as before, the figure must be compared:

accumulated foreign assets within the advanced economies themselves were something like twice as large, at nearly $60 billion. Moreover, cross-investments within the metropolitan center have been growing at a much faster rate than investments by the center in the periphery. The reason, ironically enough, has been summed up best by a marxist:

> [I]t does not make sense for the big corporations to promote large-scale capital exports to the so-called Third World. The markets are too limited there.[64]

Some marxist and radical writers protest that this is actually beside the point. It is not the rate of growth of capital exports to the periphery that indicates how important these are to the center, or even their accumulated total. Rather it is their rate of return—their contribution to the *profits* of the industries of modern capitalism. Direct investment connections with the poor countries are vital to the rich because they sustain corporate profitability. Here, according to such sources, is the real reason for the persistence of economic imperialism today.[65]

There can be no doubt that direct investment connections with the poor countries are profitable for industries of the rich. Otherwise, such investments would not occur in the first place. Likewise, there can be no doubt that these profits are important for industries of the rich. If they were not, the large multinational corporations would be unlikely to put up with the familiar risks and disadvantages of operating in what are often quite inhospitable political conditions. However, the importance of these profits ought not to be exaggerated. Magdoff insists that United States net earnings from overseas investments are "becoming an ever more important component of business profits."[66] In fact, they are doing nothing of the sort, as Table 4–9 shows. Net earnings from investments in the Third World actually declined as a proportion of total corporate profits between 1957 and 1966; even in the former year the proportion was only a meager 4.5 percent.

TABLE 4–9

*Comparison of Net Earnings from U.S. Foreign Direct Investments in Less
Developed Countries and Total U.S. Corporate Profits, 1950–1966*

	1950	1957	1966
Net earnings on foreign investments in less developed countries (in billions of dollars) [a]	0.99	2.15	3.02
Total corporate profits before taxes (in billions of dollars)	42.6	47.2	84.2
Foreign earnings as a percentage of total profits (percentage)	2.3	4.6	3.6
Addendum: foreign earnings as a percentage of total profits, according to Magdoff (percentage)	0.7	20.1	21.0 [b]

Sources: Earnings: Department of Commerce, *U.S. Direct Investments
Abroad 1966.* Profits: Department of Commerce, *The National Income and
Product Accounts of the United States, 1929–1965; Survey of Current Busi-
ness,* July 1969. Harry Magdoff, *The Age of Imperialism* (New York:
Monthly Review Press, 1969), p. 183.

[a] Includes all areas except Europe, Canada, Japan, Australia, New Zealand, and South Africa.
[b] 1965.

Compare these percentages with Magdoff's own calculations,
reproduced in the last line of Table 4–9. Why are Magdoff's results so much higher? In the first place, his figures for foreign
earnings include investments in developed as well as in less developed areas; since U.S. capital exports have gone increasingly to
industrial countries since the mid-1950s, rather than to LDCs,
this was bound to bias his calculations upward. In fact, more than
two-thirds of all American foreign investments are now located in
mature capitalist areas (overwhelmingly in Canada and Europe).
Magdoff insists that these investments be included in the analysis:
those who ignore them "do not face up to the reality of world
economic interdependence." [67] But interdependence within the
metropolitan center is not really the issue. The concern is with
the extent of interdependence between the center and the periphery—that is, the extent to which the rich countries need the
poor, not one another. For the purpose of exploring this issue,

cross-investments within the metropolitan center should be omitted. Including them in the analysis only serves to inflate the statistical calculation.

Another reason for Magdoff's higher results is that his figures include earnings on foreign portfolio investments as well as direct investments, and also earnings on investments of nonfinancial corporations, even though his data on total corporate profits exclude the latter. In addition, his data on total corporate profits are quoted after taxes rather than before. No wonder he got such high percentages.

Raw Materials

What about the role of the periphery as a prime source of vital raw materials for the metropolitan center? It is perhaps in this respect alone that the poor countries retain anything even approximating the importance attributed to them by marxist and radical writers. The industries of the rich are undoubtedly in need of access to cheap minerals, fuels, and agricultural inputs, and LDCs are a prime source of supply for such items. A number of marxists and radicals have attempted to build a complete theory out of this single need, to explain the alleged persistence of economic imperialism. The advanced capitalist nations are driven to dominate the Third World in order to ensure an uninterrupted flow of essential natural resources. In the words of one French marxist, "it is my contention that the dependence of the industrialized countries on the Third World . . . lies in the field of raw materials." [68]

It is not difficult to document the importance of imported raw materials for the industries of the rich. American industry is particularly reliant on a steady supply of foreign natural resources, as the Randall Commission staff report (cited above) emphasized. Once the United States was relatively self-sufficient in raw materials output. Today domestic supplies of most critical resources are rapidly becoming exhausted. At present this country produces all it needs of just two important metals—molybdenum and magnesium. In most other cases, as Table 4–10 shows, imports account for a strikingly high proportion of total domestic use of various inputs. Some materials, such as crude rubber, chromium, and cobalt, are entirely imported.

However, we must be careful not to exaggerate the importance of even this role of the periphery. The issue is not only

TABLE 4–10

*Relative Dependence of the United States on
Selected Imported Raw Materials, 1967*

	IMPORTS AS A PERCENTAGE OF TOTAL DOMESTIC USE
Agricultural raw materials	
Carpet wool	100
Copra	100
Crude rubber	100
Fibers	100
Gums and barks	100
Raw silk	100
Wool (other than carpet wools)	50
Minerals	
Abrasives	100
Asbestos	80
Bauxite	89
Beryllium	100
Chromium	100
Cobalt	100
Copper	21
Fluorspar	65
Gypsum	22
Iron ores and concentrates	35
Lead and zinc ores	27
Manganese ores	96
Mercury	48
Mica	99
Nickel	92
Peat	64
Platinum	99
Potash	24
Sulfur	16
Tin	60
Titanium	99
Tungsten	25

Source: Bureau of the Census, *Statistical Abstract of the United States*.

the current extent of reliance by rich countries like the United States on supplies of raw materials from the poor, as indicated by the percentage of imports in domestic use. Involved as well is the ability to find alternatives to this particular pattern of imports, as indicated by the capacity to economize on the use of foreign natural resources and/or to replace them with substitutes or with domestic production. In other words, does the current extent of reliance represent genuine "dependence of the industrialized countries on the Third World," or merely an economic convenience based on such considerations as accessibility and price? Do the center countries import raw materials from the periphery from necessity or from choice?

All the evidence suggests that it is from choice. There *are* alternatives to the present pattern of imports. The technology for systematically recovering and recycling materials, already significantly advanced, can be expected to be developed even further in this age of growing public concern over ecology. Similarly, a variety of replacements have already been invented which substitute more than adequately for imported natural resources—synthetic rubber for crude, nylon and other fibers for silk, ceramics for high-temperature steel, and so on. Further developments on this front can be expected as well. In addition, there is the vital factor of price. It is well known that the United States purchases most materials from abroad only because they happen to be the cheapest available, not because there happen to be no alternative (albeit more expensive) sources of supply at home. Exhaustion of domestic supplies of these materials means only scarcity of high-yield deposits, not scarcity in any absolute sense. There are still plenty of lower-yield deposits which could conceivably be exploited if the need arose. Moreover, technology in this area is constantly being developed, to improve the detection of new reserves and to cheapen the processing of poorer grades. In such cases reliance on imports is actually much more an illusion than a reality.

We may conclude, therefore, that not even the raw materials

of the periphery make imperialism either necessary or inevitable. The resources of the LDCs are important, and so are their markets and their investment opportunities. But they are not *as* important to the metropolitan center of advanced capitalism as the modern theory of economic imperialism insists.

To be sure, these aspects of the LDCs may be vital to certain individual corporations within the metropolitan center, or even to certain whole industries. But this possibility carries no particular significance for purposes of analysis unless it can be proved that such corporations or industries are capable of controlling, or at least substantially influencing, the foreign economic policies of their national governments. I have already made clear my reasons for believing that the relationship between business and state is not anywhere near that close. Trade and investment in LDCs are neither a requisite for the survival of mature capitalism nor an inevitable concomitant of its development. They are simply a convenience—the path of least resistance to profits, prosperity, and growth. Of course, even convenience may be sufficient excuse to take advantage of the poor countries—to distort their growth and exploit them. But that is another matter entirely, a different aspect of the problem which we take up in the following two chapters.

NOTES

1. Richard D. Wolff, "Modern Imperialism: The View from the Metropolis," *American Economic Review* 60, no. 2 (May 1970): 225.

2. For several samples see Tom Kemp, *Theories of Imperialism* (London: Dobson Books, 1967), pp. 106–120.

3. Maurice Dobb, *Political Economy and Capitalism* (London: Routledge, 1937), chap. 7. See also Dobb, *Capitalism Yesterday and Today* (London: Lawrence and Wishart, 1958), pp. 30–32.

4. Dobb, *Political Economy*, p. 231.

5. Ibid., p. 234.

6. Ibid., p. 231. Emphasis supplied.

7. Ibid., p. 235.

8. Kemp, *Theories of Imperialism*, pp. 120, 133.

9. Robert Wolfe, "American Imperialism and the Peace Movement," in K. T. Fann and Donald C. Hodges, eds., *Readings in U.S. Imperialism* (Boston: Porter Sargent, 1971), p. 313.

10. James O'Connor, "The Meaning of Economic Imperialism," in Fann and Hodges, *Readings in U.S. Imperialism*, p. 44.

11. Paul A. Baran and Paul M. Sweezy, *Monopoly Capital* (New York: Monthly Review Press, 1966). This joint effort by the two authors grew out of their earlier separate writings. See especially Sweezy, *The Theory of Capitalist Development* (1942; reprint ed., New York: Monthly Review Press, 1968) and Baran, *The Political Economy of Growth* (1957; reprint ed., New York: Monthly Review Press, 1968). For examples of other recent works that depend mainly on the Baran-Sweezy approach, see O'Connor, "Meaning of Economic Imperialism," and Michael Reich, "Does the U.S. Economy Require Military Spending?" *American Economic Review* 62, no. 2 (May 1972): 296–303.

12. Harry Magdoff, *The Age of Imperialism* (New York: Monthly Review Press, 1969). For examples of other recent works that take an approach similar to Magdoff's, see Wolff, "Modern Imperialism," and Arthur Mac-Ewan, "Capitalist Expansion, Ideology and Intervention," *Upstart*, no. 2 (May 1971): 25–41.

13. Baran and Sweezy, *Monopoly Capital*, p. 9.

14. Ibid., p. 76.

15. Baran, *Political Economy of Growth*, p. 22. Emphasis in the original.

16. Ibid., p. 23. Emphasis in the original.

17. Ibid., p. 32.

18. Ibid., p. 36.

19. Ibid., p. 39.

20. Baran and Sweezy, *Monopoly Capital*, p. 72.

21. Ibid., p. 108.

22. Ibid., p. 72.

23. Paul A. Baran and Paul M. Sweezy, "Notes on the Theory of Imperialism," *Monthly Review* 17, no. 10 (March 1966): 18.

24. Baran and Sweezy, *Monopoly Capital*, pp. 53–54.

25. Ibid., pp. 71–72.

26. See, e.g., Joe S. Bain, *International Differences in Industrial Structure* (New Haven: Yale University Press, 1966).

27. Baran and Sweezy, *Monopoly Capital*, p. 6, n. 3.

28. Ibid., p. 67.

29. Ibid., p. 88.

30. Baran, *Political Economy of Growth*, p. 106.

31. See, e.g., Herman F. Miller, *Income Distribution in the United States* (Washington: Government Printing Office, 1966), p. 4.

32. Baran and Sweezy, *Monopoly Capital*, p. 173.

33. Ibid., p. 161. Emphasis in the original.

34. Ibid., p. 213.

35. Baran and Sweezy, "Notes," p. 30.

36. Reich, "The U.S. Economy," p. 296.

37. Harry G. Johnson, *International Economic Questions Facing Britain, the United States, and Canada in the 70's* (London: British-North American Committee, 1970), p. 11.

38. Harry Magdoff and Paul M. Sweezy, "Notes on the Multinational Corporation," *Monthly Review* 21, nos. 5–6 (October–November 1969): 1–13 in each issue.

39. See, e.g., Stephen H. Hymer, "The International Operations of National Firms: A Study of Direct Investment" (Ph.D. diss., M.I.T., 1960); Raymond Vernon, "International Investment and International Trade in the Product Cycle," *Quarterly Journal of Economics* 80, no. 2 (May 1966): 190–207; Richard E. Caves, "International Corporations: The Industrial Economics of Foreign Investment," *Economica*, new ser., 38, no. 149 (February 1971): 1–27.

40. John G. Gurley, "The State of Political Economics," *American Economic Review* 61, no. 2 (May 1971): 56.

41. Magdoff, *Age of Imperialism*, p. 8.

42. Ibid., p. 12.

43. Ibid., pp. 14, 15.

44. Ibid., p. 38.

45. Harry Magdoff, "The Logic of Imperialism," *Social Policy* 1, no. 3 (September–October 1970): 27.

46. Magdoff, *Age of Imperialism*, p. 34.

47. Ibid., p. 14.

48. Harry Magdoff, "Militarism and Imperialism," *American Economic Review* 60, no. 2 (May 1970): 240, 241.

49. Arthur MacEwan, "Economics of Imperialism: Discussion," *American Economic Review* 60, no. 2 (May 1970): 246.

50. Bernard Baruch, in preface to Samuel Lubell, *The Revolution in World Trade and American Policy* (New York: Harper & Row, 1955).

51. Apparently the first source to cite the Acheson testimony in this connection was William Appleman Williams' now classic study, *The Tragedy of American Diplomacy* (New York: Dell Publishing Co., 1962), p. 235.

52. Commission on Foreign Economic Policy, *Staff Papers* (Washington: Government Printing Office, 1954), p. 224.

53. Carl Oglesby, "Vietnamese Crucible: An Essay on the Meanings of the Cold War," in Carl Oglesby and Richard Shaull, *Containment and Change* (New York: Macmillan, 1967), pp. 112–139.

54. MacEwan, "Capitalist Expansion," p. 35. See also Magdoff, *Age of Imperialism*, p. 14.

55. MacEwan, "Capitalist Expansion," p. 35.

56. See, e.g., Jack M. Behrman, *National Interests and the Multinational Enterprise* (Englewood Cliffs, N.J.: Prentice-Hall, 1970), pt. 2; Richard N. Cooper, *The Economics of Interdependence* (New York: McGraw-Hill for the Council on Foreign Relations, 1968), chap. 4.

57. Stephen Hymer, "Economics of Imperialism: Discussion," *American Economic Review* 60, no. 2 (May 1970): 243.

58. Richard J. Barnet, *Roots of War* (New York: Atheneum, 1972), p. 229.

59. Robert W. Tucker, *The Radical Left and American Foreign Policy* (Baltimore: Johns Hopkins Press, 1971), p. 61.

60. See, e.g., Gabriel Kolko, *The Roots of American Foreign Policy* (Boston: Beacon Press, 1969), chap. 1.

61. Barnet, *Roots of War*, pp. 232–235.

62. Magdoff, *Age of Imperialism*, p. 26.

63. See, e.g., Magdoff, "The Logic of Imperialism," p. 27.

64. Ernest Mandel, *Europe versus America? Contradictions of Imperialism*

(London: NLB, 1970), p. 14.

65. See, e.g., Frank Ackerman, "Magdoff on Imperialism," *Public Policy* 19, no. 3 (Summer 1971): 525–531.

66. Magdoff, *Age of Imperialism,* p. 182.

67. Magdoff, "The Logic of Imperialism," p. 23.

68. Pierre Jalée, *The Third World in World Economy* (New York: Monthly Review Press, 1969), p. 86. See also Heather Dean, "Scarce Resources: The Dynamic of American Imperialism," in Fann and Hodges, *Readings in U.S. Imperialism,* pp. 139–154.

V

THE VIEW FROM THE PERIPHERY

From the point of view of the countries of the periphery, the most important questions raised by modern marxist and radical discussions of imperialism are: (1) Do capitalist trade and investment retard or distort the development of the poor? (2) What is the significance of the economic dependence of the poor? (3) Are the poor exploited? The first of these questions will be examined here, the second and third in Chapter 6.

The Periphery

We must first ask: *Who* are the poor? What countries are included in the periphery? In theory, the group is easily distinguishable, but in practice it is virtually impossible to draw any hard and fast line between developed and less developed countries (LDCs).

Consider, for example, Table 5–1, which ranks some 127 countries in order of per capita product.[1] Income per head of population is popularly assumed to be an index of a country's level of economic development. Unfortunately, it is both superficial and misleading. By that standard, oil-producing states such as

145

Kuwait, Qatar, and Libya would have to be classified among the most favored of rich countries; south European states such as Greece, Spain, and Portugal would have to be placed among the poor. Similar borderline cases, in which the appropriate assignment is not readily apparent, are numerous. Where, for instance, would one put Hong Kong, with a per capita income level above that of South Africa? Where would one put Puerto Rico, with a per capita income above Ireland's? Where would one put Argentina or Singapore, with their relatively high income levels, or Yugoslavia or Turkey, with their relatively lower incomes?

TABLE 5-1

Estimated Gross National Product Per Capita, All Countries with Populations of One Million or More, 1969

COUNTRY	GNP PER CAPITA (U.S. DOLLARS)	COUNTRY	GNP PER CAPITA (U.S. DOLLARS)
United States	4,240	Italy	1,400
Kuwait [a]	3,320	Czechoslovakia	1,370
Sweden	2,920	USSR	1,200
Switzerland	2,700	Ireland	1,110
Canada	2,650	Hungary	1,100
France	2,460	Argentina	1,060
Luxembourg [a]	2,420	Venezuela	1,000
Denmark	2,310	Poland	940
Australia	2,300	Trinidad and Tobago	890
New Zealand	2,230	Bulgaria	860
Germany, Fed. Rep. of	2,190	Romania	860
Norway	2,160	Hong Kong	850
Belgium	2,010	Greece	840
Finland	1,980	Spain	820
United Kingdom	1,890	Singapore	800
Iceland [a]	1,850	South Africa	710
Netherlands	1,760	Panama	660
Trucial States [a]	1,590	Lebanon	580
Germany (Eastern)	1,570	Mexico	580
Israel	1,570	Yugoslavia	580
Qatar [a]	1,550	Uruguay	560
Libya	1,510	Jamaica	550
Austria	1,470	Chile	510
Japan	1,430	Costa Rica	510
Puerto Rico	1,410	Portugal	510

TABLE 5-1 (continued)

Estimated Gross National Product Per Capita, All Countries with Populations of One Million or More, 1969

COUNTRY	GNP PER CAPITA (U.S. DOLLARS)	COUNTRY	GNP PER CAPITA (U.S. DOLLARS)
Mongolia	460	Thailand	160
Albania	430	Cameroon	150
Nicaragua	380	Mauritania	140
Saudi Arabia	380	Vietnam (South)	140
Guatemala	350	Central Africa Rep.	130
Iran	350	Kenya	130
Turkey	350	Khmer Rep.	130
Malaysia	340	Yemen, People's Dem. Rep. of	120
Peru	330	India	110
Iraq	310	Laos	110
Taiwan	300	Malagasy Rep.	110
Colombia	290	Pakistan	110
El Salvador	290	Sudan	110
Zambia	290	Uganda	110
Cuba	280	Indonesia	100
Dominican Republic	280	Togo	100
Jordan	280	Afghanistan	—
Korea (North)	280	Burma	—
Brazil	270	Burundi	—
Algeria	260	Chad	—
Honduras	260	China (Mainland)	—
Syria	260	Congo, Dem. Rep. of	—
Ecuador	240	Dahomey	—
Ivory Coast	240	Ethiopia	—
Paraguay	240	Guinea	—
Rhodesia	240	Haiti	—
Tunisia	230	Malawi	—
Angola	210	Mali	—
Korea (South)	210	Nepal	—
Mozambique	210	Niger	—
Papua-New Guinea	210	Nigeria	—
Philippines	210	Rwanda	—
Liberia	200	Somalia	—
Senegal	200	Tanzania	—
Ceylon	190	Upper Volta	—
Ghana	190	Vietnam (North)	—
Morocco	190	Yemen, Arab Rep. of	—
Sierra Leone	170		
Bolivia	160		
Egypt	160		

Source: International Monetary Fund and World Bank Group, *Finance and Development*, March 1972.

Note: — Estimated at less than $100.

a Populations of less than one million.

In reality, per capita product is only an approximate index of a country's level of development. So are other similar statistical measures. Economic development is a multivariate concept; no single variable can possibly provide a definitive norm of membership in the area we call the periphery. Whether one considers product per head, demographic characteristics, social conditions, or the structure of production, anomalies are bound to arise. Some assignments are bound to seem arbitrary. This is well demonstrated by Table 5–2. Here six of the richest and most advanced countries of the world are compared along several dimensions with a random sample of 18 African, Asian, and Latin American nations. In every column there are at least one or two ambiguous borderline cases.

The first three columns consider certain demographic characteristics commonly thought to distinguish sharply between rich and poor countries. The poor, it is usually assumed, have relatively rural rather than urban populations, relatively low school enrollments, and relatively high birth rates. Yet each column displays at least one striking exception. Venezuela's population in 1960, for instance, was more urban than either Japan's or France's. Argentina had more of its eligible population enrolled in primary school than Britain, and had a lower crude birth rate than Canada. It is also commonly assumed that the saving rate is lower in LDCs (because of their lower incomes) and that their production structures are biased in favor of agriculture rather than manufacturing or services (because of their more primitive technologies). Yet in the 1960s the Ivory Coast and Malaysia both had higher savings rates than the United States. In 1965 Argentina employed a smaller proportion of its people in agriculture than did France; Libya received a smaller proportion of its gross domestic income from farming than did Japan.

Obviously it is no simple matter to define a poor country. What characterizes the periphery, first of all, is an overwhelming diversity. This is a distinctly heterogeneous collection which includes India, with over half a billion people, and Gabon, with under half a million. It includes Rwanda, with a population density in excess of 100 per square kilometer, and Libya, with a density under one. It encompasses stagnant peasant societies and dynamic industrializers, nations rich in natural resources and nations with hardly any at all. It includes political systems ranging from parliamentary democracies to military dictatorships, economic systems from free enterprise to state socialism, and social systems from the tribal to the pluralistic. It includes countries that have had an independent existence for centuries, and countries that gained their formal independence only in the last decade.

Yet it *is* still possible to speak of the "poor countries," if only in general terms and as a group. Diverse as they are, poor countries are nonetheless distinguishable from the rich. It may not be possible to define a poor country by referring to any one statistical variable, since all countries are exceptions in one way or another. But it is possible to define poor countries collectively, by referring to several or all of the variables considered in Tables 5–1 and 5–2. Every poor country shares some or most of these attributes; few rich countries share more than one or two of them. It is in this sense that we may legitimately draw a line in this world between developed and less developed countries. The gulf which separates the poor countries from the rich is enshrined in common language in the term "Third World."

The First World is the metropolitan center of advanced capitalism—the United States and Canada, the countries of western Europe, and Japan. Generally the center is understood to include *all* of the noncommunist countries of Europe, even the poorer ones along the area's Mediterranean littoral. In addition, Australia and New Zealand, as relatively high-income societies, are usually placed in this favored category. South Africa and Israel are sometimes also added, though as much for ideological as for economic reasons. The Second World is the world of communist states, understood to include not only the relatively more ad-

TABLE 5-2

A Comparison of Six Industrial Countries and Eighteen African, Asian, and Latin American Nations

	URBAN POPULATION AS % OF TOTAL POPULATION (1960)	PRIMARY SCHOOL ENROLLMENT AS % OF POPULATION AGED 5-14 (1960)	CRUDE BIRTH RATE PER 1,000 (1960)	GROSS NATIONAL SAVING AS % OF GNP (1961-1967)	PERCENTAGE IN AGRICULTURE OF: LABOR FORCE (1965)	PERCENTAGE IN AGRICULTURE OF: GROSS DOMESTIC PRODUCT (1965)
Industrial Countries						
Canada	70	84	26.7	22.6	8	6.5
France	63	74	17.9	25.7	20 (1960)	8.9
Germany	68 (1950)	69	17.5	27.5	11	4.4
Japan	63	62	17.2	36.0	27	11.2
United Kingdom	78	62	17.5	18.6	3	3.4
United States	70	83	23.7	18.6	6	3.4
Africa						
Burundi	2	17 (1965)	n.a.	3.6 (1967)	95 (1960)	72.5
Ghana	23	32	n.a.	10.9	58 (1960)	35.7
Ivory Coast	2 (1965)	31	52.5	19.5	86 (1964)	42.1
Libya	35	41	n.a.	28.6	36	5.0
Sudan	8 (1955)	11	n.a.	11.1	78	54.3
Tanzania	5 (1955)	19	n.a.	13.6	95	54.1

Asia						
India	18 (1965)	34	38.9	14.0	67	46.1
Iran	39 (1965)	28	39.3	15.6	55 (1955)	25.6
Iraq	44 (1965)	43	40.5	19.2	48 (1955)	19.6
Korea (South)	28	60	44.7	8.0	53	41.3
Malaysia	36 (1955)	58	40.9	19.5	51 (1960)	31.0
Thailand	12	59	34.7	18.4	82 (1960)	39.6
Latin America						
Argentina	60	69	23.1	19.9	18 (1960)	17.5
Bolivia	30 (1967)	38	43.0	9.0	65	22.7
Dominican Republic	30	66	41.0	9.5	57	26.0
Honduras	23	42	47.0	12.4	65	40.5
Mexico	51	54	49.6	18.4	52	14.5
Venezuela	68	70	45.1	23.9	29	7.1

Source: International Bank for Reconstruction and Development, *World Tables.*
Note: n.a. = Not available.

vanced economies of the Soviet Union and eastern Europe, but also the less advanced ones in Asia, Cuba, and Albania. Yugoslavia, similarly, is ordinarily classified among this group of countries.

This leaves all the rest, the nations of Latin America, Asia, and Africa, as well as the oceans in between—more than a hundred countries in all, populated by as many as half of the world's people and occupying more than a third of the globe's territory. This is the Third World, the periphery of poor countries which is spoken of in modern marxist and radical discussions of imperialism. These are the supposedly neocolonial societies whose development is said to be retarded and distorted by relations of trade and investment with the capitalist rich.

Neocolonialism

This brings us to the main issue—neocolonialism. *How* do economic relations with the rich retard and distort the development of the poor? [2] Marxists and radicals argue that the process of neocolonialism works in two ways—first through effects on the endowment and allocation of productive resources, and second through effects on the pattern of tastes and expenditures. Both types of effects are reflected in a structure of global prices which is systematically biased in favor of the countries of the metropolitan center. Both types have allegedly been reinforced by the rise in recent years of the multinational corporation.

Resources

Every country is endowed with a certain quantity and variety of productive resources. Resources are the things or services which, either singly or in combination, are available for producing the goods and services which satisfy final wants. The usual custom of economists is to classify factors of production into the three categories of land, labor, and capital. Land is taken to stand as a shorthand expression for natural resources of all kinds.

Labor represents human effort, both physical and mental. Capital traditionally is defined to include any nonhuman producible resource used at some point in the production process, such as machinery, buildings, inventories, and raw and semifinished materials. These three categories are supposed to be exhaustive. Together with technology—the available pool of knowledge regarding the industrial arts—the quantity and quality of resources set the overall limit to a country's "production possibilities."

To a certain extent, this traditional tripartite classification of resources is somewhat arbitrary. Other taxonomies can be imagined and, indeed, have often been employed. Some economists have insisted on a fourth category of resources called "management," to represent the special skills of organization required to mobilize and combine the other three types of factors in production. Other economists have broadened the definition of capital to include not only nonhuman but also *human* producible resources—that is, labor effort which has been improved through the advantage of education or on-the-job training. This is the notion of "human capital," quite distinct from simple labor power, which has gained wide currency in the economics literature in recent years. Another group of economists has suggested that only two categories are all we need, to distinguish between those resources that are human and those that are not (land and physical capital). For our purposes, it is not necessary to make a definitive choice among these various alternative taxonomies. It is enough merely to acknowledge that the pie can be cut up in several different ways.

According to marxist and radical writers, the effect of capitalist trade and investment on poor countries is to distort the allocation of available resources and to retard the growth of factor endowments (supplies). Production possibilities, consequently, are doubly limited. Some writers tend to stress only the role of capitalist relations in *perpetuating* the condition of poverty in the Third World. For them the problem consists mainly of the impact on the rate of increase in the *endowment* of productive resources. Most marxists and radicals, however, go further, to emphasize the role of capitalist relations not only in perpetuating but also in *generating* the condition of poverty in the Third World. They see the problem as existing at least as much in the impact on the *allocation* of productive resources.

Perhaps the most forceful exponent of this broader emphasis is marxist economist Andre Gunder Frank.[3] In Frank's view, the current condition of poverty in the Third World is no mere accident of history, no fortuitous consequence of the fact that the countries of the periphery simply happened to get a later start along the road to industrialization and economic modernization. Their condition is not just what might be called *"un*development." Frank calls it *"under*development," a form of poverty *imposed* on the poor countries by their economic connections with the capitalist rich. Poor countries are badly off, not because they have always been that way, but because they were made that way, their production structures systematically distorted and subordinated by the economies of the metropolitan center. As he wrote in 1966:

> [U]nderdevelopment is not original or traditional. . . . [C]ontemporary underdevelopment is in large part the historical product of past and continuing economic and other relations between the satellite underdeveloped and the now developed metropolitan countries. . . . [W]hen the metropolis expands to incorporate previously isolated regimes into the worldwide system, the previous development and industrialization of these regions is choked off or channeled into directions which are not self-perpetuating and promising.[4]

Unfortunately, Frank has a tendency to cast his argument in excessively doctrinaire marxist terminology:

> My thesis is that these capitalist contradictions and the historical development of the capitalist system have generated underdevelopment in the peripheral satellites whose economic surplus was expropriated, while generating economic development in the metropolitan centers which appropriate that surplus . . .[5]

Because of this intellectual bias, Frank's analysis has often been severely criticized, not least by writers who are otherwise fundamentally sympathetic to his broader point of view.[6] I have already discussed in Chapters 2 and 4 the weaknesses of the concepts of surplus value and economic surplus. Even so, Frank's type of argument can hardly be dismissed lightly. Too many writers have called attention to too many possible ways in which economic relations with the metropolitan center can generate and perpetuate poverty in the periphery.[7] These potential impacts are too numerous to ignore in a serious analytical study. As I suggested at the end of Chapter 4, one does not need to resort to elaborate intellectual abstractions—arguments about necessity or inevitability or the like—in order to find sufficient cause for the kinds of effects such writers are talking about. Convenience alone may be more than enough reason.

Trade. Consider, for instance, some potential impacts on the periphery of trade relations with the metropolitan center. Because of their head start in industrialization, the developed countries generally tend to have a competitive advantage in the export of manufactured goods, complemented by a hearty appetite for cheap imports of raw materials, fuels, and foodstuffs. At the same time, because of their considerably higher levels of income and output, the developed countries also tend to dominate in determining supply and demand in world markets for both of these types of products. Consequently, LDCs find themselves confronted with a distinctly biased structure of global prices. Concentration on one or a few primary-type exports (agriculture or extraction) is greatly encouraged, while development of home-grown manufacturing industry is more or less discouraged. The result is a decided skewness in the allocation of their resources; "one-dimensional states," they have often been called.

This skewness is an observable fact whose existence is admitted by even the most orthodox of contemporary economists. The conventional wisdom is that this is simply part of the world-wide system of specialization and division of labor, not necessarily a bad thing. According to marxists and radicals, however, it *is* a bad thing, for a variety of reasons.

In the first place, this skewness may not be in accord with the long-term dynamic competitive advantage of LDCs, even if it does seem in accord with their current, static production possibilities. The poor may be potentially capable of specializing in manufacturing with even greater efficiency than they have so far been able to achieve in their concentration on primary-type production. They do, after all, have many things working in their favor, including ready access to abundant raw materials and considerable supplies of cheap and willing labor. They may also be able to avail themselves of significant economies of scale in many lines of industrial output. Their only real problem may be the historical head start of the metropolitan center, which prevents them from breaking easily into established market patterns or denies them access to the most modern advances in technology. If this is so, then the presently skewed allocation of their resources is a *distortion* from their point of view, limiting their income and productivity below their genuine potential. This is what marxists and radicals mean when they say that relations with the center *generate* poverty in the periphery.

Furthermore, the skewness may not necessarily encourage the most rapid possible *growth* of factor endowments in the periphery. This is what marxists and radicals mean when they say that relations with the center *perpetuate* poverty in the periphery. Reliance on imports of manufactured goods may, for example, inhibit, if not altogether stifle, the development of indigenous entrepreneurial talent—the fourth factor, management. In instances where such talent may have already begun to develop, opening up of trade with the capitalist rich can actually destroy that valuable national resource; "industrial infanticide," Baran has called it.[8] Many writers cite the case of India where, prior to the arrival of the British, a flourishing textile industry had long been in existence. This industry was soon ruined by a flood of cheaper woven products from the power looms of England, and Indian entrepreneurs were forced into bankruptcy.[9] Frank has found evidence of a similar pattern of events in the economic histories of Chile and Brazil.[10]

It is not only entrepreneurial talent that can be lost when a domestic industry is ruined by the opening up of trade with the rich. Important industrial skills—forms of human capital—may be lost as well. Where such skills have only begun to develop, their accumulation may be retarded or stifled so long as the production structure is encouraged to concentrate on primary-type exports. A familiar phenomenon today is the "brain drain" out of the less developed countries, as scientists, engineers, and other highly educated professionals emigrate to the metropolitan center in search of better-paying jobs and a more stimulating work environment. Specialization in primary-type output can also lead directly to depletion of another valuable national resource—the very minerals and fuels which are being exported. By definition, these riches which lie under the soil and off the shores of poor countries are finite in supply. They are wasting assets and nonrenewable. Finally, perhaps worst of all, if specialization in primary production does produce all these effects, and thus does hold back expansion of national incomes in the periphery, it will retard the accumulation of local savings as well. Without savings the stock of productive capital cannot be readily expanded.

Investment. All of these potential impacts of trade relations on the periphery can be reinforced by the parallel effects of investment relations with the metropolitan center. Marxist and radical writers repeatedly assert that the operations of the large multinational corporations in poor countries serve only to accentuate and rigidify the skewness in the allocation of resources. In large measure this is because corporations historically have preferred to confine their investments mainly to the primary exporting sector (or the complementary transportation sector—in order to get the goods out). In most cases it is precisely these foreign corporations that have created the primary exporting sector. Specialization of foreign trade of the Third World in agricultural and extractive products usually resulted directly from the decision of foreign entrepreneurs to initiate and organize the exploitation of available natural resources.

From the point of view of the Third World, it was bad enough that such investments resulted in so skewed a resource allocation. Even worse was the tendency of the primary exporting sector to become what amounted to an independent enclave in each country, segregated from the remainder of the local economy and providing few benefits to it. Because ownership was foreign, profits generally tended to be either repatriated to the home country or reinvested only in the enclave, rather than utilized elsewhere in the host country. Since many of the workers employed in the enclave were foreign as well (owing to the technical or managerial skills required), much of the payments to labor generally tended to go abroad, either as personal savings or in payment for consumer goods available only in industrial countries. Likewise, most of the capital goods used in these operations tended to be purchased from abroad (owing to the lack of necessary manufacturing facilities and technology in the periphery). Consequently, very little of the income generated by enclave investments was apt to be left over to seep into the local economy.

To some extent, this picture has been changing in recent years. Multinational corporations are taking increasing advantage of the availability of supplies of cheap labor in poor countries to set up facilities for the manufacture or assembly of industrial products. The primary sector of the Third World now accounts for a declining proportion of total foreign investment. As one prominent Latin American radical economist has noted: "Foreign investment is gradually ceasing to be a colonial-exporting enclave and is changing the old international division of labor. . . . [F]oreign capital is turning toward the manufacturing sector." [11]

Yet even this, in the view of marxists and radicals, may only result in further generation and perpetuation of poverty in the periphery. Multinational corporations tend to have definite advantages over local enterprises in such respects as market connections, finance, and patents. Their manufacturing investments may simply suppress or ruin any nascent domestic competition. The effect therefore can be to raise even higher the barriers to development of indigenous entrepreneurial talent. In addition, whether due to force of habit or familiarity, multinational corporations tend to choose production techniques that are more appropriate to the metropolitan center (where capital is abundant relative to labor) than they are to the periphery (where capital is the relatively scarce factor). Consequently, the facilities that are established often fail to provide sufficient employment opportunities for available unemployed or underemployed workers, the effect of which can be to stunt the development of important industrial skills.

Perhaps the most frequent criticism of foreign manufacturing investment relates to its impact on the growth of the supply of capital in the periphery. Many such investments are underwritten by profits generated from past investments in the host country, or by credits or loans from banks in the host country, rather than by new capital imports from the metropolitan center. Moreover, to the extent that there are new capital imports from the center, much is spent on equipment or services bought from the center, rather than on locally available alternatives. (In large part this is due directly to the foreign investor's propensity to use production techniques more appropriate to the home country than to the periphery.) Consequently the net inflow of capital associated with new foreign investments may be quite small in absolute total.

Furthermore, any net inflow may be more than offset by the reverse outflow of dividends and interest earned on past investments in the periphery. Marxist and radical writers like to stress just how large that reverse outflow can be. In Latin

America, for instance, where American corporations are the biggest foreign investors, repatriation of profits back to the United States generally tends to run far in excess of the movement of new private U.S. capital into the region. During most of the 1950s and 1960s the reverse outflow exceeded the net inflow by as much as three to one. According to marxists and radicals, such figures amount to a process of "decapitalization" rather than capitalization. As one Latin American author states:

> Imperialism first makes its subject ill, and then it constructs the hospital in which the patient lies imprisoned and without any possibility of being cured. . . . It is a vicious circle of strangulation: loans and investments increase, and as a result the payments of amortizations, interest, dividends, and other services also increase. In order to make these payments, new injections of foreign capital that generate greater obligations are needed, and so on successively.[12]

Tastes

A country's production possibilities represent only one determinant of its overall national welfare. The other determinant is its pattern of tastes, as evidenced by the distribution of the public's total expenditures of income. Some patterns of taste enhance the development of the poor by encouraging a more efficient allocation of productive resources and/or by facilitating a more rapid growth of factor endowments. Other preference patterns will have just the opposite effect, retarding or distorting the progress of the poor. Tastes, like the quantity and quality of resources, can be greatly influenced by the nature of economic relations with the capitalist rich.

According to marxist and radical writers, this influence is inevitably misguided and malignant. Economic relations with the rich transmit to the poor a profile of preferences and desires altogether unsuited to their economic and social needs. Their distribution of expenditures does not reflect tastes which have been autonomously determined by their citizens and governments, but rather reflect the configuration of ideals and values, styles and fashions, generally associated with the system of global capitalism. This configuration, damaging to the development of the periphery, is transmitted by both trade and investment connections with the metropolitan center.

Trade transmits the configuration through what is usually called the "demonstration effect." This refers to the tendency on the part of many people in poor countries (at least those who can afford it) to attempt to emulate the consumption patterns of rich nations about which they constantly read in their press, or hear on their radio, or see for themselves on their television and in the movies. Tastes are gradually oriented away from home-grown products toward characteristically foreign types of goods. From the point of view of the needs of the periphery, this is considered distinctly bad, because it makes matters just that much worse for local infant industries trying to compete against manufactured imports from the metropolitan center. The ultimate effect may be to add to the forces inhibiting or stifling the development of indigenous entrepreneurial talent and industrial skills. The demonstration effect may result as well in a consumerist mentality which inflates the general level of consumption; that is, the average propensity to save may be considerably reduced by the determination to imitate the life style of the rich. This adds to the forces retarding growth of the capital stock in poor countries.

Investment connections reinforce these effects through what the radical economist, Stephen Hymer, has called "trickle-down marketing." [13] Once the demonstration effect has created an appetite for some commodity in the periphery, the multinational corporations producing it have an incentive to widen and consolidate the market via investment in merchandising facilities and sales promotion. (They also have an incentive to invest in assembly or manufacturing facilities closer to the market, another factor helping to explain the recent turn of foreign capital toward the manufacturing sector in LDCs.) Their aim is to facilitate the spread of a preference for their output throughout the whole of the local economy. This means that they must become involved in the international transmission of values and fashions. Peter Evans, a (nonradical) sociologist, has likened this activity to the similar role played by the Roman Catholic church in areas of the Third World:

> By introducing its wares and, even more important, by trying to convince people to consume them the manufacturing firm joins the church as an outsider helping to shape the culture of less developed countries.[14]

In the opinion of marxists and radicals, this amounts to "cultural imperialism," the destruction of local cultural autonomy; "coca-cola imperialism" it is often called. As regards the process of economic development, it may very well mean an even greater degree of skewness in the resource allocation of poor countries. As Evans summarized:

> [I]t seems plausible that multinational corporations help transmit standards of consumption which may well represent a misallocation of resources from the point of view of the welfare of the community as a whole. If this is true, then the distortion of consumer desires has a retarding effect on economic progress. . . .[15]

Classical Optimism

This is quite a bill of charges. Whether one focuses on production possibilities or on tastes, it appears that trade and investment with the rich *as a matter of course* can only result in ever greater poverty for the poor. Marxist and radical writers find remarkably little to praise in neocolonial economic relations. The potential impacts are many—and they are virtually all bad.

Ironically, such pessimism stands in stark contrast to the more optimistic view of prospects for the periphery expounded in classical imperialism theory. Most of the marxists and (liberal) radicals writing in the early part of the century emphasized the positive rather than the negative impacts of trade and investment on the poor. If anything, economic relations with the metropolitan center were expected to accelerate rather than retard or distort the development of less developed areas.

John Hobson, for instance, was convinced that the new imperialism of the late nineteenth century was good for colonial territories. In his opinion the stimulus to development in the periphery was so strong that eventually it would be the rich countries rather than the poor that would experience all the ill effects of trade and investment. For him, this was just one more reason for opposing Britain's colonial expansion overseas. The new imperialism transferred both capital and technology to areas of the periphery. It also gradually conditioned indigenous populations to a life of factory and machine work, thus effectively enhancing the endowment of labor. All this meant a considerable increase in the periphery's production possibilities. Ultimately, according to Hobson, it would also mean a serious competitive threat to the economies of the metropolitan center:

> Thus fully equipped for future international development in all the necessary productive powers, such a nation may turn upon her civilizer, untrammelled by need of further industrial aid, undersell him in his own market, take away his other foreign markets and secure for herself what further developing work remains to be done in other undeveloped parts of the earth.[16]

Hobson's predictions were echoed in the writings of other liberal critics of the new imperialism as well as in the writings of most marxists—both minority and majority views. Rosa Luxemburg, for example, thought that international expansion of capitalism would bring industrialization to the colonial periphery, and eventually competition back to the metropolitan center:

> [A]s soon as simple commodity production has superseded natural economy, capital must turn against it. No sooner has capital called it to life, than the two must compete for means of production, labour power, and markets.[17]

Lenin also argued that the new imperialism would enhance rather than limit the production possibilities of the poor. Like Hobson and Luxemburg, he expected that the transfers of capital and technology from the center would gradually lead to establishment of a viable and dynamic industrial base in areas of the periphery. He further expected that these transfers would gradually lead to a decline into decadence and atrophy by the imperialist powers themselves, as the bourgeoisie grew more and more dependent on *rentier* earnings from their overseas investments. According to Lenin, this was all part of the dialectical process of mature capitalist development. He called it the system's stage of "parasitism and decay." [18]

Where did this more optimistic view of prospects for the periphery come from? In fact, Hobson, Luxemburg, and Lenin were all simply following the lead of the so-called classical school of capitalist economics. As unorthodox as they may have been in other respects, when it came to the issue of development in poor countries the principal theorists of imperialism tended to be utterly conventional. Their ideas were borrowed directly from the earlier liberal tradition of Adam Smith and his followers.

Not that the liberal tradition paid a great deal of attention to the issue of development in the periphery. For the most part, growth problems hardly even entered into the discussions of the classical school, except as a distinctly subsidiary theme. The vast majority of Smith's followers preferred to focus on more static kinds of questions. Optimality, not development, was their central theme—finding the most efficient allocation of the existing endowment of resources, not finding the path to the most rapid growth of factor supplies. For example, probably the most prominent member of the classical school in the early decades of the nineteenth century was David Ricardo. His writings on international economics always stressed the static benefits to be gained from an improved allocation of resources. Free global trade would enable every country (and colony) to specialize in the export of those things it could produce relatively more cheaply than anyone else, in exchange for what others could produce at lower resource cost. This was his famous doctrine or law of comparative advantage (comparative costs). It was not necessary that a country be able to produce something *absolutely* more cheaply; it sufficed that each country concentrate on what it did *relatively* best. This was enough to ensure that all would gain (or at least not lose) from the international division of labor. Resources would be allocated optimally, in the most efficient manner possible. As a result incomes and productivity around the world, including in the periphery, would be raised to their maximum. Throughout the nineteenth century Ricardo's type of static approach dominated most discussions of international trade theory and policy.

However, this does not mean that the classical school was unconcerned with the more dynamic aspects of international trade theory and policy. In fact, the liberal tradition regarded trade as a particularly powerful kind of "engine of growth." In at least three ways, participation in the international economy was expected to stimulate and transmit development from the metropolitan center to the periphery.[19]

First, trade was expected to raise the capacity for saving because of the positive impact of international specialization on incomes and productivity. This in turn would permit a higher rate of accumulation of the stock of productive capital. It might also stimulate an inflow of capital, skilled labor, and technology to develop periphery sources of supply. (Though they usually assumed international immobility of factors in their theoretical analyses, nineteenth-century economists were not unaware of the vast migrations of people and capital that were in fact taking place.) All of these effects were at least implicit in the Ricardian comparative costs theory of trade.

A second element in the engine of growth, sometimes called the "productivity" theory of trade, was emphasized by John Stuart Mill, Ricardo's successor as leader of the classical school in the middle decades of the century.[20] The "more efficient employment of the productive forces of the world" Mill called the "direct economical advantage of foreign trade." But, he suggested, "there are, besides, indirect effects, which must be counted as benefits of a high order." One of the most significant of these was "the tendency of every extension of the market to improve the process of production." [21] Widening the division of labor would tend to enhance the skill and dexterity of workers, encourage technical improvements and innovations, and permit greater use of machinery. In addition, it would enable countries to capture significant economies of scale by overcoming technical indivisibilities. Mill also stressed the fundamental educative effect of foreign trade. Commercial contacts abroad would stimulate importation of industrial skills, management methods, and more advanced technologies. Even more important would be importation of a whole new way of life (see Hobson above). This consideration, he said, was "principally applicable to an early stage of industrial advancement":

> A people may be in a quiescent, indolent, uncultivated state, with all their tastes either fully satisfied or entirely undeveloped, and they may fail to put forth the whole of their productive energies for want of any sufficient object of desire. The opening of a foreign trade, by making them acquainted with new objects, or tempting them by the easier acquisition of things which they had not previously thought attainable, sometimes works a sort of industrial revolution in a country whose resources were previously undeveloped for want of energy and ambition in the people: inducing those who were satisfied with scanty comforts and little work, to work harder for the gratification of their new tastes, and even to save, and accumulate capital, for the still more complete satisfaction of those tastes at a future time.[22]

The third element in the engine of growth was emphasized by the founder of the classical school himself, Adam Smith. This was the "vent-for-surplus" theory of trade, which focused on the role of exports as an outlet for surplus production over domestic requirements. Smith observed that countries frequently had a capacity for certain lines of activity for which there was simply not enough effective demand in the home market. Resources for which there were no available alternative uses of significant economic value at home could easily be rescued from idleness or underemployment by access to foreign markets. In Smith's opinion, this was an important benefit of international trade:

> It carries out that surplus part of the produce of their land and labour for which there is no demand among them, and brings back in return for it something else for which there is a demand. It gives a value to their superfluities, by exchanging them for something else, which may satisfy a part of their wants, and increase their enjoyments. By means of it, the narrowness of the home market does not hinder the division of labour in any particular branch of art or manufacture from being carried to the highest perfection.[23]

All three of these elements were present in the liberal economic tradition, even if not emphasized in most public discussions. This was mainly because growth was not considered something to worry or wonder about in the context of the expanding economy of the nineteenth century. Growth was just something that happened—a fact of life, part of the natural order of things. As one source has noted:

> Why was this aspect neglected? Perhaps because economic growth was taken for granted, like the air we breathe. As it was going on at a pace satisfactory for both the new countries and the old, it seemed a matter of no particular interest compared with the fascinating theoretical problem of "entry into contact." Once economies had entered into contact through trade and reallocated their resources for increased specialization, what happened after that? Well, of course, they just grew and progressed, as everything did in the nineteenth century.[24]

In short, growth was inherent in the intellectual milieu. The role of trade as an engine of growth was universally accepted as axiomatic by all branches of the classical school of capitalist economics. Like the air they breathed, it was accepted by all of the principal radical and marxist theorists of imperialism as well.

The Debate

As expressed either in early imperialism theory or in the liberal economic tradition, the classical optimistic view of prospects for the periphery remained the conventional wisdom for many decades. It was also as far removed from the more modern theory of neocolonialism as it possibly could be. The two stand as extreme alternatives, antipodes in a debate of considerable consequence. Where does the truth actually lie? Can economic relations with the rich really be an engine of growth for the poor, as the older tradition maintained? Or must they necessarily retard and distort development in the periphery, as the newer marxist and radical writings insist?

The answer may be anticipated. As is so often the case in debates of this kind, the truth in fact lies somewhere between the two extremes. Economic relations with the rich may not *always* be an engine of growth for the poor, but they can certainly have that effect at times. Trade and investment need not *necessarily* result in greater poverty in the periphery, but they can certainly have that effect often enough. It all depends on the circumstances.

The Swinging Pendulum

In a sense, the modern theory of neocolonialism simply represents the furthest swing of the pendulum away from the earlier classical optimism. There is no doubt that such a swing was justified. Nineteenth-century economists tended to be a bit myopic when it came to the subject of growth. They saw growth in northern and western Europe, the heartland of advanced capitalism, in the "regions of recent settlement" in the world's temperate latitudes (including, in particular, the United States, Canada, Australia, New Zealand, and South Africa), and in

Japan after the Meiji restoration. Therefore they saw it every-where—in southern and eastern Europe, Africa, Asia, and Latin America as well. In truth, growth in these places was only rarely a fact of everyday life; stagnation, not development, was much more the natural order of things. Yet even there the classical economists took growth for granted—if not today, then surely tomorrow or the next day. Their vision of progress was unbounded.

Optimism on such a scale was clearly excessive, since the prospects for the periphery were never that favorable. It had to be only a matter of time before the classical school's unbounded vision of progress for the Third World would be called into question. Doubts first began to arise during the Great Depression of the 1930s, and then became widespread after the start of decolonization following World War II. Suddenly dozens of new nations were being created with little or no prospect for rapid economic development. Their growth, far from being taken for granted, was something to be analyzed, planned, encouraged, sustained, and consolidated. As a result, development became the preoccupation of a whole new branch of economic study, and the role of trade and investment in the development process became the subject of extensive inquiry in its own right.

Gradually the pendulum started to swing. Economists began to recognize that economic relations with the rich need not always work to the benefit of the poor. Many potentially negative impacts were identified—on allocation of resources, growth of factor supplies, and patterns of tastes. Ultimately these impacts began to appear in the writings of marxists and radicals as well. Virtually all of the negative effects now regularly enumerated in marxist and radical sources were first remarked by considerably more orthodox members of the economics profession.[25]

But the difference is that these more orthodox economists have never allowed the pendulum to swing *all* the way to the opposite extreme. Marxists and radicals choose to emphasize *only* the negative effects of trade and investment. They cannot see capitalism as anything but disadvantageous to the poor; their theories and analyses are highly deterministic. For others less categorical in orientation, capitalism can be viewed more dispassionately as a mixed blessing for the periphery. Participation in the international economy is certainly no guarantee of growth, but may still be regarded as an invitation to growth. The outcome depends especially on three circumstances—the strength of the initial stimulus to development, the strength of the various "linkages" transmitting this stimulus to the remainder of the local economy, and the local economy's overall "capacity to transform."

The Stimulus

Both trade and investment provide an initial stimulus to development in the form of additional income potentially available for expenditure in the local economy or abroad. The strength of the trade stimulus depends on the net volume of demand which foreign buyers bring to the export sector. The strength of the investment stimulus depends on the net volume of capital which foreign investors bring to the investment sector. Both volumes are highly variable.

Trade. In the nineteenth century the net volume of demand brought by foreign buyers to the export sector of what were then considered poorer countries was enormous. Economic growth in the center meant a rapidly rising level of purchases of primary-type output in the periphery. The greatest stimulus was provided by Britain, first home of the industrial revolution. Many countries were among the beneficiaries. The Netherlands, for example, gained a substantial additional income from Britain's rising level of demand for such foodstuffs as meat and cheese. Denmark gained similarly from the demand for butter, eggs, and bacon, and Sweden from timber, wood pulp, and iron ore. The United States was an early recipient of this stimulus in cotton, and most of the temperate regions of recent settlement shared in the stimulus provided by wheat, wool, and (after refrigerator ships were developed in about 1875) meat. Even tropical countries benefited significantly from British (and European) demand for foodstuffs and raw materials. One source has estimated that the exports of tropical countries rose by an average of 3.6 percent a year between 1883 and 1913, with the largest increases recorded in west and central Africa and parts of Latin America. The principal exceptions were India and the sugar colonies.[26]

Perhaps the most striking example of the trade stimulus at work in the nineteenth century was Japan. Prior to 1858 the Japanese were almost totally isolated from the rest of the world economy. After that year, as the country's self-imposed restrictions on economic contact were gradually lifted, its volume of exports increased rapidly, multiplying some seventyfold in the first dozen years. World demand for silk and tea, in particular, was exceptionally strong. As a result, Japan's national income rose by an estimated 65 percent during the transition from autarky to free trade.[27]

In the twentieth century a number of countries have benefited enormously from the stimulus of foreign trade in primary products, particularly the oil-exporting countries—Venezuela, Nigeria, Indonesia, and Iran, as well as many of the Arab states. Unfortunately, such privileged countries tend to be the exception. For perhaps the majority of LDCs today, the stimulus provided by the primary export sector seems to be weaker than it was in the nineteenth century. Economists now recognize that economic growth in the center no longer means as rapidly rising a level of demand for foodstuffs and raw materials from the periphery as it once did.

In conventional economic analysis, the connection between economic growth and demand is described by the concept of income elasticity—the percentage change of quantity demanded divided by the percentage change of income. In the nineteenth century the income elasticity of demand in the center for the agricultural and extractive output of the periphery was considerably greater than one: increases of income in the rich translated into a considerably greater than proportional rise of sales of such products by the poor. This no longer tends to be so. On average, the center's income elasticity of demand for such products now seems to be no more than about two-thirds at best; that is, a growth rate of 3 percent in the rich seems to mean no more than about a 2 percent growth rate of total demand for the primary output of the poor. This represents a relative secular decline in the overall stimulus provided through the periphery's primary export sector.

Any number of reasons for this decline have been identified.[28] Especially important is the rising share of services in the gross output of most rich countries. This automatically implies that demand for primary production will lag behind growth of income in the rich. Demand for imports of raw materials suffers specifically from the trend of industrial production in rich countries away from "light" industries (e.g., textiles), where the raw material content of finished output is high, toward "heavy" industries (e.g., engineering and chemicals) in which the raw material content is lower. Such demand has also been affected adversely by technological developments in the recovery and recycling of materials, and by inventions of numerous synthetics and other man-made substitutes for imports. Demand for imports of foodstuffs suffers specifically from agricultural protectionism in the metropolitan center, as well as from the shifting composition of consumption there from items with high import content (e.g., tropical beverages and vegetable oils) toward those with lower import content (e.g., meat and poultry).

For many poor countries, the effect of the relative secular decline of the trade stimulus in primary commodities has been an increasing "foreign-exchange gap"—that is, an increasing shortage of foreign-exchange earnings from exports to pay for the various imports needed for economic development. This effect has been compounded through a downward pressure on the terms of trade of such countries—on their export prices relative to their import prices. These countries thus find it difficult to close their foreign-exchange gap by increasing their productivity and export volume. Because of the low income elasticity of demand for primary-type output in the center, often the only significant result is a decline of export prices in the periphery, with little or no change in net foreign-exchange proceeds. In other words, productivity gains are often exported to the rich through the declining terms of trade of the poor.[29] To this extent, marxists and radicals are right to criticize the typically skewed allocation of resources in LDCs. In many instances specialization in primary production, even if in accord with static comparative costs, does limit the level of current income as well as the accumulation of factor supplies. It obviously can also accentuate the dependence of many such countries on private capital exports from the capitalist rich.

But of course it is possible to exaggerate these ill effects, The criticism ignores the possible benefits of such specialization, in particular the vent-for-surplus aspect of primary trade emphasized by Adam Smith and others. The vent-for-surplus theory of trade assumes that some resource endowments are highly specific, able to be used economically for only one or a few specific purposes. In more advanced economies such specificity of resource supply is generally rare. Their relatively highly developed price mechanisms and economic organization allow any surplus of productive capacity over domestic requirements to be equilibrated away in time by appropriate adjustments of price. The vent-for-surplus theory of trade, therefore, is not normally applicable in the conditions of the metropolitan center. In the countries of the periphery, however, conditions are different. Prices usually are less flexible than in rich countries, demand and supply less elastic, factors less mobile. Consequently, some resources do find themselves condemned to idleness or underemployment because of an insufficient home market. (These include not only land and other natural resources—minerals, petroleum, and so on—but also much of the labor force, at least in rural areas.) The vent-for-surplus theory is applicable in these conditions. Access to foreign markets may be viewed as a virtually "costless" means of stimulating domestic activity and adding to national income. This is a real benefit of specialization in primary production which marxists and radicals are prone either to overlook or forget.

Marxists and radicals also neglect the possibility that LDCs may be able to circumvent the ill effects of primary specialization by diversifying out of agriculture or extraction and into other lines of activity. Although difficult, it is not impossible for poor countries to overcome the historical head start of the rich, as well as the specificity of their own resources, and take advantage of economies of scale, cheap labor supplies, abundant raw materials, or other favorable endowments to reduce the degree of their concentration on primary-type exports. Many have already begun to do so. Mexico, Brazil, South Korea, and Taiwan, for example, have been able to shift resources increasingly out of the peasant sector and into various kinds of industrial manufacture and assembly. Certain other LDCs have been favorably placed to concentrate on the sale of specialized services of various kinds, such as banking and finance (Hong Kong, Singapore, Lebanon) or tourism (parts of the Mediterranean and Caribbean). For countries such as these, as for countries using primary exports as a vent for surplus, the trade stimulus still works effectively to make available considerable amounts of additional income.

Investment. Many of the same points hold with respect to the investment stimulus to development. In the nineteenth century the net volume of capital which investors in the metropolitan center brought to the investment sector of what were then considered poorer countries—especially countries around the edges of Europe and in the regions of recent settlement—was enormous (see Chapter 2). Such privileged countries have tended to become the exception in the twentieth century. In relative terms, there is now much less new private investment in poor countries than there used to be. The stimulus from this source has also weakened on the contemporary scene. To this extent marxists and radicals are right to criticize foreign investment for its relatively more limited contribution to the growth of the supply of capital in the Third World. But it is possible to exaggerate this problem, too.

It is certainly an exaggeration to contrast the net inflow of new capital from the center with the frequently even larger reverse outflow of dividends and interest earned on previous investments in the periphery, and to call this decapitalization. The fallacy here is like saying that investors never have the right to enjoy the profits of their own investments. As one source has noted:

> It is surely not incumbent on a reviewer to destroy this tired fallacy, beyond saying that if one makes an investment, say in ten shares of General Motors, one is not obliged to reinvest in G.M. a sum equal to the annual dividends for the rest of time, nor is one exploiting General Motors if one spends the income.[30]

By definition, decapitalization means destruction of economically productive facilities. This is hardly the reason why investors make investments, foreign or otherwise. Investments are made in order to *build* productive facilities, to expand output capacity and the potential for additional income. In the case of foreign investment, the real issue is whether the facilities thus built represent a *net* addition to the volume of capital in the host country, or simply take the place of existing facilities or of new facilities that might otherwise be built by indigenous enterprise. Does the foreign investment handicap or discourage domestic entrepreneurs from launching competing operations—for instance, by depriving them of access to bank loans or credits, or by bidding away their skilled labor force? Does it even drive them out of business altogether? If so, it adds nothing on balance to the stock of capital locally, and the eventual reverse outflow of earnings overseas does constitute a net loss to the economy of the periphery. On the other hand, if the foreign investment does not do all these things, then the effect on the capital supply on balance must be regarded as positive—as capitalization, not decapitalization—and the reverse outflow of profits must be treated as a legitimate return to the investor for the risks he has undertaken. Only the deepest pessimist would deny the latter possibility in every case. As one (nonradical) source has suggested, foreign investment "shares to a very high degree the ambiguity of most human inventions and institutions: it has considerable potential for both good and evil." [31] In many cases foreign investors bring a substantial net volume of capital to the investment sector of LDCs. To that extent the investment stimulus still works effectively.

That still leaves the problem of the foreign-exchange gap, which cannot be ignored. Superficially, an excess of dividends and interest outflows over new capital inflows appears to worsen the problem of balance-of-payments deficit for poor countries. It does so in many instances, but this result is hardly certain. Overlooked is the related effect of foreign investment on other aspects of the balance of payments—especially on the capacity to export or to replace imports out of domestic production. In many cases the net result is a narrower, not a wider, foreign-exchange gap. Even in this respect the ill effects of the investment stimulus are all too often exaggerated.

The "Linkages"

Additional income provided by trade or investment is the initial stimulus, the "invitation" to growth. Whether that invitation will actually be "delivered" depends on the second of three circumstances specified—the strength of the various linkages transmitting the stimulus to the remainder of the local economy.

Suppose that foreign trade creates a substantial and growing export sector in an LDC. Will the impulse provided by the expansion of foreign demand actually make itself felt in other economic sectors? That depends on the character of the export base itself, on such matters as the factor proportions and the types of technologies actually being used in the production for foreign markets. These determine the percentage of the value of output that will be spent at home or abroad in ways that will promote the country's domestic development.

For example, factor proportions are important because they determine the distribution of the net income generated by a rising level of exports, and therefore the pattern of expenditures on final consumption. In general, labor-intensive export industries such as peasant agriculture or light manufacturing (a relatively large share of whose costs are accounted for by wages or their equivalent) are more likely to be effective in promoting local development than such capital-intensive industries as mining, petroleum, or plantation agriculture. This is because peasants and workers tend to have a higher propensity to consume domestic goods and a lower propensity to import than large landowners or capitalists. Consequently, more of the income is spent on home production, furthering current industrial growth. In addition, to the extent that they are able to save at all, peasants and workers tend to use domestic financial institutions more than large landowners and capitalists (who are more apt to leak their funds abroad to foreign financial centers). More of the income thus becomes available locally to finance future industrial growth.

Types of technologies are important because they determine the extent to which subsidiary production stages will be promoted locally by a rising level of exports. Relatively unsophisticated production techniques in a poor country's export industries make it easier for domestic entrepreneurs to offer their services at related stages of the production process, either as suppliers of various inputs such as materials, tools, or machinery ("backward" linkage) or as marketing agents or processors of raw or semifinished output ("forward" linkage). This is a major means of transmitting the growth impulse provided by expanding foreign demand. The export base integrates fully into the local economy, playing the role of "leading sector" in a takeoff into self-sustaining development. Highly sophisticated industrial techniques in the export base, borrowed directly from the metropolitan center, are more apt to discourage than encourage production linkages either backward or forward. The sector is likely to remain segregated from the local economy, rather than be integrated into it, and sources in the center rather than at home will be relied upon for inputs, processing, and marketing.

Unfortunately, both the factor proportions and types of technologies used in the export industries of LDCs are frequently apt to be unfavorable to their long-term growth prospects. Most economists have now come to realize this. Export sectors concentrated on primary-type output often provide, at best, only a weak transmission belt for the stimulus of foreign demand. Much export-oriented agriculture (apart from some peasant crops like cocoa, jute, or rice) and most extractive industries tend to be more intensive in capital than in labor; many of these, particularly mining and petroleum, also employ only the most sophisticated types of technologies in production. The result is that often relatively little of the impulse provided by expanding foreign demand actually carries over into promotion of domestic development.

To this extent marxists and radicals are again right to criticize the typically skewed allocation of resources in the Third World. They are equally right in criticizing the parallel effects of investment relations in this respect. Foreign investments from the metropolitan center, for all the net volume of capital they may bring to the periphery, are frequently even more apt to be intensive in capital rather than in labor, and to involve sophisticated types of technology appropriate to the home country rather than to the periphery. This was usually the case with the traditional enclave type of investment in agriculture or extraction. Marxist and radical writers like to point out that it is also often the case with the increasing number of multinational corporate investments in the manufacturing sector of poor countries. Finally, to the same extent, such writers are right to criticize trade and investment relations for their impact on taste patterns in most poor countries. As a result of the demonstration effect and trickle-down marketing, more of the income generated by economic connections with the rich is apt to be spent on imports, and perhaps less will be saved, than would otherwise be likely.

However, marxists and radicals have a tendency to exaggerate these ill effects, too. Weak though they may be in many instances, some of the linkages provided by the character of the export or investment base can be quite strong. Case studies have shown that even in the most classic types of extractive industries (whether foreign or domestically owned), the stimulus to domestic development provided through local consumer expenditures and forward and backward production linkages has often grown to be remarkably vigorous.[32] In time, investors do respond to obvious environmental differences by adapting their technologies and factor proportions. There is also much evidence that, in the long run, the impacts of trade and investment relations on taste patterns in poor countries are not as misguided and malignant as marxists and radicals insist. One source has stressed how imports "reconnoiter and map out the country's demand; they remove uncertainty and reduce selling costs at the same time, thereby bringing perceptibly closer the point at which domestic production can economically be started." [33] Others stress the incentive side of the demonstration effect—the inspiration of greater work effort and production as well as new consumer preferences and desires. People may be moved by foreign trade or trickle-down marketing not only to buy more but also, as Mill said, "to work harder for the gratification of their new tastes, and even to save." [34] This can often more than offset the demonstration effect on the consumption side.

Finally, it is important not to overlook the role played by the fiscal mechanism in poor countries in strengthening the linkages leading from the stimulus of trade or investment. Even if the export or investment sector does not become an integrated part of the local economy, it must pay taxes, and these revenues can be used by the government to promote further economic development at home. Throughout most areas of the Third World the fiscal mechanism is being used increasingly in precisely this fashion. The share of profits going to the state, particularly from extractive investments, has been rising regularly in recent years.[35] This share may still not be as large, or expanding as rapidly, as it might, and governments may not be utilizing the revenues of taxation as effectively as they might. But so long as such revenues are forthcoming and put to use for development purposes, they serve to facilitate the carry-over from the foreign trade or investment base, whatever its specific character.

The "Capacity to Transform"

The linkages provided by the character of the export or investment base ensure that the initial invitation to growth will be delivered. There is still the question of whether that stimulus, once transmitted, will elicit any response. This depends on the third of the three circumstances specified—the local economy's overall "capacity to transform."

Capacity to transform refers to an economy's ability to react to change (originating at home or abroad) by reallocating resources and otherwise adapting the domestic structure of production. At the most general level, this is a matter of the economy's overall receptivity to market signals. The greater that receptivity, the more likely it is that growth stimuli carrying over from the export or investment sector will actually result in development in other sectors or activities. If the environment is truly hospitable, even a small stimulus transmitted through weak linkages will produce significant economic progress. When there are formidable domestic impediments that limit receptivity to change, even a great stimulus transmitted through strong linkages will have little penetrative power.

In the nineteenth century, the capacity to transform was obviously high in such areas as northern and western Europe, the regions of recent settlement, and Japan. This helps to explain why the classical economists were so myopic about growth: their unbounded vision of progress was an understandable generalization from the relatively small sample of happy cases they knew best. In the twentieth century it has become clear that, for a variety of social and cultural reasons, these were really special cases in history. The vast majority of mankind, then as now, lived in societies committed to more traditional values and verities. Their amenability to economic adaptation was quite minimal. This was not recognized by the classical school of economics, but is now taken for granted by most contemporary economists.

Indeed, for some contemporary economists this has become the main explanation for the frequent failure of trade or investment to act as an engine of growth in the periphery.[36] Such sources stress the many formidable domestic impediments to change in LDCs, the market "imperfections" which severely limit the capacity to transform. These include immobility of resources, rigidity of prices, monopolistic tendencies in both factor and goods markets, lack of relevant information, absence of entrepreneurial talent, inadequate money and credit institutions, and insufficient transportation and communications facilities—all acting to reduce a poor economy's receptivity to signals from the marketplace. If these imperfections are serious enough, they will block development no matter how powerful the invitation to growth resulting from participation in the international economy.

Marxist and radical writers also stress the limited capacity to transform of LDCs, but they differ from more orthodox economists in their explanation of these imperfections. Conventional analysis emphasizes the force of sociocultural habits and customs—the lack of receptivity or active hostility to change on the part of traditional social organization. Marxists and radicals criticize this attitude as bordering on the racist. In Magdoff's words: "The crucial obstacles to the needed changes are not to be found in the innate nature of the people, or in special features of their culture, or in their religion. The obstacles, instead, are located in the social institutions under which people live."[37] In short, the obstacles are in participation in the international economy itself, which restricts economic adaptability in the periphery. It is not that the domestic environment is genuinely inhospitable to market signals, but that the poor are prevented from responding to these signals by their economic connections with the rich. Limited factor mobility, price rigidity, and all the rest are said to be the direct result of the metropolitan center's destructive competitive power in trade and investment markets. Through the various impacts described earlier, the large multinational corporations effectively suppress the capacity to transform in the economies of the periphery.

Once again marxists and radicals are right in their criticism to some extent, and likewise they have a way of exaggerating the ill effects. Undoubtedly many of these negative impacts on the capacity to transform do occur. For example, the monopolistic powers of many multinational corporations do often inhibit local price flexibility, or the diffusion of information, or the development of indigenous entrepreneurial talent. Even so, it is misleading to concentrate on such impacts alone. This makes a caricature of the facts.

First, it is hardly racist to call attention to sociocultural differences between countries. While traditional social organization in most poor countries may not be quite as unreceptive to change as is often supposed, the resistance is there and can hardly be denied. Qualitative differences between the economic institutions, attitudes, and behavioral norms of rich and poor countries have been remarked often enough.[38]

Besides, there are positive as well as negative impacts to keep in mind. One, the vent for surplus which trade offers as an offset to traditional market imperfections, has already been mentioned. A second is the fundamental educative effect of participation in the international economy emphasized by Mill and others. Try as they might, multinational corporations cannot monopolize forever their knowledge of technologies, industrial skills, management methods, and so on. Eventually (though not necessarily very quickly) such information begins to seep into less developed economies—particularly through the effect of foreign investment on the mobilization of resources—to help break down factor immobility and price rigidity, and help build up indigenous entrepreneurial talent and economic infrastructure. The incentive side of the demonstration effect also eventually tends to assert itself to help inspire greater work effort and new attitudes. All of this enhances the capacity to transform of poor countries, and can smooth the operation of the international engine of growth.

Polarization and Spread

In conclusion, it appears that economic relations with the rich are rather risky for the poor. Participation in the international economy might turn out to be quite beneficial, or it might be just the opposite. The initial stimulus provided by trade or investment could turn out to be not very great; the linkages to the remainder of the local economy could be weak; the economy's capacity to transform could be low. Any one of these circumstances could conceivably short-circuit the engine of growth and retard or distort the development of poor countries. Modern marxist and radical writers, therefore, are by no means entirely wrong. But neither were the classical optimists. Both views take in a piece of the truth.

The real issue is what conventional economic analysis refers to as the problem of "agglomeration." Historically, growth has always been decidedly uneven, beginning in certain centers of economic strength and then radiating various pressures and tensions outward. These pressures and tensions may or may not result in parallel growth elsewhere. In some respects, growth tends to polarize centripetally in the original center of strength, reflecting the economies inherent in locating as many activities as possible in a single place (agglomeration). In other respects growth tends to spread centrifugally into less developed areas in the periphery, reflecting the diseconomies of spatial agglomeration. Both polarization and spread are cumulative, self-reinforcing processes, and both operate simultaneously.[39]

Polarization reflects the advantages of a head start. An early start gives an area experience, control of the latest technologies, a developed infrastructure, and a reserve of productive capital (human as well as nonhuman). It also gives the area an opportunity to exploit all available economies of scale. Accordingly, it can mean a definite competive superiority in many lines of trade. Other things being equal, producers in less developed areas will be thwarted and driven out of business, while capital and labor in peripheral areas will be attracted to migrate to the more highly developed center. The tendency will be for growth to concentrate cumulatively.

But this will not be the only tendency. There will be a simultaneous disposition for growth to spread cumulatively, reflecting the fact that there are also disadvantages to beginning first. In particular, costs of production have a way of rising eventually in an early starter as compared with less developed areas, partly because of congestion and overcrowding of industry on a limited resource base, partly because of the effect of rising income levels on the market price of labor. Consequently, producers in the periphery will benefit from the growing diffusion of demand for less expensive imports of raw materials, foodstuffs, and consumer items; areas of the periphery will also benefit from an outflow of capital from the center in search of cheaper supplies of labor, aiming to establish production facilities in those lines of output for which the center has no special advantage. In this latter respect, latecomers enjoy the distinct advantages of being able to learn from the experiences of the early starter, and of not being weighed down with an outmoded industrial plant.

Obviously other things are not equal. Growth in a core area generates positive as well as negative impacts on peripheral areas. This is the important fact that modern marxists and radicals are prone to overlook or forget when they talk of neocolonialism. Like the classical optimists, they suffer from a bit of myopia about growth. Their outlook is much too deterministic. All they see is polarization—industrial infanticide, brain drain, decapitalization of the poor. What they fail to see is spread—the benefits of import demand from the rich, capital inflows, borrowings of skills and technologies, and so on. Participation in the international economy need not, on balance, be bad for LDCs. It all depends on the relative strength of the two cumulative processes.

A priori, it is impossible to know which of the two processes is apt to be the stronger. In every instance the outcome will be determined by a host of detailed circumstances. There is no necessity, no inevitability. Capitalist traders and investors are just going about their business—buying and selling, investing their capital, and trying to make a profit—and LDCs may, incidentally, either gain or lose as a result.

NOTES

1. A word of caution here is necessary. Measurement and comparison of national per capita products are notoriously difficult and imprecise. In many countries estimates of GNP as well as population are subject to a wide margin of error; an additional source of error or bias is introduced by the process of conversion from local currency values into U.S. dollars. For a brief discussion of some of the problems inherent in these kinds of calculations, see Everett E. Hagen, *The Economics of Development* (Homewood, Illinois: R. D. Irwin, 1968), chap. 1.

2. Here is another word of caution. In the ensuing discussion, development will be taken to be synonymous with economic growth—i.e., as mean-

ing expansion of output and income on either a gross or per capita basis—even though the two concepts are not theoretically identical. Development is really much broader in meaning, involving changes which are social and political as well as narrowly economic. Growth per se does not measure development. However, development requires resources and growth supplies them. Therefore, growth can be regarded as a useful measure of the *capacity* for development. In other words, growth can be regarded as a *necessary* condition for development, even if not as a *sufficient* condition. It is in this sense that the two concepts will be treated as synonymous.

3. See, e.g., Andre Gunder Frank, *Capitalism and Underdevelopment in Latin America*, rev. ed. (New York: Monthly Review Press, 1969); Frank, *Latin America: Underdevelopment or Revolution* (New York: Monthly Review Press, 1969).

4. Frank, "The Development of Underdevelopment," in Frank, *Latin America*, pp. 4, 11.

5. Frank, *Capitalism and Underdevelopment*, p. 3.

6. See, e.g., Susanne Bodenheimer, "Dependency and Imperialism: The Roots of Latin American Underdevelopment," in K. T. Fann and Donald C. Hodges, eds., *Readings in U.S. Imperialism* (Boston: Porter Sargent, 1971), pp. 168–169.

7. There is not enough space to cite all of the many marxist and radical authors who have written on aspects of this problem. Only a representative sample can be listed, including (in addition to Frank) Paul A. Baran, *The Political Economy of Growth* (1957; reprint ed., New York: Monthly Review Press, 1968), chaps. 5–7; Paul M. Sweezy, *Modern Capitalism and Other Essays* (New York: Monthly Review Press, 1972), chaps. 1–2; Pierre Jalée, *The Pillage of the Third World* (New York: Monthly Review Press, 1968); Michael Barratt Brown, *After Imperialism*, rev. ed. (New York: Humanities Press, 1970); Thomas E. Weisskopf, "Capitalism, Underdevelopment and the Future of the Poor Countries," in Jagdish N. Bhagwati, ed., *Economics and World Order* (New York: Macmillan, 1972), pp. 43–77; Stephen H. Hymer and Stephen A. Resnick, "International Trade and Uneven Development," in Jagdish N. Bhagwati, Ronald W. Jones, Robert A. Mundell, and Jaroslav Vanek, eds., *Trade, Balance of Payments and Growth* (Amsterdam: North-Holland Publishing Co., 1971), pp. 473–494. See also Fann and Hodges, *Readings in U.S. Imperialism*, and Robert I. Rhodes, ed., *Imperialism and Underdevelopment: A Reader* (New York: Monthly Review Press, 1970).

8. Baran, *Political Economy of Growth*, p. 174.

9. See, e.g., ibid., pp. 144–150.

10. See Frank, *Capitalism and Underdevelopment*.

11. Theotonio Dos Santos, "The Changing Structure of Foreign Investment in Latin America," in James Petras and Maurice Zeitlin, eds., *Latin America: Reform or Revolution?* (Greenwich, Conn.: Fawcett, 1968), p. 97.

12. Eduardo Galeano, "Latin America and the Theory of Imperialism," in Fann and Hodges, *Readings in U.S. Imperialism*, p. 217.

13. Stephen H. Hymer, "The Efficiency (Contradictions) of Multinational Corporations," *American Economic Review* 60, no. 2 (May 1970): 444–445, and "The Multinational Corporation and the Law of Uneven Development," in Bhagwati, *Economics and World Order*, pp. 125–126. See also

Peter B. Evans, "National Autonomy and Economic Development: Critical Perspectives on Multinational Corporations in Poor Countries," in Robert O. Keohane and Joseph S. Nye, eds., *Transnational Relations and World Politics* (Cambridge: Harvard University Press, 1972), pp. 332–335.

14. Evans, "National Autonomy," p. 332.

15. Ibid., p. 335.

16. John A. Hobson, *Imperialism: A Study* (Ann Arbor, Mich.: University of Michigan Press, 1965), p. 308.

17. Rosa Luxemburg, *The Accumulation of Capital* (London: Routledge, 1951), p. 402. For a useful discussion, see George Lee, "Rosa Luxemburg and the Impact of Imperialism," *Economic Journal* 81, no. 324 (December 1971): 847–862.

18. V. I. Lenin, *Imperialism, The Highest Stage of Capitalism* (Peking: Foreign Languages Press, 1965), p. 118.

19. The phrase "engine of growth" was coined in 1938 by twentieth-century English economist Dennis Robertson. See D. H. Robertson, "The Future of International Trade," in American Economic Association, *Readings in the Theory of International Trade* (Philadelphia: Blakiston, 1950), p. 501. For some recent discussions of the dynamic aspects of classical trade theory, see, e.g., Hla Myint, *Economic Theory and the Underdeveloped Countries* (London: Oxford University Press, 1971), chaps. 5–7; Gerald M. Meier, *The International Economics of Development* (New York: Harper & Row, 1968), chap. 8; Richard E. Caves, " 'Vent for Surplus' Models of Trade and Growth," in Robert E. Baldwin et al., *Trade, Growth, and the Balance of Payments* (Chicago: Rand McNally, 1965), pp. 95–115.

20. See John Stuart Mill, *Principles of Political Economy* (1848; reprint ed., London: Longmans, Green, 1936), bk. III, chap. 17, sec. 5, p. 581.

21. Ibid.

22. Ibid.

23. Adam Smith, *The Wealth of Nations* (New York: Modern Library ed., 1937), p. 415. Further along in the same paragraph, Smith anticipated Mill's productivity theory of trade: "By opening a more extensive market . . . [trade] encourages them to improve its productive powers, and to augment its annual produce to the utmost, and thereby to increase the real revenue and wealth of the society."

24. Ragnar Nurkse, *Equilibrium and Growth in the World Economy* (Cambridge: Harvard University Press, 1962), p. 284.

25. Many orthodox economists took their cue from the work of Professor John Williams of Harvard University during the interwar period. See J. H. Williams, "The Theory of International Trade Reconsidered," in American Economic Association, *Theory of International Trade*, pp. 253–271. For an excellent review of the subsequent literature, see Meier, *International Economics of Development*, chap. 8.

26. W. Arthur Lewis, *Aspects of Tropical Trade, 1883–1965* (Stockholm: Almqvist and Wiksell, 1969), p. 8.

27. See J. Richard Huber, "Effect on Prices of Japan's Entry into World Commerce after 1858," *Journal of Political Economy* 79, no. 3 (May/June 1971): 614–628.

28. See, e.g., Nurkse, *Equilibrium and Growth*, pp. 294–295.

29. This proposition forms the central core of a prominent theory of

economic development and trade generally known as the "Prebisch-Singer thesis," after economists Raul Prebisch and Hans W. Singer. See, e.g., H. W. Singer, "The Distribution of Gains Between Investing and Borrowing Countries," in Richard E. Caves and Harry G. Johnson, eds., *Readings in International Economics* (Homewood, Ill.: Richard D. Irwin, 1968), pp. 306–317; R. Prebisch, "Commercial Policy in the Underdeveloped Countries," *American Economic Review* 49, no. 2 (May 1959): 251–273. For a useful review of the Prebisch-Singer thesis, see A. S. Friedeberg, *The United Nations Conference on Trade and Development of 1964* (Rotterdam: Rotterdam University Press, 1970), chap. 3.

30. Charles P. Kindleberger, "Magdoff on Imperialism," *Public Policy* 19, no. 3 (Summer 1971): 533.

31. Albert O. Hirschman, *How to Divest in Latin America, and Why*, Princeton Essays in International Finance No. 76 (Princeton: International Finance Section, 1969), p. 3.

32. See, e.g., Raymond F. Mikesell et al., *Foreign Investment in the Petroleum and Mineral Industries* (Baltimore: Johns Hopkins Press, 1971).

33. Albert O. Hirschman, *The Strategy of Economic Development* (New Haven: Yale University Press, 1958), p. 121.

34. Mill, *Principles of Political Economy*, p. 581.

35. See, e.g., Raymond Vernon, "Foreign Enterprises and Developing Nations in the Raw Materials Industries," *American Economic Review* 60, no. 2 (May 1970): 122–126.

36. See, e.g., Meier, *International Economics of Development*, chap. 8, and A. G. Kenwood and A. L. Lougheed, *The Growth of the International Economy, 1820–1960* (London: George Allen and Unwin, 1971), chaps. 8, 9.

37. Harry Magdoff, "The Impact of U.S. Foreign Policy on Underdeveloped Countries," *Monthly Review* 22, no. 10 (March 1971): 5.

38. See, e.g., Theodore Geiger, *The Conflicted Relationship* (New York: McGraw-Hill, 1967), esp. chap. 3.

39. The two processes were independently identified in the late 1950s by Albert Hirschman and Gunnar Myrdal. See Hirschman, *Strategy of Economic Development*, chap. 10, and Myrdal, *Economic Theory and Under-Developed Regions* (London: Duckworth, 1957), chap. 3. The term "polarization" is Hirschman's (Myrdal called it "backwash"); the term "spread" is Myrdal's (Hirschman called it "trickling-down"). Hirschman put much more emphasis on the spread effect of international trade and investment; Myrdal, like today's marxists and radicals, believed that the polarization effect tended to predominate.

VI

DEPENDENCE AND EXPLOITATION

According to the modern theory of neocolonialism, the skewness in the allocation of resources in poor countries not only holds back the growth of their income and production possibilities; even worse, it forces them into a position of economic dependence on the countries of the metropolitan center. This is the familiar "dependencia" model, especially stressed by Latin American marxists and radicals.[1] Economic dependence is alleged to result from the material needs of international capitalism. It is also supposed to lead, in turn, to the economic exploitation of the periphery. These allegations of marxist and radical theory form the subject of the present chapter.

My position in this chapter (as in the previous chapter) will be partially in accord with marxist and radical discussions, and partially agnostic. I agree that most poor countries are economically dependent on the capitalist rich; about that there can be little doubt. For that matter, such dependence in many ways may actually be intensified by the working of the international capitalist economy. But there can be considerable doubt about the related allegations which marxists and radicals derive from the dependency model. Economic dependence is not necessarily

189

a condition perpetuated simply because of the presumed material needs of international capitalism, and exploitation is not a necessary consequence of the condition of economic dependence. Both allegations miss the real meaning of the dominance-dependence relationship between rich and poor countries.

Dependence

The notion of economic dependence is widely used in discussions of the international economy, yet it is rarely defined explicitly. Most sources (whether radical or marxist, or more orthodox) are apt to be vague about the matter. Generally they seem to have in mind some kind of a "conditioning situation," in which the possibilities for economic progress in a nation (the options for behavior) are determined and largely limited by constraints imposed from the outside. In fact, this involves two separate and quite distinct aspects. First, it implies a high measure of sensitivity to external forces: dependent economies are unable to avoid being influenced by events elsewhere. Second, it involves a high measure of irreversibility of impact: dependent economies are unable to override the influence of events elsewhere. Both aspects are essential to the notion of dependence. Together they mean that foreign economies have an implicit veto power over the capability of domestic decision-makers (private or official) to direct the development of the local economy. What happens at home depends on what happens abroad. As one (radical) source has put it, as objectively as anyone might:

> By dependence we mean a situation in which the economy of certain countries is conditioned by the development and expansion of another economy to which the former is subjected. The relation of interdependence between two or more economies, and between these and world trade, assumes the form of dependence when some countries (the dominant ones) can expand and be self-sustaining, while other countries (the dependent ones) can do this only

as a reflection of that expansion, which can have either a positive or a negative effect on their immediate development.[2]

Dependence is a matter of degree rather than of kind: economies are more or less dependent, rather than absolutely dependent or not. Short of autarky, there is no such thing as perfect economic independence. It is also clear that dependence, like economic development (see Chapter 5), is a multivariate concept, involving a number of different dimensions: economies may be more dependent in some respects, less so in others. There is no single variable by which degree of dependence may be measured.

The notion of dependence actually encompasses a wide variety of economic variables. Among the most important are structural characteristics of national production and foreign trade, such as the share of trade in GNP and the commodity and geographic concentration of exports and imports. The share of trade in GNP determines the sensitivity of the domestic economy to external forces in general. The more "open" an economy is—the higher the proportion of its income accounted for by foreign trade—the greater will be its overall dependence on conditions of supply and demand abroad. In an open economy, a decline of demand abroad for exports will have a large multiplier impact on the level of internal production and income; similarly, a decline of import supply will have considerable impact on the level of internal prices. Commodity and geographic concentration of trade determine the sensitivity of the domestic economy to specific external forces. An economy whose trade is well diversified, in terms of both products and trading partners, will not be unduly affected by variations of supply or demand in the markets for individual goods or of individual countries. But an economy whose trade is concentrated in just a few commodities traded with just a few other countries will (unless it enjoys monopoly or monopsony power) be highly dependent on what happens in each specific market.

Other important variables encompassed by the notion of dependence relate to the role of external capital and manpower in the national economy—characteristics such as the share of private capital inflows and foreign aid in the total level of new investment, the share of foreign enterprise in the ownership of domestic productive capacity, and the share of foreign personnel in jobs of high skill and influence. These features are important because they directly constrain the decision-making capabilities of indigenous private enterprise as well as of the national political authorities.

Taking all of these variables into account, we can get a fair idea of what is ordinarily meant by the notion of economic dependence—just as in Chapter 5, by taking into account all the variables considered in Tables 5–1 and 5–2, we could get a fair idea of what is ordinarily meant by the notion of economic development. It was noted then that every poor country tends to share some or most of the attributes of underdevelopment. Now we may perceive the same thing about the attributes of economic dependence. Virtually every poor country tends to share some or most of the characteristics of dependence, even if not all of them. As a group, despite their great diversity, the LDCs tend to be largely dependent on the dominant economies of the metropolitan center. About this there can be little doubt.

For example, most LDCs have a relatively high share of foreign trade in GNP. There are exceptions: India, with its large size and comparatively diversified production structure, has a lower ratio of trade to GNP than Belgium; Brazil, similarly, has a lower ratio than Japan. However, for the overwhelming majority of countries in the Third World, a high measure of openness is a familiar, if unfortunate, fact of life. This is especially true if one considers only the monetized portion of less developed economies, which in many cases is concentrated almost exclusively in production for export to the capitalist rich.

Paralleling this, most LDCs also tend to have a relatively high degree of both commodity and geographic concentration in their foreign trade. Again there are exceptions, particularly among the larger or more industrially advanced LDCs. But for most poor countries, large-scale trade diversification is a luxury that they have not yet been able to afford. Most still concentrate heavily on just one or a few primary-type exports—e.g., petroleum (many of the Arab states), tin (Malaysia, Bolivia), copper (Chile, Zambia), bauxite (Guyana, Jamaica), cocoa (Ghana, Ivory Coast), bananas (Ecuador, Central America), and sugar (Philippines, Dominican Republic, Mauritius). The majority also maintain just one or a few principal trading partners among the capitalist rich—such as the United States (most of Latin America) or one of the other former colonial powers like Britain (much of the Commonwealth) or France (the French Community).

Capital and manpower coming from the capitalist rich tend to play a prominent role in the operation of the national economy of most LDCs, supplying a significant proportion of new capital, owning much of the existing productive capacity, and occupying many of the most influential positions in production and management.

In short, most LDCs tend to have all of the characteristics of economic dependence; virtually all share at least some of them. To this extent, the modern theory of neocolonialism is perfectly correct (see Chapter 3). Even conventional analysis accepts that behind the veil of nominal political sovereignty, LDCs still lack much of the substance of real economic independence; despite decolonization, relations with the advanced capitalist countries still spell dominance for the metropolitan center, dependence for the nations of the periphery. Conventional analysis also believes that these relations may actually intensify economic dependence on the center; the theory of neocolonialism is also correct in this respect (though not, as usual, to the extent that marxist and radical discussions assume). In many ways the working of the international capitalist economy strengthens the implicit veto power of the rich over the development of the poor. About this, too, there can be little doubt.

The root of the poor's dependence lies in the skewed allocation of their resources. This forces them to rely on trade with the capitalist rich for access to most types of goods, services, and technologies, and to rely on a relatively narrow range of exports to pay for their needed imports. The result is that the progress of their economies is highly conditioned by what happens in a few external markets. This leads to the problem of the foreign-exchange gap discussed in Chapter 5, as well as to reliance on inflows of foreign capital to fill the gap in payments balances.

Many LDCs have tried to cut down on their reliance on foreign capital, and ease the problem of the foreign-exchange gap, by promoting policies of import substitution. Using a variety of protective devices (e.g., tariffs, quotas, subsidies, even multiple exchange rates), they have tried to replace all but the most essential imports with domestic production and thus save on scarce foreign exchange. Unfortunately, such programs may actually increase, rather than decrease, the dependence of the poor. Import-substituting industries themselves are apt to require imports, whether of capital goods or of raw materials and intermediate inputs. Poor countries frequently find that their need for foreign exchange on balance is raised, rather than lowered, by protection of domestic "infant industries"—especially after the first, relatively simple phase of import substitution is completed. In the beginning it is not too difficult to replace a wide range of foreign consumer goods, and even some capital goods, with inexpensive domestic alternatives. Eventually, however, a point of diminishing returns is reached as the process moves toward more complex and capital-intensive substitution activities. To achieve economic viability, these activities require a much larger home market than most LDCs can generally provide. Beyond this point, therefore, import substitution tends to breed little more than inefficiency and misallocation of resources, with scarce foreign exchange being wasted rather than saved.

Import substitution may also increase dependence by heightening the degree of sensitivity to *fluctuations* of foreign-exchange receipts. By replacing all but the most essential imports, LDCs leave themselves little room for maneuver in the event of a sudden crisis of the balance of payments. Suppose foreign-exchange earnings drop for some reason. When imports include a margin of nonessential consumer goods, foreign purchases can be temporarily compressed without slowing the pace of domestic activity. But when the only imports are essential raw materials and capital goods, there is no way of avoiding a negative impact on the growth rate or level of employment in the home economy (unless the country has substantial foreign-exchange reserves or access to foreign credit). As one source has noted, "prior to import substitution a decline in imports implied mainly a tighter belt for consumers; after import substitution a reduction of imports meant unemployment and a lower rate of growth."[3]

Besides this, the working of the international economy may intensify the dependence of the poor in two ways—through the operations of the large multinational corporations in the Third World, and through the policies and programs of home governments in the metropolitan center.

Multinational corporations influence the degree of dependence of the poor mainly via the nature of their investments and related activities. Operations in the Third World (whether in the primary sector or in manufacturing) confront managers of the large multinationals with a complex problem of organization and control. This problem has been well described by Hymer:

> Multinational corporations are torn in two directions. On the one hand, they must adapt to local circumstances in each country. This

calls for decentralized decision making. On the other hand, they must coordinate their activities in various parts of the world and stimulate the flow of ideas from one part of their empire to another. This calls for centralized controls. They must therefore develop an organizational structure to balance the need to coordinate and integrate operations with the need to adapt to a patchwork quilt of languages, laws, and customs.[4]

This is not an easy balance to strike. From the point of view of the corporation, adaptation to local circumstances is an inconvenience. Even if circumstances dictate transferring a certain amount of decision-making responsibility—at least for day-to-day operations—to branches or subsidiaries in the Third World, the necessity will at best be tolerated. The corporation's basic instinct is to centralize, not decentralize. To the extent possible, investments in LDCs are treated as part of an interlocking global structure of production, not as autonomous or independent entities. Multinationals try to avoid placing all stages of the production process—from research and development, to extraction, to refining and processing, to fabrication, to sales and servicing—within a single LDC. More typically, one or a few stages are located in one country, other stages elsewhere, with the highest levels of decision-making authority reserved for the corporation's central headquarters. A division of labor is created among countries, reflecting the vertical integration of the corporation's various business operations.

From the point of view of the individual LDC, such a division of labor spells dependence; Hymer calls it the "New Imperial System."[5] The LDC does not have full control over an important part of the productive capacity located within its own borders. Vital stages of the production process are not accessible to it. The foreign firm must be relied upon in some crucial regard or other—for technology, refining or processing, marketing outlets, or finance. What happens to the local venture will depend on decisions taken elsewhere. To this extent, marxists and radicals are right when they criticize multinational corporations for subordinating the national economies of the periphery.

Marxists and radicals are right in another respect. In their operations in the Third World, multinational corporations create clientele groups whose interests, privileges, and status are directly derived from their ties to foreign enterprise. Some of those clients act as wholesalers—assembling, sorting, and standardizing commodities that they purchase as middlemen from small peasant or household producers. Others function as suppliers of local materials or marketing agents for local sales, or cater to various other needs of the multinationals and their managements. All gain their incomes from the activities of foreign business; all have a vested interest in maintaining and perpetuating the multinational corporation's pre-eminent role in the local economy. Marxists and radicals have good reason, therefore, to criticize these clientele groups as a kind of economic "fifth column" in LDCs. Baran has called them the "comprador element of the native bourgeoisie." [0]

However, as usual, marxists and radicals have a way of exaggerating these ill effects. Not *all* local ventures are unable to function autonomously; not *all* local groups are co-opted by foreign enterprise. Inevitably there are beneficial spin-offs from the operations of the multinationals, in the form of new lines of output created, new industrial skills trained, new entrepreneurial talent stimulated—all acting to reduce somewhat the skewness in LDC resource allocation. In other words, inevitably there are spread effects as well as polarization, decentralization as well as the centralized hierarchy of Hymer's "New Imperial System." The activities of multinational corporations may intensify the dependence of poor countries in many ways, but they do not do so in *all* ways.

Home governments in the metropolitan center may also influence the degree of dependence of the poor through the nature of their foreign economic policies and programs. An obvious example is tariff policy—especially policy affecting the structure (not just the average height) of tariffs. Rich countries typically tend to escalate or "cascade" their tariff structures by stages of production. Rates are usually made low or zero on imports of raw materials and fuels, higher on semimanufactures, and highest of all on final products. Naturally this tends to bias the opportunities for development through trade in the periphery toward exploitation of natural resources. Reallocation of resources toward processing and fabrication is automatically discouraged, even though it might potentially be more in accord with the region's overall comparative advantage.

These effects are often compounded by other instruments of trade policy in the metropolitan center. Protective devices such as mandatory import quotas, so-called "voluntary" export quotas, and production subsidies, all administered on behalf of weak and inefficient home industries, act as deterrents to industrial development in the periphery. At the same time, many rich countries make it a policy to offer commercial preferences to selected LDCs on their exports of primary products—in the form of commodity purchase agreements, tariff or quota preferences, and so on. This is particularly true of some of the former colonial powers in their relations with ex-colonies (e.g., the Commonwealth Sugar Agreement). The result is to provide yet one more incentive to the ex-colonies to perpetuate the skewed allocation of their resources.

These effects are further compounded by the foreign-investment policies of the metropolitan center. The governments of the rich typically provide many incentives to their corporations to invest in areas of the periphery, including insurance, guarantees, tax breaks, and even low-cost loans. One consequence of these programs is an increase in the already prominent role of external capital and manpower in the operation of LDC economies.

Finally there are the foreign-aid programs of the metropolitan center. Most aid-giving agencies—not just national agencies such as the United States Agency for International Development (A.I.D.), but also international agencies such as the World Bank and its affiliates, the International Monetary Fund (I.M.F.), and various regional development banks—tend to attach conditions to their offers of economic assistance to LDCs. These conditions relate to various aspects of the general economic policies of the recipients—policies with respect to such matters as tariffs, exchange rates, wages, prices, credit, taxation, and nationalization. According to the agencies themselves, such conditionality (or "leverage," as it is also known) is necessary to ensure that aid grants and loans are used efficiently. From the recipients' point of view, the conditions represent a constraint on their decision-making capabilities—an implicit veto made explicit. The "good performance" that is demanded may simply heighten their dependence on the economies of the rich.

For instance, the I.M.F. often makes its assistance, which is provided for purposes of balance-of-payments support, conditional upon policies of "monetary stabilization." In addition to credit restraint, this term is frequently interpreted to require such measures as liberalization of trade or currency restrictions, or reduction of state intervention in economic affairs. Such measures may well have the effect of reinforcing the skewness of resource allocation in the Third World. Similarly, the World Bank often makes its assistance, which is provided for purposes of long-term capital creation, conditional upon a hospitable attitude toward private foreign-investment activity. The Bank actually has a policy of refusing loans to any country that resorts to nationalization of foreign-owned assets without "adequate" compensation. Under the Hickenlooper amendment, the United States Government is legally bound to do the same in the event of seizure of American-owned assets. These policies too may act to bolster the existing international division of labor.

Foreign aid is also frequently used as a device to promote exports from donor to recipient countries. Magdoff quotes a former president of the World Bank as saying: "Our foreign aid

programs constitute a distinct benefit to American business. . . .
Foreign aid provides a substantial and immediate market for
U.S. goods and services. . . . Foreign aid stimulates the development of new overseas markets for U.S. companies." [7] Accordingly, even in this respect foreign aid may be criticized for its
possible contribution to the continued dependence of the poor.
One radical writer calls it "merely the smooth face of
imperialism." [8]

In all these respects, marxists and radicals are right to criticize the policies and programs of governments in the metropolitan center. However, once again, they have a way of exaggerating the ill effects. Not *all* of the actions of the rich add to the
external constraints on the poor. The "good performance" demanded by aid-giving agencies has often turned out to be in
the periphery's own long-term interest; many recipients have
ultimately been willing to admit this. Likewise, trade policies of
the metropolitan center have frequently led to the promotion of
infant industrialization in less developed areas, rather than
always to its discouragement. In the so-called "Kennedy Round"
of global trade negotiations concluded in 1967, the poor countries were entirely excused from any obligation to reciprocate
for tariff cuts agreed upon by the more advanced capitalist nations. Similarly, in more recent years most of the advanced nations have extended comprehensive, generalized tariff preferences to the LDCs for their exports of processed or fabricated
items. Examples such as these indicate that while the home
governments of the rich do in many ways intensify the dependence of the poor, they, like multinational corporations, do not
do so in *all* ways.

The Significance of Dependence

It seems clear that most poor countries are economically dependent on the rich. Furthermore, in many ways (though not
all) the working of the international capitalist economy clearly

intensifies that condition of dependence. The question to consider now is: What is the significance of this economic dependence?

It should be emphasized first that there is no necessary connotation of shame in the notion of dependence. Dependence is simply the price one pays for the benefit of a division of labor. Independence is possible only in isolation. Dependence follows automatically from participation in any system of interrelationships. It is the logical corollary of interdependence. This is as true of the individual family as it is of the family of nations. All participants are dependent to a greater or lesser extent.

But there, of course, is the catch: "to a greater or lesser extent." Like Orwell's equals, in any system of interrelationships, even though all participants are dependent, some may be more dependent than others. The interdependence may be asymmetrical, following directly from the multivariate character of the dependence concept. Some participants are dependent in many respects, others in only a few. Here is the key to real understanding of the relations between poor and rich countries in the international economy today. It is not that the poor are dependent, the rich independent. The rich are also dependent within the system. (This has important implications, as we shall see below.) It is just that they are dependent to a much lesser extent.

The dependence of the rich within the system is acknowledged even by marxist and radical writers. In fact, this is precisely what the various lines of argument discussed in Chapter 4 were all about. The view from the metropolis *stresses* the dependence of the rich on the poor—for export markets, for investment outlets, for sources of raw materials. Indeed, if anything, the view tends to *exaggerate* the extent of this dependence. As I have already argued, the periphery can be considered important to the center, without being necessary. Unfortunately, this qualification can be of only minor comfort to the poor, for whom it implies even less relative bargaining strength within the system than they might otherwise be able to apply.

According to most marxist and radical writers, this asymmetry of interdependence, this dominance-dependence relationship between the rich and the poor, is a direct consequence of the historical development of capitalism. That is what much of Chapter 5 was all about—what the theory of neocolonialism calls the distortion of development, the generation of poverty, and Frank calls the "development of underdevelopment." As one source has put it:

> The "dependencia" analysis maintains that one of the essential elements of the development of capitalism has been, from the outset, the creation of an international system which brought the world economy under the influence of a few European countries, plus the United States from the late nineteenth century onwards. Development and underdevelopment, in this view, are simultaneous processes: the two faces of the historical evolution of the capitalist system.[9]

I have already conceded much to this particular perspective on the past. Above I said that the root of the poor's dependence lies in the skewed allocation of their resources, and in Chapter 5 I said that the reason for this skewness lies in the biased global structure of capitalist prices. To this extent capitalism can be held responsible as the cause of the present dependent condition of the poor. There are also other factors one might consider; cause and effect are never a simple matter in the "seamless web of history." For example, there is the historical head start toward industrialization of what is now regarded as the world economy's metropolitan center. Accident of time and place though this may have been, it was bound (through the economies of spatial agglomeration) to bias the development of those who came later, whatever the nature of the international system. In addition there is the narrow resource base in most of what is now regarded as the periphery. Lacking much in the way of physical or human capital (to say nothing of a capacity to transform), the poorer countries were bound to look to specialization in trade as a form of "escape" from the disadvantages of their smallness. Both of these factors must share some of the responsibility for the present asymmetry of interdependence between rich and poor.

However, that is not really the issue that concerns us here. Our problem is not to understand why in the past the poor became dependent to a greater extent than the rich. The problem is to understand why that dominance-dependence relationship is still perpetuated, even intensified, in the present. Marxists and radicals insist that it is perpetuated because of the presumed needs of international capitalism—that this motivation explains the true significance of the poor's economic dependence. It is at this point that the "dependencia" model diverges most sharply from more conventional analysis, as one radical source has pointed out:

> Although capitalist development theory admits the existence of an "external" dependence, it is unable to perceive underdevelopment in the way our present theory perceives it, as a consequence and part of the process of the world expansion of capitalism—a part that is *necessary to* and integrally linked with it.[10]

Can this really be the explanation? To answer, we must consider separately the motivations of the two chief agents influencing the degree of dependence of the periphery—the large multinational corporations and the home governments of the metropolitan center.

As far as the multinational corporations are concerned, there can be little doubt that marxist and radical writers are right. Multinational enterprises are principally motivated by the material needs of capitalism (if not they, then who?)—by the profit incentive and the traditional capitalist imperative of expansion. As pointed out in Chapter 4, being profit-making institutions, the multinationals are opportunistic. They seek out the paths of least resistance to corporate gain and oligopoly power, and if these paths happen to lie through the economies of the periphery, then so much the worse for the periphery. It is not the corporation's worry if the development of the poor is incidentally distorted or subordinated in the process. Its worry is solely to survive in the competitive struggle of the marketplace. The economies of the periphery will figure in its calculations, but only insofar as these directly or indirectly further the corporation's own objectives.

Specifically, the corporation is motivated by a desire to preserve the gains derived from any monopolistic advantages that it may enjoy vis-à-vis its competitors. According to the modern theory of oligopolistic competition, this more than anything explains why enterprises go multinational in the first place (see Chapter 4). A firm develops some type of monopolistic advantage, whether in technology, refining or processing, marketing, or finance. It then seeks to defend or expand its oligopoly power by exploiting this advantage, wherever it can and for as long as it can. This is why the corporation's basic instinct is to centralize, rather than decentralize, its various business operations. By encouraging a vertical integration of activities, it ensures maintenance of conditions in which its aid and participation continue to be essential. In other words, all of its monopoly profits continue to be perpetuated—even if, for the periphery, the only thing perpetuated is dependence.

On the other hand, as far as the home governments of the metropolitan center are concerned, marxists and radicals are clearly wrong. The governments of the rich are not principally motivated by the material needs of capitalism, despite numerous arguments to the contrary. The issue has already been discussed at length in Chapter 4. The foreign economic policies and programs of the rich are not explicable exclusively, or even mainly, in terms of profits or corporate performance. The economies of the poor are not distorted or subordinated by them in order to serve the economic interests of the bourgeoisie. The relationship between business and state, to repeat, is not that close.

What does motivate the state, I have argued, are predominantly broader and more long-range considerations—the needs of politics, power, and national prestige. These represent the real explanation of the policies and programs of the rich. The authorities are concerned first about the security of the nation. All government actions are conditioned by this basic interest, especially including actions in the economic sphere (e.g., ensuring access to vital raw materials sources). If the security of the nation will be served by distorting or subordinating the economies of the periphery, then (once again) so much the worse for the periphery.

As it happens, most economic relations between rich and poor countries are conducted through private business channels. As I have said, private business has a selfish interest of its own, parallel to what is often the government's interest, in perpetuating the dependence of the periphery. Therefore, it often happens that the interests of the political authorities and the large corporations tend to coincide, and accordingly official policies and programs end up enhancing private monopoly profits. However, insofar as this does occur, it seems to be mainly because business can be made to serve the will of the state, not vice versa. (It also frequently happens that official policies and programs do not end up enhancing private monopoly profits.) This is where the marxists and radicals go wrong. Corporate trade and investment are the means of government policy in this connection, not the end.

This explains the true significance of the economic dependence of the poor. Though arising out of the pursuit of profit by business, it is perpetuated by the state for an entirely different set of reasons. Marxists and radicals are right in suggesting that the governments of the metropolitan center still exert a kind of imperial dominance over the economies of the periphery, despite decolonization and the spreading of formal political sovereignty. But they are wrong in charging that the governments do this because of the needs of international capitalism. In fact, governments seem to do it primarily because of the broader security interests of the nation. They harness the motivations of multinational enterprise to serve their own strategic ends: trade and investment—to say nothing of foreign aid—become the vehicle by which public political (not merely private economic) goals are attained. Marxists and radicals are sufficiently perceptive to see all the symptoms. Their diagnosis of the condition, however, tends to be misleading.

Exploitation

This leaves us with one last question: Are the poor exploited? Marxists and radicals insist that they are. In their view, the very existence of dependence implies exploitation, this being integral to the needs of international capitalism; in the words of one writer, "the world system is inherently exploitative." [11] However, in this respect too their diagnosis is unfortunately misleading. That the less developed are asymmetrically dependent on the more developed does not mean that they are necessarily worse off as a result. That capitalism works to perpetuate and intensify the condition of dependence does not mean that there will necessarily be a net loss for those who are dependent.

Dependence may be rightfully resented by those who are dependent. Dependence means that considerable decision-making capability is arrogated by foreigners who have no claim to represent or even understand the specific interests of the nation. In a real sense, dependence impugns the national integrity; the country is treated like a child in the family of nations, its ability to shape its own destiny seriously impaired. This has nothing to do with how the decision-making capability is used—whether or not it is employed ostensibly "for the nation's own good" (as parents in an individual family employ their decision-making capability ostensibly "for the child's own good"). It has to do only with the fact that the nation itself is unable to control the decisions that affect its future development. Anyone who believes in the principle of self-determination (as I do) cannot but take exception to this kind of situation, where some nations are able to exercise an implicit veto over the actions or policies of others. Nations are not children. Dominance and dependence may be unavoidable in the world as we presently know it (see Chapter 1), but that hardly makes the condition any less unpalatable for those who are dependent. Every nation should have the right to make its own mistakes.

If marxists and radicals would only stop here, one could hardly quarrel with their argument. Their hearts are plainly in the right place. Regrettably, they do not stop here, but go on to suggest that there is a second and even more compelling reason to resent the dependence of the poor. That is the charge of exploitation, having to do precisely with the matter of how the decision-making capability is used. In the individual family the capability may indeed be used for the child's own good. In the family of nations, however, according to the theory of neocolonialism, it cannot possibly be used for the good of the dependent country. Decisions made by foreigners cannot be more beneficial than alternatives that might be adopted by the country itself in a relationship of less asymmetrical interdependence. In short, the country cannot avoid losing so long as it remains dependent within the world system. Exploitation must follow from the working of the international capitalist economy:

> The hierarchy of nations which make up the capitalist system is characterized by a complex set of exploitative relations. Those at the top exploit in varying degrees all the lower layers, and similarly those at any given level exploit those below them until we reach the very lowest layer which has no one to exploit. . . . Thus we have a network of antagonistic relations pitting exploiters against exploited. . . .[12]

Opportunity and Necessity

What can we say about such a charge? To begin with, one must distinguish carefully between *opportunity* for exploitation and *necessity* for exploitation. The former may be conceded without having to concede the latter. In fact, the opportunity for exploitation always exists in any relationship of asymmetrical interdependence; even conventional economic analysis accepts the truth of that. Dependence automatically implies a measure of influence for the dominant participant. The source of its influence is its control over that for which the dependent participant relies on it. For example, suppose A depends on B for the supply of something of value, such as machinery. B can then influence A through its ability to control—and *in extremis* to halt—the sale of machinery to A. True, B may do itself harm in the process. But if A requires the machinery to a greater extent and cannot locate alternative sources of supply, then B's influence over A is effective. Even in the absence of effective control of the sale of any important commodities or services to A, B can exercise effective influence over A if, alternatively, it either provides essential markets for A's production, or supplies A with vitally needed investments or foreign aid. With respect to each of these kinds of relationship, A is continuously exposed to the potential threat of a stoppage by B. Herein lies the essence of national power in the international economy. As Albert Hirschman pointed out in his classic study of economic influence, "the power to interrupt commercial or financial relations with any country, considered as an attribute of national sovereignty, is the root cause of the influence or power position which a country acquires in other countries. . . ." [13]

Such an influence or power position obviously gives a country an opportunity for exploitation. But does this mean that the country will necessarily *make use* of its opportunity? That is another matter entirely. Basically, it depends on what one means by exploitation. According to some writers, the word simply means "utilization for one's own advantage or profit." If that is the meaning we choose, then we must conclude that exploitation is one of the most ubiquitous of all human conditions, for only saints and fools ever enter into interrelationships with absolutely no thought of some sort of personal aggrandizement. Ordinary mortals—and nations—naturally expect something of value, some advantage or profit, to result from social intercourse. Otherwise, they would be hermits.

A more reasonable definition of exploitation would add the adjective "unfair": exploitation means *"unfair* utilization for one's own advantage or profit"; in other words, an "unfair" allocation of value (an "unjust" bargain). This means, of course, that there can be no such thing as an objective definition of exploitation. The word "unfair" implies an ethical or value judgment, so it follows that only a *normative* definition of exploitation is possible. There can be no agreement on the empirical question of whether exploitation even exists unless there is prior agreement or consensus on the conceptual question of the relevant normative beliefs.

We have now arrived at a crucial juncture, the point at which neocolonialism theory and conventional analysis once again begin to part company. For between marxist and radical writers on the one hand, and more orthodox economists on the other, there is no agreement on the relevant normative beliefs. Marxists and radicals tend to believe in the inevitability of conflict of interests, at least under capitalist conditions. Because antagonism is natural in a free-enterprise system, someone—some individual, group, or nation—is thought always to win, someone else is thought always to lose, within the context of a capitalist economy. This is the fundamental world view of all marxist and radical economic theory.[14] It follows directly from the labor theory of value of Karl Marx, described in Chapter 2, which alleges that the labor power of workers produces more in value than it receives in wage payments, the resulting surplus value being appropriated by the owners of the means of production. As one young marxist has written, "capitalist relations in all cases result in exploitation."[15]

Marxists and radicals thus believe that if an opportunity for exploitation exists, it will be used. This applies as well to international relations as it does to relations within nations:

> If it is in the very nature of things for one group of men to exploit others within their own country, then it is clearly normal, natural and right for this class to search for ways in which it can enrich itself by exploiting people abroad as well. This is a very natural progression and there is nothing mysterious about it.[16]

Accordingly, marxists and radicals believe that any asymmetry of interdependence between nations will inevitably result in "unfair" utilization of those who are dependent by those who are dominant. This is essentially the same world view that lay behind the Gallagher-Robinson conception of the nineteenth-century "imperialism of free trade": a system based on the formally equal treatment of inherent unequals, it was thought, was bound to be operated exclusively to the advantage of those who were most powerful, in that case primarily the British.[17] The modern theory of neocolonialism merely updates Gallagher and Robinson to encompass an "imperialism of free investment" (and foreign aid) as well. The system is still thought to be operated exclusively to serve the interests of its strongest and most advanced constituents, now the Americans along with the Western Europeans and Japanese. International inequality necessarily implies a net loss for those who are less equal; the system still offers nothing but an "unjust" bargain to the poor.

More orthodox economists are unimpressed by this marxist-radical world view—and with good reason. The view treats dependence and exploitation as identical concepts; in other words, it is tautological, and like most tautologies, tends to beg what are really the main issues. The basic question is not whether the interests of individuals, groups, or nations may be in conflict under capitalist conditions. Of course they may be. The question is whether such interests, even if not exactly harmonious, may nevertheless be *reconcilable* to everyone's advantage (or at least to no one's disadvantage) within the economic system. Conventional analysis is based on the belief that divergent interests may be so reconcilable, and there is good reason to suppose that this alternative view of the world is not at all unreasonable. The system is not lacking in elements of harmony and cooperation. Even if all participants are not inherent equals, it does not follow that superiority will necessarily be *actively affirmed* (see Chapter 1). Even if all participants do not always gain from capitalist relations, it does not mean that someone must necessarily lose *by definition*. Whether exploitation exists is still an empirical question, not a foregone conclusion.

The point may be made more firmly in the language of the theory of games. Game theory was originally created by mathematician John von Neumann and economist Oskar Morgenstern to provide a new approach to analysis of economic problems.[10] Relations within the economic system can be viewed as a sort of "game"—a strategical, competitive interaction between two or more "players." The behavior (strategy) of each player is based upon an expectation concerning the behavior (strategy) of all the others, with the final outcome ultimately determined by the actions of all the players taken together. Some games are "zero-sum"; that is, the sum of winnings is always zero (a loss being a negative win). What one player gains is what another player loses. In such games the interests of the players are diametrically opposed and utterly irreconcilable. Other games are "nonzero-sum" ("general games"). The sum of winnings may be greater than (or less than) zero, and all players may gain (or lose) simultaneously, though not necessarily always in the same proportions. In such games the interests of the players are neither completely irreconcilable nor entirely harmonious. Such games are characterized, simultaneously, by elements of both competition and cooperation, conflict and harmony. As von Neumann and Morgenstern put it, "the advantage of one group of players need not be synonymous with the disadvantage of the others. In such a game moves—or rather changes in strategy—may exist which are advantageous to both groups." [19]

The contrast between neocolonialism theory and conventional analysis is precisely this difference between zero-sum and non-zero-sum games. Marxists and radicals believe that conflict is the only element in interactions within a capitalist context. Orthodox economists insist that there are elements of harmony and cooperation as well. The latter view seems a much closer approximation to reality; after all, that is what the condition of interdependence is all about. As one student of game theory has written: "Games with both cooperative and competitive elements are generally . . . encountered more frequently in everyday life than pure competitive games." [20] Once one goes beyond parlor games such as poker or chess, it is hard to find relevant examples of game situations where the sum of winnings is necessarily zero. In most real-life situations, players share certain interests even as they compete against each other. Their competition concerns the question of shares—how the pie will be sliced. What they have in common is an interest in seeing to it that the pie will be available, and will be as large as possible—in other words, that the sum of winnings will be positive rather than negative. A union and management negotiating a new labor contract, for instance, may differ over the proper wage for workers, but share an interest in avoiding a crippling strike. A customer and salesman may differ over the proper price of a used automobile, but share an interest in consummating the final sale. Two business partners may differ over the proper division of profits, but share an interest in keeping their joint enterprise from failing. Two nations may differ over the proper way in which to organize international economic relations, but share an interest in the benefits of a global division of labor.

A crucial requirement in all these game situations is a rational strategy for behavior. Each player must develop a strategy based on his perception of his own bargaining strength within the system of interrelationships. The outcome of the game as a whole—the size of the pie as well as the distribution of shares —will be determined by the relative bargaining strength of all the players taken together. The greater the number of players, the more complex the game will become, the more numerous the possible strategies, and therefore the more uncertain the outcome. In fact, there will be as many possible outcomes as there are combinations of strategies and bargaining strengths.

How, then, are we to define what we mean by exploitation? If the concept is to have any meaning, it must be in terms of "opportunity cost" (broadly understood)—that is, in reference to all conceivable alternative outcomes within the context of the game. Some particular organization of relationships may be considered exploitative if the absolute benefit to one of the participants—its wage or price or profit or income (or however else benefit is defined)—falls below what could realistically be obtained if relations were organized differently. Exploitation exists, in other words, whenever the terms of the bargain are inadequate, inadequacy being determined by reference to the entire range of alternative opportunities foregone.

Two points must be made particularly clear in this definition. First, it bears repeating that exploitation is determined by reference to the *entire* range of alternative opportunities. The problem is not simply one of a *single* alternative foregone, such as, for example, perfect competition. Some (more orthodox) sources prefer to define the concept in this narrower way: exploitation consists merely of any deviation from the free-market solution, owing to the exercise of monopoly or monopsony power. As one writer has said, "imperialist exploitation consists in the employment of labor at wages lower than would obtain in a free bargaining situation; or in the appropriation of goods at prices lower than would obtain in a free market. Imperialist exploitation, in other words, implies non-market constraint." [21] This just brings us back to where we started—to the problem of the relevant normative beliefs. Is perfect competition really the only possible standard of what is "fair" or "just"? Is the exercise of monopoly or monopsony power always likely to be "unfair" or "unjust?" Marxists and radicals would surely not agree, and neither, for that matter, would I. Certainly perfect competition may yield the greatest efficiency for a given volume and variety of resources. In other words, perfect competition may be optimal from the point of view of production for final use. But is perfect competition also optimal from the point of view of distribution among final users? Does perfect competition also yield the greatest *equity* for a given volume and variety of resources? That depends on how income is distributed—on how the ownership of resources is allocated among participants. Frequently that allocation owes as much to force of political or military coercion, or to tradition, as it does to the force of the marketplace. And even the force of the marketplace may yield a distribution of output among final users that is anything but "fair" or "just." In short, the free-market solution can turn out to be anything but equitable. That is why opportunity cost must be defined broadly in terms of all conceivable alternatives, not just in terms of the single standard of perfect competition.

The second point that bears repeating is that exploitation is determined by reference to the *absolute* benefit that each participant receives. The problem is not simply one of disproportionality, of who benefits *relatively* most from this particular organization of relationships. Some (more orthodox) sources prefer to define the concept in this narrower way,[22] but this may not necessarily mean a net loss for the participant. Such a definition overlooks that the pie itself, not just each of the slices, can vary in size in a nonzero-sum game. Rationally, it should be only the absolute magnitude of the benefit that matters, not the proportional share. A quarter of a large pie may represent a greater absolute gain than half or more of a smaller one. Such a bargain can hardly be called "unjust" (even though the participant's position of greater relative inferiority may subjectively entail some sense of wounded pride). The allocation of value cannot really be called "unfair."

Using this definition of exploitation, we can derive four particularly useful analytical concepts.

1. *Exploitation loss* (*EL*). Define the absolute benefit the exploited participant receives from the present organization of relationships as x. Similarly, define the benefit he could realistically receive from his best alternative opportunity as y. The difference $(y - x)$ measures the degree of exploitation suffered by that participant—his "exploitation loss."

2. *Exploitation gain* (*EG*). Define the absolute benefit the exploiting participant receives from the present organization of relationships as w, and the benefit he could realistically receive from his best alternative opportunity as v. The difference $(w - v)$ measures the degree of exploitation imposed by that participant —his "exploitation gain." It should be noted that in a nonzero-sum game, EG need not equal EL (except by accident).

3. *Cost of escape* (*CE*). To avoid EL, the exploited participant must effect a transition to a new organization of relationships. Necessarily, this involves some cost—what we may term the "cost of escape." If the present value (actuarial value) of CE is less than that of EL, then the participant will modify his strategy and try to alter the outcome of the game. But if CE exceeds EL, then no change will occur: it simply does not pay for him to try to escape from the status quo, despite the loss from exploitation. This explains why exploitation often persists for long periods in real-life situations.

4. *Cost of maintenance* (*CM*). To preserve EG, the exploiting participant must prevent a transition to a new organization of relationships. This also involves some cost—what we may term the "cost of maintenance." As above, it should be noted that in a nonzero-sum game, CM need not equal CE (except by accident). If the expected value of CM is less than that of EG, the participant will stick to his strategy and try to prevent any

alteration of the outcome of the game. But if CM exceeds EG, change will occur: it simply does not pay for him to try to maintain the status quo, despite the gain from exploitation. This explains why it is so important in real-life situations to distinguish between the opportunity for exploitation and the necessity for exploitation. Despite a positive EG, the opportunity for exploitation will not necessarily be used if CM is greater still. Superiority will not be actively affirmed. The element of harmony in the game will predominate, and the divergent interests of the participants will be reconciled.

Clearly, all four of these variables are crucial to the outcome of any nonzero-sum game. No one of the four is apt to remain unchanged for very long. In fact, the magnitude of each is likely to increase or decrease considerably through time as a result of flux and change in the system. Modifications can occur in the number of players, or at least in the variety of opportunities open to any player to enter into alliances or coalitions; in the legitimate authority of any of the players to use direct force or coercion in order to get his way; in the monopoly or monopsony power that any of the players can effectively exercise; in the general ability to communicate or in the access of any particular player to information; in the resource base available to any of the players; in tastes or technology; or even merely in the personalities or value structures of the players involved. Any of these changes can influence the relative bargaining strength of one or more of the players. Accordingly, despite the force of inertia, the final outcome of the game itself is apt to be altered quite frequently. The system as a whole will have to constantly adjust to the inconstancy (as well as the uncertainty) of conditions.

The Empirical Question

Let us now return to the theory of neocolonialism. Is it true, as charged, that the world system is inherently exploitative—that the poor nations are necessarily exploited by the rich? Such an empirical question is not easy to answer, even *after* having reached agreement on the relevant normative beliefs. Nonetheless, certain presumptions are suggested as a result of the conceptual discussion just concluded.

First, international economic relations in general can legitimately be analyzed in game-theoretic terms. The international economy is in fact a nonzero-sum game. The pie consists of the gains from specialization and a global division of labor, including not only the static benefits to be derived from improved allocation of resources, but also the more dynamic impacts of the international engine of growth (i.e., greater capacity for saving, "productivity" effects, and vent for surplus). The size of the pie, as well as the distribution of shares among all participating nations, is determined by the organization of relationships prevailing at the moment, which is, in turn, determined by the balance of national bargaining strengths within the system as a whole.

Second, the present organization of international economic relations reflects the considerably greater bargaining strength of the dominant capitalist nations. Therefore, an opportunity for exploitation does undoubtedly exist in the asymmetry of interdependence that is perpetuated by the system.

However, it does not thereby follow that all LDCs are exploited as a result. The present organization of international economic relations does not necessarily represent an "unjust" bargain for all who are dependent. Recall the conclusion of Chapter 5. Participation in the international capitalist economy, I pointed out, *can* result in a net loss for the poor, but it can also have precisely the *opposite* effect. If the circumstances are right, economic relations with the metropolitan center may act as an enormously powerful engine of growth in the periphery. In fact, there can be little doubt that for some LDCs the impact —in terms of income and product per capita—has been quite beneficial.

I should immediately hasten to add a qualifying note. I do not mean to suggest that exploitation is nonexistent in the present organization of international economic relations. Quite the contrary; I have little doubt that for some LDCs the impact of economic relations with the metropolitan center has been highly detrimental. For many, the negative effects of trade and investment have far outweighed any positive effects they may have experienced, leaving them with scarcely anything but stagnation to show for their dependent role in the world economy. Moreover, even among those who have gained on balance, the benefit until now, in absolute terms, may not have been nearly so great as they might realistically have expected had relations been organized differently. Exploitation, in these cases, does not seem an inappropriate description. But it is hardly appropriate to generalize from these experiences, as marxists and radicals do, to the experience of the Third World as a whole.

I mean to suggest that exploitation is not *inherent* in the present organization of international economic relations. Capitalism does not *necessarily* make victims of all the poor, even if it does make them dependent. The theory of neocolonialism, in this respect, is simply not supported by the evidence. That outlook is still much too deterministic.

There are some LDCs for whom the present organization of relations can very reasonably be described as the "best of all possible worlds." In terms of conceivable or realistic alternatives to trade and investment as they currently exist, some of these countries could hardly do as well otherwise. (Because the pie is so large, their absolute benefit is commensurately greater, even if their proportional share may be smaller than they would prefer.) This is especially true of many of the smallest of the LDCs, for whom participation in the international capitalist economy has always represented the only realistic hope of "escape" from the disadvantages of a narrow resource base. Though dependent, such countries are able to reap virtually all of the marginal gains from trade between themselves and the metropolitan center by exporting at world-market prices far above the average cost of production at home, while importing at world-market prices far below the average cost of domestic substitutes. Conventional analysis has long recognized this advantage of small size in foreign trade. A small country can export and import all it likes without worrying about any deleterious influence this may have on its international terms of trade.

However, there are also many LDCs for whom the present organization of relations cannot reasonably be described as favorable—countries that have lost rather than gained as a result of their dependent status, or have gained less than they otherwise might. These countries *are* victims of capitalism; they may even form a majority of the Third World. They are of course the sample from which neocolonialism theory draws its generalizations, and even if the theory is wrong about its generalizations, the question still remains: Is it right about this sample? Are *these* countries condemned to be victims of capitalism, even if all LDCs are not? Marxists and radicals pessimistically suggest that they are; the argument is implicit in their deterministic assertions about inherence and necessity. However, in this respect their theory is simply not supported by the evidence.

In fact, the evidence is strong that there are fundamental forces at work in the world capitalist economy operating to reduce on balance, or even eliminate, the exploitation of many poor countries by the rich (even if the dependent condition of the poor is perpetuated and intensified). These are the same forces, arising at the international level, described in Chapter 2 in connection with the trend of the distribution of income at the national level. Although as in the domestic economy, the "natural" tendency of the system is in many ways to intensify the dependence of the poor, this tendency is frequently offset by the emergence of powerful counterpressures reflecting basic changes in the underlying power structure of capitalism. One change is the improved relative income status of many initially inferior participants; another is the implicit veto gained by many of the same participants as a result of the increasingly intricate interdependence of all concerned. Both changes (examples are provided below) are entirely endogenous to the operations of the political-economic system; both enhance the relative bargaining strength of many of those who are dependent.

Once again I hasten to add a qualifying note. I do not mean to suggest that all those who are dependent will necessarily find their relative bargaining strength gradually enhanced through time. For some, the situation may never improve at all; it may even deteriorate further. Capitalism is by no means a system of benevolence for all. What I do mean to suggest is that the blanket pessimism of marxists and radicals regarding the reformative capacity of international capitalist society is hardly more justified than their traditional pessimism regarding the reformative capacity of domestic capitalist society. For practical reasons the world economy, like any nonzero-sum game, shows a remarkably high degree of flexibility in the face of changing conditions. Consequently, for many poor countries there is a definite prospect of an increasingly favorable outcome within the global system of interdependent relationships.

One force working in this direction is decolonization itself. Marxists and radicals, as I pointed out in Chapter 3, attach no particular importance to the ebbing of the new imperialism after World War II. In their opinion the transfers of formal sovereignty have been more illusion than reality. Effective sovereignty allegedly still remains where it has always been, with the former colonialists—partly because of the continued economic dependence of the former colonies (a point conceded above), and partly because of the composition of the governments that have been created to take over after the former colonists leave. According to marxist and radical sources, most successor regimes are mere tools in the hands of international capitalism. Being made up of the same clientele groups that Baran called the "comprador element of the native bourgeoisie," they have a strong interest in fortifying and perpetuating the status quo, and therefore an incentive to run their countries primarily for the benefit of the rich. As Baran put it, the poor "are no longer outright colonies of the capitalist powers but are managed for them by local comprador administrations." [23]

The best answer to Baran has been suggested by British socialist John Strachey:

> No impartial observer would wish to deny that it is possible to carry on the imperialist control and exploitation of an underdeveloped country without retaining it as, or making it into, a direct and formal colony. . . . Every experienced imperialist will tell Professor Baran, however, that such indirect rule and exploitation is by no means the same thing as possession of the country in question as a direct colony. Once an even nominally sovereign local government is established, forces are invariably set in motion which tend in the direction of genuine independence. Imperialist control can go on, often for some time, but it becomes more and more precarious. To say that the advent of even partial independence makes no difference is a grotesque oversimplification.[24]

Decolonization makes a difference because it removes the legitimate authority previously enjoyed by colonialists to use direct force or coercion in order to get their way. No longer can they simply order a former colony to do as it is told; no longer can they simply trade and invest on a straightforward "take-it-or-leave-it" basis. Now they must use more subtle and indirect means of compulsion or persuasion in order to achieve the same ends. They must offer bribes, lures, and incentives—for example, lower prices on their own exports, greater market access for their imports, better terms on investments, and more and cheaper foreign aid. In other words, they must pay: to preserve their gains within the system (EG), they must bear a higher cost (CM). This, in essence, is what "every experienced imperialist" would be trying to tell Professor Baran.

Furthermore, once decolonization is accomplished, two additional forces soon come into play. The first is change in the make-up of the governments of the former colonies. Even if most successor regimes are initially not much more than "comprador administrations," they do not usually stay that way for very long. This is what Strachey means by imperialist control becoming "more and more precarious." Eventually, whether by revolution or by more democratic methods, groups other than the clients of the rich begin to take over the reins of authority. These new rulers may merely be more nationally minded bourgeoisie, they may be liberal reformers or democratic socialists, or they may be communists or military populists. Numerous examples of all of these can be found throughout the Third World. What is important about them is that they represent a modification in the personalities or value structures of crucial players in the game. A change of government denotes a change in the country's subjective evaluation of the costs involved in altering the present organization of relationships. The more radical or nationalistic the new regime happens to be, the less importance it will attach to the cost of transition (CE) in relation to the country's overall exploitation loss (EL).

The second additional force is the increase in the variety of opportunities available to the former colonies to enter into alliances and coalitions. Colonial status obviously focuses a nation's international relations predominantly on one metropolitan imperial power. Decolonization enables a country to look further afield, to increase its room for maneuver by taking advantage of rivalries among the rich. Already many ex-colonies have begun to seize this opportunity for diversification in their trade and investment connections; economic alliances and coalitions have been formed with a number of other advanced capitalist countries, or even with communist countries. True, most LDCs still remain more concentrated geographically in their relations than they might prefer, but many have managed to become considerably less dependent on a single market and source of supply than they used to be, and are consequently a good deal less sensitive to specific external forces. By definition, this implies both a lower CE and a higher CM. For former colonies, options for behavior have been increased; for former colonizers, it now costs more to maintain the traditional organization of relationships.

Former colonies can also enter into alliances and coalitions with each other. Acting in isolation, individual nations in the periphery have relatively little potential for bargaining strength vis-à-vis the metropolitan center. Acting in unison, they can enhance their bargaining strength substantially, especially if together they exercise any power as monopolists or monopsonists in particular world markets. Dependence, I have emphasized, is a two-way street. The poor are not entirely lacking in their own sources of leverage. Since the rich are also dependent within the system in certain respects, they can be harmed as well by an interruption of various commercial or financial relations. Collective action along these lines has always been the key to the redistribution of income gains at the national level (see Chapter 2). Increasingly, LDCs are discovering that it is the key to redistributing the benefits of the international economy as well. Once again, the effect is to lower CE and to raise CM.

In this regard, perhaps a turning point was reached with the first United Nations Conference on Trade and Development, held in Geneva in 1964. Before UNCTAD I (subsequent sessions were held in New Delhi in 1968 and Santiago in 1972), the LDCs had not particularly distinguished themselves in articulating their discontents in the international economy. In Geneva, however, for the first time they managed to achieve a real measure of unity in confrontation with the rich. Organized in the so-called Group of 75 (now known as the Group of 77, though almost a hundred nations are actually included), they articulated a list of demands that far exceeded the usual pleas for more aid on easier terms. Subsequently, UNCTAD itself was reorganized as a permanent institution of the United Nations, functioning principally as a lobby for the interests of the Third World. It is significant that in the years since 1964 many of the demands of the poor have been at least partially met. These include suspension of the periphery's reciprocity obligations in the Kennedy Round and the generalized tariff preferences mentioned above; some agreements in the field of commodity trade; and a scheme for compensatory finance within the I.M.F. to protect LDCs against unanticipated short-falls of export receipts.

Another instructive example in this regard is the Organization of Petroleum Exporting Countries (O.P.E.C.), consisting of the governments of seven Arab states plus Iran, Indonesia, Nigeria, and Venezuela. Formed in 1960 as a kind of producers' cartel, O.P.E.C. in recent years has enjoyed great success in increasing its membership's gains from international trade in oil. Production has been lifted, prices have been raised, and the share of governments in the revenues of the multinational oil companies has risen very sharply. In early 1972, O.P.E.C. was even able to obtain an agreement from the companies to compensate them in full for the December 1971 devaluation of the dollar (the currency in which oil prices are posted). As one expert has written, O.P.E.C. "has demonstrated the potential power of a group of developing nations against the international companies, which have hitherto been able to 'play off' each of the countries against the others." [25]

Thus, many forces have been at work in the international economy, operating to shift the balance of national bargaining strengths in favor of the LDCs. For many poor countries there is a prospect of reduction, perhaps even elimination, of their EL. Not that the rich, consequently, are going to roll over cooperatively and play dead; they are unlikely to give up their EG without a struggle. Indeed, they can be expected to do everything within their power, for as long as they can, to preserve the status quo. But the rich will in many instances gradually lose both the means and the incentive to do anything like that—the means, because CE is constantly declining, and the incentive, because CM is constantly rising. That is the reason why one can be more optimistic about the outcome for the poor than marxists and radicals are prone to be.

Again, the example of O.P.E.C. is instructive in this regard. The greatest weapon possessed by governments of the producing countries is the threat of nationalization of local production facilities. Comply with our demands, the international companies are told, or we will take over the oil fields and run them ourselves. In response, the companies have tried to maintain their traditional leverage over the governments by holding onto control of later stages of the vertically integrated production process. If their facilities are seized by national enterprises, they say, they will refuse access to their refineries and channels of distribution, the producing countries will be unable to process or market what they manage to pump out of the ground. However, in practice the companies have found that this leverage, like oil itself, is a wasting asset. Countries that have nationalized production facilities—such as Algeria, Iraq, and Libya—have in fact found that it is possible to get along on their own. Some have been remarkably successful at turning the tables on the companies, and playing each of them against the others. Others have managed to bypass the companies altogether, making deals directly with the governments of consuming countries, or even processing and marketing through countries of the Soviet bloc. For the producing countries this represents a decline of CE. For the oil companies, the only way to preserve the status quo is to pay a higher CM. Can there be any doubt that the outcome will be elimination of all exploitation gains by the companies?

Of course, it can be argued that the oil industry is a unique situation. Production is concentrated in a relatively small number of countries, demand is intense and rapidly growing, and substitutes are few and expensive. (It should be noted that the cost of providing substitutes—e.g., oil from shale or coal, or nuclear power—sets the upper limit to the gains oil-producing countries may hope to achieve at the expense of the companies and consuming countries.) Few other industries provide so favorable an opportunity for the poor. But there are few other industries that provide no opportunity at all. For instance, in many industries, production is even more highly concentrated than it is in oil, e.g., in copper, where just four countries account for the bulk of world exports (Chile, Peru, Zaire, and Zambia); in tin, where just three exporting countries predominate (Bolivia, Malaysia, Thailand); or in lead, where there are also just three major exporters (Australia, Mexico, Peru). These and similar situations clearly allow a great deal of room for increasing the bargaining strength of the periphery through collective action. That is what really matters. Despite their asymmetrical dependence, the poor are not condemned to perpetual exploitation by the international capitalist economy. Many of them may now be victims, but it is neither necessary nor inherent in the system that they all remain victims forever.

NOTES

1. See, e.g., Theotonio Dos Santos, "The Structure of Dependence," in K. T. Fann and Donald C. Hodges, eds., *Readings in U.S. Imperialism* (Boston: Porter Sargent, 1971), pp. 225–236, and Susanne Bodenheimer, "Dependency and Imperialism: The Roots of Latin American Underdevelopment," in Fann and Hodges, pp. 155–181.
2. Dos Santos, "The Structure of Dependence," p. 231.
3. Daniel M. Schydlowsky, "Latin American Trade Policies in the 1970s," *Quarterly Journal of Economics* 86, no. 2 (May 1972): 271.
4. Stephen H. Hymer, "The Efficiency (Contradictions) of Multinational Corporations," *American Economic Review* 60, no. 2 (May 1970): 445. See also Hymer, "The Multinational Corporation and the Law of Uneven Development," in Jagdish N. Bhagwati, ed., *Economics and World Order* (New York: Macmillan, 1972), p. 127.
5. Hymer, "Efficiency (Contradictions)," p. 446; "The Multinational Corporation," p. 114.
6. Paul A. Baran, *The Political Economy of Growth* (1957; reprint ed., New York: Monthly Review Press, 1968), p. 195. A comprador was a Chinese merchant engaged in trade with foreigners.
7. Harry Magdoff, *The Age of Imperialism* (New York: Monthly Review Press, 1969), p. 176. The former World Bank president was Eugene Black.
8. Teresa Hayter, *Aid as Imperialism* (London: Penguin, 1971), p. 7.

9. Osvaldo Sunkel, "Big Business and 'Dependencia': A Latin American View," *Foreign Affairs* 50, no. 3 (April 1972): 520.

10. Dos Santos, "The Structure of Dependence," p. 231. Emphasis supplied.

11. Robin Jenkins, *Exploitation: The World Power Structure and the Inequality of Nations* (London: MacGibbon and Kee, 1970), p. 43. Similarly, Paul Sweezy has written that trade and investment relations between rich and poor countries "are fundamentally exploitative." See Paul M. Sweezy, *Modern Capitalism and Other Essays* (New York: Monthly Review Press, 1972), p. 13.

12. Paul A. Baran and Paul M. Sweezy, *Monopoly Capital* (New York: Monthly Review Press, 1966), p. 179.

13. Albert O. Hirschman, *National Power and the Structure of Foreign Trade* (Berkeley: University of California Press, 1945), p. 16.

14. For a skillful explanation and defense of this world view, see Sweezy, *Modern Capitalism and Other Essays*, chap. 4.

15. Tom Kemp, *Theories of Imperialism* (London: Dobson, 1967), p. 169.

16. Felix Greene, *The Enemy: What Every American Should Know About Imperialism* (New York: Vintage Books, 1971), p. 102.

17. For an interesting application of the Gallagher-Robinson conception to the history of British commercial relations with Portugal, see S. Sideri, *Trade and Power: Informal Colonialism in Anglo-Portuguese Relations* (Rotterdam: Rotterdam University Press, 1970). Sideri concludes: "Free trade is the mercantilism of the strongest power" (p. 6).

18. For a clear and concise introduction to what game theory is all about, see Morton D. Davis, *Game Theory* (New York: Basic Books, 1970).

19. John von Neumann and Oskar Morgenstern, *The Theory of Games and Economic Behavior* (Princeton: Princeton University Press, 1953), p. 540.

20. Davis, *Game Theory*, p. 66.

21. David S. Landes, "The Nature of Economic Imperialism," *Journal of Economic History* 21, no. 4 (December 1961): 499.

22. See, e.g., Edith Penrose, "The State and Multinational Enterprises in Less-Developed Countries," in John H. Dunning, ed., *The Multinational Enterprise* (London: George Allen and Unwin, 1971), pp. 232–233.

23. Baran, *Political Economy of Growth*, p. 205.

24. John Strachey, *The End of Empire* (New York: Frederick A. Praeger, 1964), pp. 198–199.

25. Peter R. Odell, *Oil and World Power* (London: Penguin, 1970), p. 92.

VII

TOWARD A GENERAL THEORY
OF IMPERIALISM

It is now time to pull all the strands of the argument together. Chapter 1 suggested that there are two issues of particular importance to any study of the subject of imperialism: (1) the *form* of dominance-dependence relationships, and (2) the *force(s)* giving rise to and maintaining them. These are the very meat of analysis. Subsequent chapters focused on several alternative forms of imperial relations—classical maritime imperialism (Chapter 2), political imperialism (Chapter 3), and modern economic imperialism (Chapters 4–6). This final chapter will focus on the question of underlying, motivating forces. Is there a common "taproot" (again borrowing John Hobson's word) to all of the various forms of imperialism?

What the Taproot Is Not

Marxists and radicals have no doubt that there is indeed a common taproot to the various forms of imperialism, and it is to be found in the presumed material needs of international capitalism. However, as the present study demonstrates, there

229

is remarkably little evidence to support this point of view. The strictly economic interpretation of imperialism is substantiated neither by logic nor by the facts.

At the level of logic, there is little validity to any of the economic theories that have been developed by marxist or radical writers. Chapter 2 showed the intellectual weaknesses of the original underconsumption hypothesis as well as of Marx's alternative concept of the rising organic composition of capital. Chapters 4–6 showed the parallel weaknesses of the several contemporary lines of argument derived from these early approaches. None of the theories considered in these chapters can prove that economic imperialism is necessary or inevitable as part of mature capitalist development, or that poor countries are necessarily retarded or exploited. The theories are all much too highly deterministic.

Neither is there much validity to any of these theories at the level of empirical observation. These weaknesses were also shown in Chapters 2 and 4–6. The nations of the periphery have rarely assumed the importance ascribed to them as markets or investment outlets, or even as sources of raw materials. This was true during the era of the new imperialism; it is equally true during the modern era of decolonization and the multinational corporation. In fact, for many LDCs economic relations with the metropolitan center have actually proved to be enormously beneficial in economic terms. The gains of the international capitalist economy do not all necessarily go to the rich.

All through history there have been innumerable examples of imperialism having nothing to do with the international capitalist economy or the presumed needs of its most advanced constituents. Chapter 2 pointed out that some of the most aggressive imperial powers of the late nineteenth century could in no way be described as mature capitalist societies. (It was also pointed out that some of the most mature capitalist societies could in no way be described as aggressive imperial powers.) Chapter 3 indicated that the political form of imperialism both antedates and postdates the development of modern capitalism. Empires were known long before the industrial revolution began; empires still persist even where capitalism has been swept away. The behavior of the Soviet Union today in eastern Europe and elsewhere certainly qualifies for description as imperialistic.

In short, marxist and radical theories of economic imperialism do not stand up to close analytical scrutiny. All that needs to be said about them has by now been said. As intellectual constructs, they are like elaborate sand castles—a few waves of the incoming tide, and much of their substance gradually dissolves and washes away.

What the Taproot Is

Does this mean that there is no common taproot of imperialism—that it is impossible to account for all of its various forms within a single analytical framework? On the contrary, evidence is strong that a single theme does effectively explain each major variation. That theme, to recall Richard Hammond's phrasing (see Chapter 2), is "the good old game of power politics."

Power Politics

Power politics figured prominently in Chapter 2 as a guide to explaining imperial behavior in the nineteenth century, before as well as after the revival of formal empire-building around 1870. It also appeared in Chapter 3 as a principal motive for more contemporary forms of political imperialism, and in Chapters 4 and 6 as the basic force behind modern economic imperialism. In all these variations, major emphasis was laid on considerations of politics, power, and national prestige. I suggested that the condition of international inequality has been actively affirmed by dominant nations because of the strategic needs of the state, not the commercial or financial needs of private business.

Not that the theme of power politics is particularly original in this connection. The political interpretation of imperialism has often been stressed by nonmarxist or nonradical writers, as previous chapters have indicated. As the British economic historian, W. H. B. Court, stated: "It is reasonable to believe that man is a political as well as an economic animal." [1] However, with only a few exceptions, most political interpretations of imperialism have unfortunately tended to be more superficial than profound. Most scholars writing in this vein have relied more on the hasty generalization or the pithy aphorism than on thorough and reasoned analysis. A prime example is Hans Morgenthau, who has written: "What the precapitalist imperialist, the capitalist imperialist, and the 'imperialist' capitalist want is power, not economic gain." [2] Taken in context, the idea is simply stated rather than explained: this is an obiter dictum, not an argument. The same is true of Raymond Aron's reference, cited in Chapter 2, to the nation's "will to power," and of Court, who speaks of the "temptations to domination." [3] Consider also American economic historian David Landes, who speaks of the "logic of dominion":

> It seems to me that one has to look at imperialism as a multifarious response to a common opportunity that consists simply in a disparity of power. [4]

I agree that this is the way to look at imperialism, but it is hardly *all* one has to look at. Remarks such as these share the common virtue of being pointed in the right direction, but they also share the common vice of not going far enough. To gain a truly complete comprehension of this complex and "multifarious" phenomenon, one must ask what lies behind this logic of dominion, this will to power. It is not enough to assert simply, as Robert Tucker does, that "dominion is its own reward." [5] That by itself is no more enlightening than to assert the contrary, as marxists and radicals in effect do, that dependence is its own punishment. Neither is it enough to assert simply, as Landes does, that "whenever and wherever such disparity [of power] has existed, people and groups have been ready to take advantage of it." [6] That by itself is no more convincing than the "dependencia" model, which also confuses opportunity and necessity. The real question is *why* people and groups have been ready to take advantage of a disparity of power. Why do nations exercise a will to power? Why do they yield to the temptations to domination? Here is where we approach the real nub of the matter.

In essence, this is the same question that has intrigued students of international relations at least since the days of Aristotle and Plato. It is the central problem of all international political theory, the problem of the cause of war and conflict among nations. Many different answers have been offered, perhaps more than could be fully comprehended by any single scholar in a lifetime. In his classic *Man, the State and War*, Kenneth Waltz comprehended as many as any scholar might, and suggested that all causes could usefully be ordered under three broad headings: (1) within man; (2) within the structure of the separate nation-states; or (3) within the structure of the system of nation-states. [7] The first of these three images of international relations stresses defects in the nature and behavior of man; the second, defects in the internal organization of states; and the third, defects in the external organization of states (the state system). Together they exhaust all possible explanations (unless, of course, one cares to entertain metaphysical or extraterrestrial hypotheses).

Marxist and radical theories of imperialism clearly fall under the second of Waltz's headings. They are all variations on the same image of international relations; indeed, as Waltz himself notes, they "represent the fullest development of the second image." [8] Nations exercise a will to power because they are organized internally along capitalist lines. Domination and conflict among nations are the direct result of the defects in social and economic structures within nations. The alternative theme

I have suggested, by contrast, falls under the third of Waltz's headings. The "good old game of power politics" focuses deliberately on the state system itself, rather than on systems within states. The logic of dominion, I wish to argue, derives directly from the defects in the external organization of states.[9]

National Security

As we know it, the state system consists of a relatively small number of separate national constituents—150 or so social collectivities, each organized within a particular constitutional order prevailing over some specific geographical terrain. The principal characteristic of the system is that each constituent claims the right to exercise complete sovereignty over its own internal affairs. As Waltz summarizes it: "The circumstances are simply the existence of a number of independent states that wish to remain independent."[10] The principal consequence of the system is that no constituent can claim the right to exercise even partial sovereignty over the external affairs of nations. No body of law, no rules, can be enforced in the realm of international relations. There is no automatic harmony, no automatic adjustment of interests. Each state is the final judge of its own ambitions and grievances. The system as whole, though interdependent, is formally in a condition of anarchy.

What is significant about this condition, from our point of view, is that in anarchy there can be no such thing as absolute security. No state can afford, without risk, to take its own national survival for granted. Uncertainty prevails. With every state left to its own devices, all are free to use force at any time to achieve their individual objectives. Therefore, all must be constantly prepared to counter force with force, or pay the price of weakness. All must be able to defend themselves against outside attack and to protect themselves against outside control, to be concerned, in other words, with self-preservation. It is in this sense that one scholar has written that "the basic objective of the foreign policy of all states is preservation of territorial integrity and political independence." [11] Preoccupation with national security is the logical corollary of the state system as we know it.

At a more immediate level, the practical problem facing each state is to translate the basic objective of national security into an operational strategy of foreign policy. This is no easy matter, for two reasons. First, the state itself is not a unitary policymaker. Much of international political theory, unfortunately, has traditionally regarded the state more or less in this way. Foreign policy has been treated as if it were the reasoned product of farsighted and creative leadership—concerted, purposive action arising out of a rational perception of the fundamental interests of the state. In fact, nothing could be further from reality; the political processes out of which policies normally spring are just not that simple. The state is not the proverbial "black box" but a social collectivity, a society of groups of all kinds, many with extensive foreign as well as domestic interests, and each with its provisional conception of the overall national interest related ideologically to its own special interest. To the extent that interest is institutionalized, particular interest expresses itself with political power, and out of governmental processes of tension and conflict the foreign policy of the state emerges—a consensus of purposes and actions that are essentially the end products of a system of domestic power relationships.

Marxists and radicals have always shown the keenest awareness of this domestic background of foreign policy. Indeed, the very idea is inherent in the traditional marxist theory of class, which takes for granted that the purposes and actions of the state abroad will reflect directly the system of power relationships at home. The only difference is that in the marxist scheme of things the power system is monopolized by a monolithic capitalist class, with the result that foreign policy equates the conception of overall national interest with the particular interest of the bourgeoisie. That, of course, is what leads marxists and radicals to concentrate on Waltz's second image of international relations: the defect derives directly from the internal organization of the state, which exists solely to guarantee a given set of property relations.

The weaknesses of the traditional marxist theory of class have already been discussed in Chapters 2 and 4. It is enough simply to repeat here that, in advanced capitalist countries at least, political rule in practice has been a good deal more pluralistic than the theory would have us believe. Governmental processes have operated to reconcile the conflicting interests of all groups with bargaining power within the system. Consequently, state action abroad usually turns out to be less monolithic than marxists and radicals generally allege. Often, in fact, it seems to be random, haphazard, or even irrational. Foreign policy will frequently take the form of an uneasy compromise as a result of deadlocked judgments. Sometimes a nation will adopt no foreign policy at all, but will instead, owing to indecision, or unwillingness or inability to act, simply drift with the force of events.

The second reason why translation of the basic security objective into an operational strategy is not easy is that the concept of national security is not a precise or well-defined guide for action. In fact, it is highly ambiguous. The presence or absence of external threats to a state's independence and territory can never be measured objectively. This must always remain a matter of subjective evaluation and speculation. National security is measured by the absence of *fear* of external threats, and fear is an obviously idiosyncratic element in international affairs. For reasons only partly explained by special interest, groups within nations and even nations themselves differ widely in their reaction to the same external situation. It is not surprising, therefore, that they differ as well in their choice of preferred foreign-policy strategy.

Furthermore, the concept of national security is usually interpreted to imply not only protection of national independence and territorial integrity, but also preservation of minimum national "core values." Tucker distinguishes between physical security per se, and security "in the greater than physical sense." [12] For the nation as for the individual, mere physical survival is not normally valued highly unless accompanied by cultural survival as well. Nations have been known to risk biological extinction through war rather than risk cultural extinction in peace. Even short of war, they tend to design and implement their foreign policies to protect not only their sovereignty and borders, but also a certain range of previously acquired values, such as rank, prestige, material possessions, and special privileges. The difficulty for foreign policy is that such values—security "in the greater than physical sense"—are by definition subjective. Not only are nations and groups within nations likely to differ in their estimation of the range of values considered "basic", that range is apt to prove elastic over time even for any single nation or group.

Finally there is the problem of what constitutes the "nation" that this concept of security is all about. I have referred in Chapter 1 to the elusive meaning of the word nation. Being a sociocultural and perceptual phenomenon, the nation is neither clearly definable nor necessarily stable in terms of either space or time. Nations are not always conterminous with the geographical boundaries of states (despite the convenience of the expression nation-state). Accordingly, there is a legitimate ambiguity regarding just what it is that foreign policy is meant to preserve: Whose territorial integrity? Whose political independence? This ambiguity only serves to heighten the general uncertainty prevailing in the system as a whole. National survival, to repeat, cannot ever be taken for granted.

The Role of Power

Despite all these difficulties, the nation must at least *try* to develop an operational strategy of foreign policy. It must attempt to define, for the purpose of guiding its own actions, a set of proximate foreign-policy goals and objectives. To see how this is done, it will be useful to draw an analogy between the behavior of states in the international arena and that of competing firms in an oligopolistic market. Both situations are particularly apt examples of a nonzero-sum game in operation.

Like the community of nations, the oligopolistic market is characterized by interdependence and uncertainty. The competitors are sufficiently few for the behavior of any one to have an appreciable effect on at least some of its rivals; in turn, the actions and reactions of its rivals cannot be predicted with any degree of certainty. The result is an interdependence of decision-making which compels each firm to be noticeably preoccupied with problems of strategy and gamesmanship. The oligopolist's principal worry, I pointed out in Chapter 6, is to survive in the competitive struggle of the marketplace. He must scrutinize his every move for its effects on the long-term market position of the firm, its implications concerning the firm's future freedom of action, and the probable countermoves of all rivals. Rarely is any move undertaken that is likely to threaten the existence of the enterprise.

For the individual oligopolist, a position of monopoly would obviously be preferable to the uncertainty and risk of his current status. But the goal of total market domination is not operative in the competitive strategies of many firms, for even apart from the constraint of antitrust legislation, each oligopolist knows that his rivals, singly or collectively, are also strongly armed with the weapons of competition—price reductions, aggressive advertising, product improvement, and so on. Oligopolistic corporations do occasionally attempt to improve their position or dominate a large part of the market by means of such predatory policies as price-cutting, monopolizing raw materials or distributive outlets, or tying arrangements. However, most oligopolists prefer to rely on less aggressive strategies that are correspondingly less likely to provoke challenge and retaliation. Some of the larger firms seem content to settle for a position of previously acquired pre-eminence, perhaps considerably short of total dominance, but acknowledged by at least a part of the market as one of price leadership. Their strategy is to maintain their position, not augment it. Smaller enterprises find security in associating themselves publicly with the acknowledged price leader and conforming readily to the latter's observed market behavior. Others, both large and small, enter tacitly or explicitly into collusive arrangements for setting prices and dividing markets; their strategy is to ensure individual survival through mutual compromise and accommodation. Another group adopts a policy of maximum independence, eschewing any consultation or prior agreements with groups of rivals in the process of deciding on their output and prices; their strategy is to ensure survival through neutrality.

There are many variations on these few themes, but the point is that they represent the basic poles of conduct in an oligopolistic market. They also represent the basic strategies of conduct in the game of international relations: predation, preservation of existing hegemonies, association with a great power, compromise agreements and alliances, and neutrality. What determines the choice of basic strategy? Clearly, a multitude of variables is operative. In an oligopolistic market, the ideological inclinations and moral convictions of the corporate management are not unimportant, nor are expectations concerning psychological and commercial developments elsewhere in the market. But undoubtedly most important is the relative bargaining strength that the firm can exercise within the system as a whole —in other words, the general market power it can bring to bear to achieve its ends.

The main problem is for the individual firm to choose a set of proximate goals consistent with the resources at its disposal (its market power). A small firm with little public enthusiasm for its product, no monopoly of any raw material or distributive outlets, and no special access to financial backing, is hardly in a position to elect a policy of immediate market domination.

Such behavior, however psychologically gratifying, would not be rational. Much more rational would be a policy of slow accumulation of market power through price "followership," or perhaps tacit collusion. Conversely, a large firm in a dominant market position cannot adopt a policy of maximum independence since its actions have such an immediate effect upon, and hence are so closely watched by, all of its rivals. For such a firm, predation or accepting the role of price leader would be more rational choices.

Firms in the marketplace tend to be much more rational in their behavior than states in the international arena. I have already emphasized that foreign policy, being largely the product of an internal political process, often seems anything but rational. All kinds of variables enter into its determination. Nevertheless, as trustee of the interests of the national community, the government must steer the state away from destruction; national survival is its first responsibility. Therefore, even though there is a wide latitude for irrational elements in foreign policy, that latitude is not without limits. Small, poor states cannot rationally aspire to dominate the world; large, rich states cannot effectively isolate themselves. The proximate goals of foreign policy must fit the resources available, however tenuously. Ultimately, national power sets the limits to the state's choice of a strategy of foreign policy, just as market power sets the limits to the oligopolist's choice of a strategy of competition.

The key word is choice. In a situation of competition, interdependence, and uncertainty, the survival of any one unit is a function of the range of alternative strategies available to it. The oligopolistic firm with only one strategic option leads a precarious existence: if that strategy fails to result in profit, the firm will disappear. Likewise, the state with only one strategic option can never feel truly secure: if that strategy fails, the state will disappear, be absorbed by others, or, more likely, be compelled to abandon certain of its national core values. For both the firm and the state, the rational solution is to broaden its range of options—*to maximize its power position,* since power sets the limits to the choice of strategy:

> [S]o long as the notion of self-help persists, the aim of maintaining the power position of the nation is paramount to all other considerations.[13]

This does not mean that more power must be accumulated than is available to any of one's rivals, or that this power must be used coercively. It only implies that power must be accumulated *to the extent possible* in order to maximize the range of available strategies. In a nonzero-sum game, the crucial imperative is always to make the most of one's relative bargaining strength. This is the conduct we observe of firms in an oligopolistic market. To the extent that governmental processes are rational, it is also the conduct we observe of states in the international arena.

Dominance and Dependence

We are nearing the end of the argument. It remains only to ask what constitutes national power, and what determines the extent to which it can be accumulated.

Essentially, power represents the ability to control or at least influence the behavior of other nations. Such an ability need not actually be exercised; it need only be acknowledged by one's rivals to be effective. The ability derives from the interdependence which is inherent in the international state system. As pointed out in the last chapter, interdependence is often asymmetrical, thus automatically implying a measure of influence for those who are the dominant participants. Albert Hirschman spoke of the power to interrupt relations of a specifically commercial or financial nature; we might now speak of any type of relations between nations. *Ceteris paribus,* the greater a state's ability to threaten stoppage of relations which are considered of vital importance by others, the stronger will be its power position in the international arena. Conversely, the more exposed a state is to interruption of relations which it regards as essential—the more dependent it is on others—the weaker will be its power position in the international arena.

It follows that if a state is to enhance its national security, it must, to the extent possible, try to use its foreign policy to *reduce* its dependence on others. At the same time, in order to counterbalance forms of dependence that cannot be avoided, it must try to enhance its *net* power position by *increasing* its own influence on others—that is to say, its *dominance* over them. This means that *imperialistic behavior is a perfectly rational strategy of foreign policy*. It is a wholly legitimate and logical response to the uncertainty surrounding the survival of the nation.

But, of course, there is a limit to the extent to which a state can behave in this way. This is determined by the entire range of resources available or potential, particularly those resources that have been or could be placed at the disposal of the nation's foreign-policy makers. Dependence can be reduced, and dominance over others increased, only insofar as national resources permit. Foremost among these is the military establishment—the organizational and physical entity that wages war. However, national power is more than just "forces in being"; it is a function of all the nation's other resources as well—its industries, population, geographic location and terrain, natural resources, scientific, managerial, and diplomatic skills, and so on. In addition, it is a function of the resources available to the nation's principal rivals, for power is potent only insofar as it balances or outweighs power elsewhere. What truly matters is not so much influence in absolute terms as influence in relation to that of others. In a nonzero-sum game, strategy depends on the player's *relative* bargaining strength.

In short, resources available or potential determine the *cost* of alternative foreign policies. Imperialism may be a rational strategy for behavior, but only as far as costs permit. As Robert Tucker writes, in his important recent book, *The Radical Left and American Foreign Policy* (1971), "it is apparent that the costs of imperialism to the collective must be taken into consideration." [14] That explains why it is misleading to speak simply of the temptations to domination. As in Chapter 6, it is necessary to distinguish between opportunity and necessity. Tempting though it may be to take advantage of disparity of power, nations will not actually yield to the temptation unless the benefits (however perceived) exceed the costs (however perceived). International inequality may be a fact of life, but it will not be actively affirmed unless, in some meaningful sense, it pays.

For example, I emphasized above that the definition of what constitutes a nation's "core values," being subjective, is often apt to prove elastic over time, particularly if the nation's available resource base is growing at all rapidly. Again quoting Tucker, "the interests of states expand roughly with their power." [15] It is a familiar phenomenon that military bases, security zones, foreign investments, commercial concessions, and so on, which may be sought and acquired by a state to protect basic national values, themselves become new national values requiring protection. The process works very much like the imperialism of the "turbulent frontier" described in Chapter 2. The dynamic of expansion acquires its own internal source of generation. Pushed to its logical conclusion, such an expansion of the range of national interests to include more and more marginal values would not stop short of the goal of total world domination. Yet in practice, at any single moment in history, world domination has rarely figured in the operational foreign-policy strategies of nations. The reason is, simply, that the cost was far too high.

When the cost is not too high (in relation to benefits), superiority over dependent nations will be actively affirmed. Then it is perfectly logical to behave in an imperialistic fashion—to subordinate, influence, and control others. Tucker said that "dominion is its own reward."[16] We now see that this means that dominion is prized because it maximizes the collectivity's range of choice in the international arena. It makes both territorial integrity and political independence more secure in an insecure and uncertain world. Above all, it enables a country to preserve the entire range of values that it has come to consider basic. As Tucker also remarks, one of the main reasons for imperialism

> must be sought in the variety of motives that have always led preponderant powers to identify their preponderance with their security and, above all, perhaps, in the fear arising simply from the loss of preponderance itself. The belief that the loss of preponderance must result in a threat to the well-being of the collective, and this irrespective of the material benefits preponderance confers, is so constant a characteristic of imperial states that it may almost be considered to form part of their natural history.[17]

The Taproot of Imperialism

Tucker is perhaps putting it a bit strongly when he speaks in terms of "natural history." This smacks of the determinism of marxism and its "iron laws." But there can be no doubt that this and his other remarks point in the right direction. Though he too tends to rely more than he should on the hasty generalization and the pithy aphorism, Tucker makes an important contribution to our understanding of the imperialism phenomenon. He identifies many of the elements of the problem, and goes far enough to suggest a final answer to the question of what lies behind the nation's will to power. That answer, he says, must be found in the "dynamics of state competition," "the compulsions of the international system":[18]

> It is not only the division of humanity into the rich and the poor that gives rise to the various forms of unequal relationships the radical equates with imperialism. It is also the division of humanity into discrete collectives.[19]

In short, the answer must be found in the character of the international political system. Other writers, following their own lines of argument, have arrived at precisely the same conclusion. British economist Lionel Robbins (now Lord Robbins), for instance, said very much the same thing:

> There are inherent in the fundamental principles of national collectivism certain basic assumptions which make conflict with other national units almost inevitable. . . . The ultimate condition giving rise to those clashes of national economic interest which lead to international war is the existence of independent national sovereignties. Not capitalism, but the anarchic political organization of the world is the root disease of our civilization. . . . [T]he existence of independent sovereign states ought to be justly regarded as the fundamental cause of conflict.[20]

Similarly, in a 1944 essay American economist Jacob Viner wrote that "war is a natural product of the organization of peoples into regionally segregated political groups." [21] Historian E. M. Winslow, using almost identical phraseology, also argued that "imperialism is a political phenomenon":

> [T]he organization of peoples into regionally segregated political groups is the most potent cause of modern war.[22]

Here is the real taproot of imperialism—*the anarchic organization of the international system of states*. Nations yield to the temptations to domination because they are driven to maximize their individual power position. They are driven to maximize their individual power position because they are overwhelmingly preoccupied with the problem of national security. And they are overwhelmingly preoccupied with the problem of national security because the system is formally in a condition of anarchy. *The logic of dominion derives directly from the existence of competing national sovereignties.* Imperialism derives directly from this crucial defect in the external organization of states.

Some Possible Objections

This completes the main body of the argument. We have now constructed a single analytical framework within which it is possible to account for all of the various forms of imperialism discussed in previous chapters. The remainder of this chapter will be devoted to an examination of some possible objections to the theme I have developed.

Too Narrow

One possible objection might be that the theme depends too much on a single explanatory variable. Chapter 2 emphasized that most social theories which attempt to reduce reality to a single causative factor can be seriously faulted on grounds of excessive consistency and limited applicability. Some readers might argue that the same seems true of the political interpretation of imperialism. The explanation seems *too narrow*.

However, this would not be a valid objection. Although the explanation depends ultimately on a single causative factor, this does not mean that the theme thereby does serious violence to the complexity of reality. While I have argued that the key to understanding the behavior of nations is their preoccupation with national security, I have also argued that what actually guides the actions of governments is their operational strategy of foreign policy—and this comprises a whole set of proximate goals and objectives. Therefore, imperialism can arise for any number of practical reasons, not just for a single one (such as, for instance, material need). At a more immediate level, the explanation depends on a multiplicity of operationally causative factors. In this sense, the political interpretation is not at all limited in analytical applicability. It is sufficiently comprehensive to encompass virtually all possible subtypes or special cases. Viner put the point best (read *imperialism* for *war*):

In my view, therefore, war is essentially a political phenomenon, a way of dealing with disputes between groups. Every kind of human interest which looks to the state for its satisfaction and which involves real or supposed conflict with the interests of other peoples or states is thus a possible source of contribution to war. Every kind of interest which can conceivably be served by successful war will be in the minds of statesmen or will be brought to their attention. Given the existence of nation-states, the factors which can contribute to war can be as varied as the activities, the hopes and fears, the passions and generosities and jealousies, of mankind, in so far as they are susceptible of being shared by groups and of being given mass expression.[23]

Too Broad

This suggests an alternative objection. Perhaps, rather than being too narrow, the explanation is really *too broad*. This objection, converse to the first, is frequently stressed by marxist and radical writers. By allowing for such a multiplicity of causative factors, they say, the political theme gets so lost in ambiguity and vague generalities that it is devoid of any genuine analytical value. As one young radical argues: "By associating imperialism with a phenomenon that has characterized international political relations since the beginning of time, this conception is so broad as to deprive the term 'imperialism' of any specific meaning." [24] Or as Magdoff puts it: "This interpretation, correct or incorrect, is at so high a level of abstraction that it contributes nothing to an understanding of historical differences in types and purposes of aggression and expansion. It is entirely irrelevant. . . ." [25]

The best answer to this objection has been suggested by Tucker:

That a general interpretation of expansion may contribute little to an understanding of historical differences in types of expansion is no doubt true. It does not follow, however, that general explanations are therefore irrelevant. All that follows is that specific cases cannot be understood in their specificity merely by applying to them other-wise valid general explanations.[26]

In other words, a general theme does not relieve the analyst of responsibility for identifying the specific causes of particular historical variations. But it does give him a common thread with which to sew them all together in the "seamless web of history." The proper test of a social theory is not whether it is at a higher or lower level of abstraction, but whether the theory offers a useful insight into a variety of historical experiences. On the evidence of the present study, the political interpretation of im-perialism does just that. The economic interpretation favored by marxists and radicals, on the other hand, fails to pass the test.

Too Shallow: I

A third possible objection might fault the political interpreta-tion for being not too narrow or too broad, but *too shallow*. Marxists and radicals frequently stress this objection. The prob-lem is not in attributing imperialism to the anarchy of the inter-national state system, but in not going deeper, to ask what lies behind that anarchic organization of relations. As one young marxist writes, "it is necessary to ask more fundamental questions —about why nations struggle for power or come into conflict with one another, why they seek to increase their rank in the international system." [27]

As we shall see below, there may be some validity to this objection, but *not* for the reasons that marxists and radicals typi-cally suggest. What these writers see lurking behind the anarchy of international relations is, of course, the omnipresent hand of business. Nations come into conflict, and seek to increase their rank in the system, because of the selfish desires of private enter-prise. To quote the same marxist: "The struggle for power is now seen for what it is—the ideological mask of monopoly capital." [28] These writers are suggesting, in effect, a return to Waltz's second image of international relations: the objection merely paraphrases the traditional marxist theory of class. However, by now the flaws of this discredited theory of politics should be more than clear. In fact, the approach makes the error of inverting ends and means. Governments do not play "the good old game of power politics" for the sake of corporate interests. All the evidence of the previous chapters indicates that the situation is, rather, the reverse—corporations being influenced to play the international power game, whenever possible, in ways that will serve government interests. If governments come into conflict over economic issues, it is because they are concerned about the security of the nation, not because they are trying to protect the security of corporate profits.

The question of the connection between economics and politics in the behavior of nations is an old one in the study of international relations. It would be rash to try to provide a definitive answer here. For the purposes of this study, it is enough to emphasize two particular points. First, there can be no doubt of the *importance* of strictly economic factors to any conception of what constitutes national security. Security depends on power, and power depends on resources. Consequently, it is only natural that nations would define their minimum core values to include at least some values that are obviously economic in nature, such as investments, commercial and financial concessions, and so on. To this extent, there is little point in distinguishing at all between economics and politics in a discussion of international relations, since both are essential elements in the perpetual struggle for survival.

However, this does not mean that economic factors are therefore the ultimate *driving force* in the struggle for survival. This is the second point to be emphasized. To assume that economics is the end rather than the means of international politics, it is necessary to make one of two key assumptions. One must assume either that governments exist exclusively to serve the interests of the bourgeoisie, a view which is now discredited, or that national security is sought for no other reason than to enhance the nation's income and material possessions, a view which is equally indefensible. Greed is hardly the sole motivation of state action in the international arena. Nations, and the people in them, appreciate many objects of value for their own sake, apart from their transferability into current consumption or future wealth. These include international rank and prestige, and even the nation's domestic culture and religion, its "way of life" and language. (Consider, for instance, France's determined efforts to promote use of the French language in international organizations and around the globe.) They even include the exercise of power itself. All go into the conception of what constitutes national security.

This suggests why marxists and radicals are so misleading when they try to explain, for example, U.S. policy in Vietnam. Some writers, as indicated in Chapter 4, have tried to find a specific economic motivation for our prolonged military involvement (so reminiscent of the bloody "sporting wars" of Bismarck's day). However, even many marxists and radicals concede that such "scandal" or "devil" theories are hardly persuasive. For someone like Magdoff or MacEwan, the real explanation is much more subtle, having to do with concern over the system as a whole, rather than with a particular set of interests. As MacEwan puts it:

> In terms of particular interests, there is simply not much at stake for U.S. business in Vietnam.
>
> However, in terms of the general interest of maintaining South Vietnam as part of the international capitalist system, there is very much at stake. . . . *What is at stake in Vietnam is not just a geographic area but a set of rules, a system.*[29]

I could not agree more with MacEwan's concluding sentiment. What is at stake in Vietnam *is* a set of rules, a system in which the United States enjoys an exceptional position of preponderance. But does this mean that the capitalist system is the ultimate driving force of policy, as MacEwan and others like him consequently argue? Not at all; with that sentiment I could not be more in disagreement. It means that the system is viewed as the necessary means to achieve other ends—specifically, to protect the whole range of national values that America, in its preponderance of power, had come to consider "basic." Defeat for our clients in Vietnam, it was somehow decided, would threaten our national security "in the greater than physical sense." As Tucker summarized:

> The threat held out by Vietnam was real. It was not America's physical security that was threatened, but the security of an economic and social system dependent upon the fruits conferred by America's hegemonial position. A world in which others controlled the course of their own development, and America's hegemonial position was broken, would be a world in which the American system itself would be seriously endangered. To prevent this prospect from materializing, to reveal to others what they can expect if they seek to control the course of their own development, the United States intervened in Vietnam.[30]

Too Shallow: II

This brings us to a fourth possible objection to the political interpretation of imperialism, which can perhaps be best phrased in the form of a question: Would a socialist (or communist) America have done the same thing? Marxists and radicals argue that it would not have. More generally, they argue that no socialist state would have done the same thing. Imperialistic behavior would be impossible, *by definition*, in a world of socialist states. The argument is implicit in the modern economic theory of imperialism. As one young radical has written: "Imperialism is capitalism which has burst the boundaries of the nation-state. . . . [The] two phenomena are inseparable: there can be no end to imperialism without an end to capitalism and to capitalist relations of production."[31]

In effect, this line of argument simply repeats the third objection above, that the political interpretation is *too shallow*. The question still involves what lies behind the anarchy of the international state system, with the answer still framed in terms of Waltz's second image of relations. The only difference is that in this instance the logic is reversed. Instead of insisting on the reasons why survival of capitalism must necessarily mean perpetuation of imperialism, the converse is implied—that the demise of capitalism must mean the end of imperialism. Socialism would correct the basic defects in the internal organization of states. Accordingly, in a socialist world there could be no serious problems of war or international conflict. No state would have reason to fear for its territorial integrity or political independence. No nation's security, physical or otherwise, would be threatened by any of its neighbors.

The fallacy of this sort of logic should be clear. As Waltz puts it: "To say that capitalist states cause war may, in some sense, be true; but the causal analysis cannot simply be reversed, as it is in the assertion that socialist states mean peace." [32] It is necessary to supply some sort of proof, at the level either of logic or of empirical observation. Unfortunately, marxists and radicals can do neither.

At the level of empirical observation, it is difficult to prove that socialist states mean peace, especially since the record shows very much the opposite. The Soviet Union in particular, as I have already emphasized, has obviously been guilty of imperialistic and warlike behavior—not only in relation to its sphere of influence in eastern Europe through the years since World War II, but especially, in more recent years, in relation to its Chinese neighbor in the Far East. Marxists and radicals retort that this demonstrates nothing. If the record shows "social imperialism," it is for one of two reasons—either because no socialist state in a predominantly capitalist world is free to realize its true nature, or because the "social imperialists" are no longer truly socialist. Magdoff has written that in his opinion the imperialism of the Soviet Union is simply a symptom of the degree to which the Russians have departed from socialism and adopted some form of sociocapitalism.[33] For Magdoff, as for most marxists and radicals, it is impossible to conceive of imperialism persisting in a world of *genuine* socialism.

This suggests that the proof must be sought at the level of logic. However, here, too, marxists and radicals have a difficult time. If conflict and war are to be ended, it must be because there is some automatic harmony, some automatic adjustment of interests. Where would this come from in a world of *genuine* socialism? The usual answer is from the change in the attitudes of men and institutions. With all states becoming socialist, the elements of competition in the system would be eliminated. Cooperation, harmony, and mutual collaboration would become the hallmark of international relations. The minimum interest of each state in its own self-preservation would become the maximum interest of them all. The strategical game, in a sense, would be finished forever.

Merely to state the answer is to make obvious the utopian quality of the marxist and radical argument. It assumes a possibility of the existential perfection of all players in the game that goes far beyond anything the evidence of history would lead us to believe is feasible. In effect, it simply assumes the past to be irrelevant in projecting into the future: men and institutions are viewed as they might become, rather than as they have been. Ultimately, as Tucker notes, it "rests on the assertion—a tautology—that if men are tranformed they will then behave differently." [34]

But would socialist states behave all that differently? Such a leap of faith is courageous, even touching, but it is hardly a persuasive tool of intellectual debate. In fact, a strong case in logic can be made that socialist states would not behave differently; indeed, they might behave in even a worse fashion. Once sovereign states become socialist and take over the means of production within their borders, all distinctions between territorial jurisdiction and property ownership disappear. As a result, the inherent inequality of nations becomes a permanent source of potential disharmony in the system. A political element is injected into all important forms of international economic relations. Any dispute over commercial or financial interests automatically implies a measure of friction between states; if disputes are serious enough, they might even achieve the status of *casus belli*. Within a single nation, economic conflicts are ultimately resolvable through the fiscal mechanisms of the state or through legislative or judicial processes. Between nations, however, these same conflicts are ultimately resolvable (in the absence of world government) only through force or the threat of force.

The situation just described bears a striking resemblance to classic laissez-faire capitalism as outlined in traditional marxist analysis. Like a nation organized along capitalist lines, a world system of socialist states would consist of a number of "sovereign" property owners, all formally "equal" partners in a network of "free" exchange relationships. According to marxist analysis, at the national level these conditions necessarily lead to dominance for capitalists (who own the means of production), dependence for workers (who have correspondingly less control over resources other than their own labor power), and exploitation of the latter by the former. By analogy, it may be argued that the same outcome would obtain at the international level—dominance for large, rich countries, dependence for small, poor ones, and exploitation of the latter by the former. Of course, it is possible that cooperation among socialist states would act to moderate and limit the antagonisms generated by international differences of wealth and development; socialism is intended to be a humane system, after all. But it is improbable that mutual collaboration would succeed in eliminating tensions entirely. As one scholar has pointed out:

> [T]he "fraternal assistance" and "mutual aid" allegedly informing the relations among Socialist states do not essentially change the character of these relations, but leave them, in Marxian terms,

fairly and squarely at the level of typical capitalist relations. . . . The point is that nations *cannot help but be* self-regarding, as long as their position is that of owners of property in a wider community characterized by economic interdependence.[35]

Too Shallow: III

This leads us to a fifth, and final, possible objection, which can also be phrased in the form of a question: *Why is it* that nations cannot help but be self-regarding? Why must the world community be divided into distinct, and potentially antagonistic, national units? In effect, this objection also faults the political interpretation of imperialism for being *too shallow.* The existence of separate national collectivities is simply assumed. The deeper question is: Why do these horizontal distinctions persist?

Marxists and radicals are unable to give a truly satisfactory answer to this question, since the focus of their analysis is generally directed toward a different kind of distinction—not the horizontal division of mankind into nations, but vertical division into classes. Here, they insist, is the true source of conflict. If horizontal group diversity tends to persist, it is only because of the antagonisms generated by the warfare between classes, between capitalists and workers; the idea is inherent in the marxist class theory of politics. Conversely, if class warfare is ended by the coming of socialism, all conflicts and tensions will be eliminated in the international arena as well. As Marx himself put the point: "Is the whole inner organization of nations, are all their international relations anything else than the expression of a particular division of labor? And must not these change when the division of labor changes?"[36] In other words, nations are self-regarding only because they are capitalist. Will they not stop being self-regarding as soon as they stop being capitalist?

Once again, merely to state the argument is to make obvious its utopian quality. All the evidence of history argues to the contrary. Horizontal distinctions in human society have prevailed since long before capitalism came into existence, in fact since the birth of time; they have persisted long after capitalism has been overthrown. As even Soviet spokesmen now willingly admit, national differences seem every bit as enduring in this world as class distinctions, if not more so. Certainly the experience of communism in more than a dozen nations since World War II has demonstrated that the centrifugal pull of national identity is at least as strong as the centripetal attraction of socialist fraternity. The leap of faith implied in the marxist and radical analysis is simply not justified by the facts.

What accounts for the persistence of national differences in this world? Unfortunately, *no* satisfactory answer is possible here. To account fully for the phenomenon would require at least another entire volume, drawing at a minimum on the combined insights of sociology, anthropology, and psychology. All that is possible here is to note that for whatever reasons one might conceivably imagine, men have always preferred to group themselves into distinct national units, and seem content to continue doing so. Separate nations are *a given fact,* and what characterizes them, as I pointed out in Chapter 1, is a feeling of homogeneity. This means not only that the members of a nation feel a sense of belonging to one another; more significantly, they feel little or no sense of obligation to others. Accordingly, as members of national collectivities, men find it most convenient to reconcile their own internal conflicts and tensions, whenever possible, mainly at the expense of outsiders. This is the meaning of "self-regarding." Foreigners don't vote, but nationals do. Even the most genuine socialist nation, maintaining the highest standards of justice and equity at home, is apt to act with less justice and equity in most of its relations abroad. The best definition of a nation I have ever seen is: "A people with a common confusion as to their origins and a common antipathy to their neighbors." [37]

This implies that there is some validity to the objection that the political interpretation of imperialism is too shallow. In this sense, it *is* too shallow. By concentrating on Waltz's third image of international relations, it takes the persistence of self-regarding nations for granted, and therefore takes the nature and behavior of man for granted. But what is suggested now is that it is precisely with the nature and behavior of man that we ought to be most concerned—in other words, Waltz's first image. In the end, it is a question of the defects in ourselves, not in our national or international systems—our selfishness, our aggressiveness, our prejudices. We cannot relieve ourselves of the blame merely by blaming "society." Real solutions are never as simple as that.

> The fault, dear Brutus, is not in our
> stars,
> But in ourselves . . .
>
> SHAKESPEARE

NOTES

1. W. H. B. Court, *Scarcity and Choice in History* (London: Edward Arnold, 1970), p. 193.
2. Hans J. Morgenthau, *Politics Among Nations*, 3rd ed. (New York: Alfred A. Knopf, 1960), p. 51.
3. Court, *Scarcity and Choice*, p. 194.
4. David S. Landes, "The Nature of Economic Imperialism," *Journal of Economic History* 21, no. 4 (December 1961): 510.
5. Robert W. Tucker, *The Radical Left and American Foreign Policy* (Baltimore: Johns Hopkins Press, 1971), p. 151. To be fair to Tucker, he does go further than authors such as those previously cited, to ask what lies behind the logic of dominion. In fact, in many respects his analysis of the imperialism phenomenon anticipates the substance of my own argument.
6. Landes, "Nature of Economic Imperialism," p. 510.
7. Kenneth N. Waltz, *Man, the State and War* (New York: Columbia University Press, 1959).
8. Ibid., p. 125.
9. A considerable part of the subsequent argument is adapted from an earlier essay of mine in my book, *American Foreign Economic Policy: Essays and Comments* (New York: Harper & Row, 1968), pt. 1.
10. Waltz, *Man, the State and War*, p. 209.
11. Nicholas Spykman, *America's Strategy in World Politics* (New York: Harcourt, Brace & Jovanovich, 1942), p. 17.

12. Tucker, *The Radical Left*, pp. 62–63.
13. Frederick S. Dunn, *Peaceful Change* (New York: Council on Foreign Relations, 1937), p. 13.
14. Tucker, *The Radical Left*, p. 114.
15. Ibid., p. 73.
16. Ibid., p. 151.
17. Ibid., p. 69.
18. Ibid., pp. 11, 38.
19. Ibid., p. 143.
20. Lionel Robbins, *The Economic Causes of War* (London: Jonathan Cape, 1939), pp. 95, 99, 104.
21. Jacob Viner, "Peace as an Economic Problem," in Viner, *International Economics* (New York: The Free Press, 1951), chap. 16, p. 247.
22. E. M. Winslow, *The Pattern of Imperialism* (New York: Columbia University Press, 1948), p. 237.
23. Viner, "Peace as an Economic Problem," p. 248.
24. Susanne Bodenheimer, "Dependency and Imperialism: The Roots of Latin American Underdevelopment," in K. T. Fann and Donald C. Hodges, eds., *Readings in U.S. Imperialism* (Boston: Porter Sargent, 1971), p. 171.
25. Harry Magdoff, *The Age of Imperialism* (New York: Monthly Review Press, 1969), p. 13.
26. Tucker, *The Radical Left*, p. 78.
27. Robin Jenkins, *Exploitation: The World Power Structure and the Inequality of Nations* (London: MacGibbon and Kee, 1970), p. 166.
28. Ibid., p. 167.
29. Arthur MacEwan, "Capitalist Expansion, Ideology and Intervention," *Upstart*, no. 2 (May 1971): 36. Emphasis in the original.
30. Tucker, *The Radical Left*, p. 52.
31. David Horowitz, *Empire and Revolution: A Radical Interpretation of Contemporary History* (New York: Random House, 1969), p. 38.
32. Waltz, *Man, the State and War*, p. 157.
33. Private correspondence to the author, January 30, 1971.
34. Tucker, *The Radical Left*, p. 145.
35. R. N. Berki, "On Marxian Thought and the Problem of International Relations," *World Politics* 24, no. 1 (October 1971): 103. Emphasis in the original.
36. As quoted in ibid., p. 82.
37. Herman Harmelink III, in a letter to *The New York Times*, January 12, 1972, p. 38.

SELECTED BIBLIOGRAPHY

CHAPTER I

THE MEANING OF IMPERIALISM

Daalder, Hans. "Imperialism," in *International Encyclopedia of the Social Sciences*, vol. 7. New York: Macmillan and The Free Press, 1968, pp. 101–109.

Galtung, Johan. "A Structural Theory of Imperialism." *Journal of Peace Research*, no. 2 (1971): 81–117.

Koebner, Richard. "The Emergence of the Concept of Imperialism." *The Cambridge Journal* 5, no. 12 (September 1952): 727–741.

——, and Schmidt, Helmut D. *Imperialism: The Story and Significance of a Political Word, 1840–1960.* Cambridge: Cambridge University Press, 1964.

Lichtheim, George. *Imperialism.* New York: Frederick A. Praeger, 1971.

Morgenthau, Hans J. *Politics Among Nations*, 3rd ed. New York: Alfred A. Knopf, 1960, Chapter 5.

Plano, Jack C., and Olton, Roy. *The International Relations Dictionary.* New York: Holt, Rinehart and Winston, 1969, Chapter 5.

Thornton, A. P. *Doctrines of Imperialism.* New York: John Wiley & Sons, 1965.

CHAPTER II

CLASSICAL IMPERIALISM

Blaug, Mark. "Economic Imperialism Revisited." *Yale Review* 50, no. 3 (March 1961): 335–349.

Boulding, Kenneth E., and Mukerjee, Tapan, eds. *Economic Imperialism*. Ann Arbor, Mich.: University of Michigan Press, 1972.

Chamberlain, M. E. *The New Imperialism*. London: The Historical Association, 1970.

Daalder, Hans. "Capitalism, Colonialism and the Underdeveloped Areas: The Political Economy of (Anti-) Imperialism," in Egbert de Vries, ed., *Essays on Unbalanced Growth: A Century of Disparity and Convergence*. The Hague: Mouton & Co., 1962, pp. 133–165.

Fieldhouse, D. K. "'Imperialism': An Historiographical Revision." *Economic History Review*, 2nd ser., 14, no. 2 (December 1961): 187–209.

————, ed. *The Theory of Capitalist Development*. London: Longmans, 1967.

Galbraith, John S. "The 'Turbulent Frontier' as a Factor in British Expansion." *Comparative Studies in Society and History* 2, no. 2 (January 1960): 150–168.

Gallagher, John, and Robinson, Ronald. "The Imperialism of Free Trade." *Economic History Review*, 2nd ser., 6, no. 1 (August 1953): 1–15.

Hammond, Richard J. "Economic Imperialism: Sidelights on a Stereotype." *Journal of Economic History* 21, no. 4 (December 1961): 582–598.

Heimann, Eduard. "Schumpeter and the Problems of Imperialism." *Social Research* 19, no. 2 (June 1952): 177–197.

Hovde, Brynjolf J. "Socialist Theories of Imperialism Prior to the Great War." *Journal of Political Economy* 36, no. 5 (October, 1928): 569–591.

Kemp, Tom. *Theories of Imperialism*. London: Dobson, 1967, Chapters 1–6.

Koebner, Richard. "The Concept of Economic Imperialism." *Economic History Review*, 2nd ser., 2, no. 1 (August 1949): 1–29.

Landes, David S. "The Nature of Economic Imperialism." *Journal of Economic History* 21, no. 4 (December 1961): 497–512.

Lichtheim, George. *Imperialism*. New York: Frederick A. Praeger, 1971, Chapter 7.

Neisser, Hans. "Economic Imperialism Reconsidered." *Social Research* 27, no. 1 (Spring 1960): 63–82.

Robinson, Ronald, and Gallagher, John. *Africa and the Victorians.* New York: St. Martin's Press, 1961.

Schuman, Frederick L. *International Politics,* 4th ed. New York: McGraw-Hill, 1948, Chapter 9.

Stretton, Hugh. *The Political Sciences.* New York: Basic Books, 1969, Chapter 4.

Winslow, E. M. "Marxian, Liberal, and Sociological Theories of Imperialism." *Journal of Political Economy* 39, no. 6 (December 1931): 713–758.

————. *The Pattern of Imperialism.* New York: Columbia University Press, 1948.

Wright, Harrison M., ed. *The "New Imperialism."* Boston: D. C. Heath, 1961.

Zimmerman, Louis J., and Crumbach, F. "Saving, Investment and Imperialism: A Reconsideration of the Theory of Imperialism." *Weltwirtschaftliches Archiv* 71, no. 1 (1953): 1–19.

CHAPTER III

THE TRANSITION TO MODERN IMPERIALISM

Bronfenbrenner, Martin. "Radical Economics in America: A 1970 Survey." *Journal of Economic Literature* 8, no. 3 (September 1970): 747–766.

Lichtheim, George. *Imperialism.* New York: Frederick A. Praeger, 1971, Chapter 8.

Lindbeck, Assar. *The Political Economy of the New Left.* New York: Harper & Row, 1971.

Strachey, John. *The End of Empire.* New York: Frederick A. Praeger, 1964, Chapters 8, 9, 13, 19, and 20.

CHAPTER IV

THE VIEW FROM THE METROPOLIS

Baran, Paul A. *The Political Economy of Growth.* New York: Monthly Review Press, 1968.

————, and Sweezy, Paul M. *Monopoly Capital.* New York: Monthly Review Press, 1966.

————. "Notes on the Theory of Imperialism." *Monthly Review* 17, no. 10 (March 1966): 15–31.

Barnet, Richard J. *Roots of War.* New York: Atheneum, 1972, Chapters 6–8.

Dobb, Maurice. *Political Economy and Capitalism.* London: Routledge, 1937, Chapter 7.

"Economics of Imperialism," a symposium. *American Economic Review* 9, no. 2 (May 1970): 225–246.

Fann, K. T., and Hodges, Donald C., eds. *Readings in U.S. Imperialism.* Boston: Porter Sargent, 1971.

Kemp, Tom. *Theories of Imperialism.* London: Dobson, 1967, Chapter 7.

Kolko, Gabriel. *The Roots of American Foreign Policy.* Boston: Beacon Press, 1969.

MacEwan, Arthur. "Capitalist Expansion, Ideology and Intervention." *Upstart,* no. 2 (May 1971): 25–41.

Magdoff, Harry. *The Age of Imperialism.* New York: Monthly Review Press, 1969.

————. "The Logic of Imperialism." *Social Policy* 1, no. 3 (September–October 1970): 20–29.

————, and Sweezy, Paul M. "Notes on the Multinational Corporation." *Monthly Review* 21, nos. 5, 6 (October–November 1969): 1–13 in each issue.

Miller, S. M.; Bennett, Roy; and Alapatt, Cyril. "Does the U.S. Economy Require Imperialism?" *Social Policy* 1, no. 3 (September–October 1970): 13–19.

O'Connor, James. "The Meaning of Economic Imperialism." In *Readings in U.S. Imperialism,* edited by K. T. Fann and Donald C. Hodges. Boston: Porter Sargent, 1971.

Sweezy, Paul M. *The Theory of Capitalist Development.* New York: Monthly Review Press, 1968.

Tucker, Robert W. *The Radical Left and American Foreign Policy.* Baltimore: Johns Hopkins Press, 1971, Chapter 3.

CHAPTER V

THE VIEW FROM THE PERIPHERY

Baran, Paul A. *The Political Economy of Growth.* New York: Monthly Review Press, 1968, Chapters 5–7.

Brown, Michael Barratt. *After Imperialism,* rev. ed. New York: Humanities Press, 1970.

Caves, Richard E. " 'Vent for Surplus' Models of Trade and Growth." In Robert E. Baldwin et al. *Trade, Growth, and the Balance of Payments.* Chicago: Rand McNally, 1965, pp. 95–115.

Dos Santos, Theotonio. "The Structure of Dependence." *American Economic Review* 60, no. 2 (May 1970): 231–236.

Fann, K. T. and Hodges, Donald C., eds. *Readings in U.S. Imperialism.* Boston: Porter Sargent, 1971.

Frank, Andre Gunder. *Capitalism and Underdevelopment in Latin America.* New York: Monthly Review Press, 1969.

————. *Latin America: Underdevelopment or Revolution.* New York: Monthly Review Press, 1969.

Hirschman, Albert O. *The Strategy of Economic Development.* New Haven: Yale University Press, 1958, Chapter 10.

Hymer, Stephen H. "The Efficiency (Contradictions) of Multinational Corporations." *American Economic Review* 60, no. 2 (May 1970): 441–448.

————. "The Multinational Corporation and the Law of Uneven Development." In *Economics and World Order,* edited by Jagdish N. Bhagwati. New York: Macmillan, 1972, pp. 113–140.

————, and Resnick, Stephen A. "International Trade and Uneven Development." In *Trade, Balance of Payments and Growth,* edited by Jagdish N. Bhagwati, Ronald W. Jones, Robert A. Mundell, and Jaroslav Vanek. Amsterdam: North-Holland Publishing Co., 1971, pp. 473–494.

Jalée, Pierre. *The Pillage of the Third World.* New York: Monthly Review Press, 1968.

Kenwood, A. G., and Lougheed, A. L. *The Growth of the International Economy, 1820–1960.* London: George Allen and Unwin, 1971, Chapters 8, 9.

Meier, Gerald M. *The International Economics of Development.* New York: Harper & Row, 1968, Chapter 8.

Myint, Hla. *Economic Theory and the Underdeveloped Countries.* London: Oxford University Press, 1971, Chapters 5–7.

Myrdal, Gunnar. *Economic Theory and Under-Developed Regions.* London: Duckworth, 1957, Chapter 3.

Prebisch, Raul. "Commercial Policy in the Underdeveloped Countries." *American Economic Review* 49, no. 2 (May 1959): 251–273.

Rhodes, Robert I., ed. *Imperialism and Underdevelopment: A Reader.* New York: Monthly Review Press, 1970.

Sideri, S. *Trade and Power: Informal Colonialism in Anglo-Portuguese Relations.* Rotterdam: Rotterdam University Press, 1970.

Singer, Hans W. "The Distribution of Gains Between Investing and Borrowing Countries." *American Economic Review* 40, no. 2 (May 1950): 473–485.

Weisskopf, Thomas E. "Capitalism, Underdevelopment and the Future of the Poor Countries." In *Economics and World Order*, edited by Jagdish N. Bhagwati. New York: Macmillan, 1972, pp. 43–77.

CHAPTER VI

DEPENDENCE AND EXPLOITATION

See the Selected Bibliography for Chapter V.

CHAPTER VII

TOWARD A GENERAL THEORY OF IMPERIALISM

Robbins, Lionel. *The Economic Causes of War*. London: Jonathan Cape, 1939.
Tucker, Robert W. *The Radical Left and American Foreign Policy*. Baltimore: Johns Hopkins Press, 1971.
Viner, Jacob. "Peace as an Economic Problem." In Viner, *International Economics*. New York: The Free Press, 1951, Chapter 16.
Waltz, Kenneth N. *Man, the State and War*. New York: Columbia University Press, 1959.
Winslow, E. M. *The Pattern of Imperialism*. New York: Columbia University Press, 1948, Chapter 9.

INDEX